(continued from front flap)

With the introduction of EX-1, the hypothetical computer devised for the development of this book, the instructional aspects of programming enter the stages of actual program writing. Subsequent chapters detail EX-1 arithmetic operations, programming techniques, input-output for the EX-1, and advanced fixed point techniques.

There is a chapter which introduces the details of a typical modern giant computer, and following sections detail higher level language, and programming systems. The book concludes with a series of appendices which provide reviews of operations with exponents, absolute magnitude and relation symbols, mathematical insights into conversion rules, powers of two, and EX-1 instruction list.

In all, this book offers an excellent and easily mastered foundation for programming of all modern high speed digital computers, as well as a firm basis for the pursuit of more advanced work in the field.

Introduction to Computer
Programming 2nd edition

Donald I. Cutler

Programming Instructor
System Development Corporation

Prentice-Hall, Inc.
Englewood Cliffs, New Jersey

A man may, without being proficient in any science,
and indeed with only the most limited knowledge of
a small portion of it, yet make himself useful to
those who are most instructed.

CHARLES BABBAGE
Life of a Philosopher—1864

Library of Congress Catalog Card Number 79-160256
Printed in The United States of America.
C-47961
Permission is granted to any agent of the UNITED STATES
GOVERMENT to quote from this work in whole or in part,
excepting any previously copyrighted material.

Current printing (last digit):
10 9 8 7 6 5 4 3 2 1

PRENTICE-HALL INTERNATIONAL, INC., *London*
PRENTICE-HALL OF AUSTRALIA, PTY., LTD., *Sydney*
PRENTICE-HALL OF CANADA, LTD., *Toronto*
PRENTICE-HALL OF INDIA (PRIVATE) LTD., *New Delhi*
PRENTICE-HALL OF JAPAN, INC., *Tokyo*

To my wife, Dorisruth Hambley Cutler

and

To my children, Dennis Edward
Rebecca Ellen
Estheruth

Introduction

There are two different kinds of computers—*digital computers* and *analog computers*. The former operate on the same principle as an abacus (that is, by counting). The latter operate on the same principle as a slide rule or thermostat (that is, by measuring).

This book will be concerned only with digital computers and the programming languages used with them.

The electronic characteristics of specific computers are often referred to as *hardware*. The computer programs which operate within the computer are often referred to as *software*. We will not be concerned to any great extent with hardware but we will with software.

A book attempting to deal with programming in a generalized fashion, so that it is applicable to all computers, is perhaps ideal in concept, but a trifle difficult to achieve. This is especially so if we wish to do more than just *talk* about programming. Therefore, we will go about learning to program in the same general manner as if we were learning to drive a car.

When someone learns to drive, he picks a specific car, gets into it, and proceeds to learn (usually with the help of a teacher). After he has mastered that particular car, other makes and models are no longer mysteries to him. He will perhaps need a slight adjustment period with other autos, but he will expect to find such things as brakes, a motor, and wheels.

We will approach the learning of computer programming in a similar manner. We will learn programming by actually programming a specific computer. This computer—*called the EX-1*—is a hypothetical or nonexistent machine. In this manner, many of the details can be eliminated or simplified while major computer characteristics are maintained.

DONALD I. CUTLER

v

Contents

Introduction to Computer Programming

CHAPTER ONE

Beginnings

I. EVOLUTION OF COMPUTERS

Man's attempts to use machines as an aid to computation are almost as old as the hills.

What is thought to be a 3500-year-old Neolithic computer is located in England and is known as Stonehenge. It consists of a group of huge stones arranged in a circular manner such that the stones and sun can be used to predict astronomical phenomena.

The fascinating story of the decoding of this ancient computer mystery is told in a book entitled *Stonehenge Decoded*. In this book Gerald Hawkins tells how he used a modern high-speed digital computer to help unravel the mystery of Stonehenge.

The antiquity of computing devices is also illustrated by the following report:

2000-Year-Old Computer

Divers exploring an ancient wreck off the Greek island of Antikythera recently discovered a device which has all the earmarks of a computer. Dr. Derek J. DeSolla Price, of the Princeton Institute of Advanced Study, estimated that the machine was about 2000 years old, thought its craftsmanship compared favorably with the best of modern Europe. The bronze or brass instrument contains delicate clock-like parts, including finely cut gear wheels. Configurations on the device indicate the seasons, signs of the zodiac, phases of the moon, time of sunrise and sunset, and other astronomical data. It is believed to have been used as early as 82 B.C. to compute planetary orbits.[1]

A detailed account with pictures of this ancient Greek computer may be found in the June 1959 issue of *Scientific American*.

Another example of an early-developed aid to computation is the abacus. This device originated in the Orient in pre-history, and was introduced in Europe at about the time of Marco Polo.

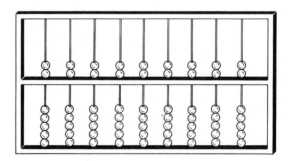

Even today, the abacus is used in parts of the world. Races have been won by abacus operators in competition with operators equipped with desk calculators.

In 1642 a French mathematician named Blaise Pascal invented a calculating machine which could add. He was quite precocious and is said to have worked out independently by the age of twelve a great number of the propositions of plane geometry. By the age of sixteen he had worked out the fundamentals

---

[1] *System Development Corporation Santa Monica Weekly Bulletin*, Volume 3, No. 5.

of conic sections almost as we know them today. He discovered the fluid law of physics which bears his name. Perhaps his most important writing is *Thoughts on Religion*, which is interesting reading even today.

Another calculator which could multiply as well as add was designed by the German mathematician Leibnitz in 1673.

These machines, although practical, never "caught on," because of deficiencies in the state of the art of machine manufacturing.

In the 1830's a great step forward was made in computer science by an Englishman named Charles Babbage. He envisioned a machine which could be given in advance all of the instructions which would be needed to solve a particular mathematical problem. This is in contrast with the desk calculator which employs human intervention at every step of a calculation.

Charles Babbage was a very colorful individual. The story of his life makes fascinating reading. In some ways he was quite eccentric and comical, yet many of his ideas were brilliant. When I read of his exploits, I could not help but compare him with Benjamin Franklin. Both were inventors of great versatility and both were practical philosophers. There seemed to be many parallels in their personalities and life.

Babbage was first led to consider calculating machines because of the prodigious job of calculating navigation tables. The first machine that he worked on was called a Difference Engine. It was never completed; but had it been, it would have consisted of about two tons of novel brass, steel, and pewter clockwork made to precise standards as nothing before it ever had been.

Babbage's efforts were severely handicapped by the state of machine tools in his day. To proceed with his work on the machine, he had to develop techniques in machine design, mechanical drawing, and operations research. Part way through with the development of his Difference Engine, he envisioned a new and much more powerful machine.

This he called the Analytical Engine. He intended to build it so that it could make decisions between two possible courses of action. To work on this machine, however, would mean starting anew. His backer, the British government, did not especially appreciate this turn of events. This led Babbage to enter the field of government subsidy of science with renewed vigor.

Babbage tried many different methods to finance the Analytical Engine. One plan called for writing novels. Another involved building a machine which would play Tic-Tac-Toe and touring the country to exhibit it at towns for a fee. In this latter plan, however, his friends convinced him that a midget, General Tom Thumb, was the current rage and that competing would be an unprofitable folly.

Babbage carried on a private war with street organ-grinders. He maintained that they disturbed his right to quiet. He also pointed out errors in Tennyson's poems.[2] His range of interests was very broad.

Babbage's machines were never completed because they had to be constructed with gears, levers, pulleys, and other mechanical contrivances. Had he lived in the age of the vacuum tube and transistor, he undoubtedly would have seen his machines work.

He was genius and a man who was about a hundred years ahead of his time. He lived to be almost eighty and died a somewhat bitter old man. One cannot help but compare him with another famous failure—Columbus. As we all know, he never reached the East by sailing west.

Summing up Babbage's contributions, we may list the following:

1. The machine should perform all arithmetic operations.
2. The list of instructions (computer program) which the machine will use to solve a particular problem will be fed into it on punched cards.
3. The machine should store partial results to be used in later stages of computation.
4. The machine should be able to decide between two courses of action, depending upon the results of a computation.

___

Problem 1.0

Make a book report on:
  Charles Babbage and His Calculating Engines (Selected Writings by Charles Babbage and Others), edited and with an introduction by Phillip, and Emily Morrison, New York: Dover Publications, Inc., 1961.

___

The first automatic computer actually built was completed in 1944 at Harvard University. It was called the Harvard Mark I Computer. The counters used in this machine were mechanical; however, it did employ electromagnetic relays to control its operation. In size it is only one-tenth as big as the machine conceived by Babbage.

___

[2]When Babbage read Tennyson's poem "The Vision of Sin," he wrote the poet: "In your otherwise beautiful poem there is a verse which reads, 'Every moment dies a man, Every moment one is born.' It must be manifest that, were this true, the population of the world would be at a standstill. In truth the rate of birth is slightly in excess of that of death. I would suggest that in your next edition of the poem you have it read, 'Every moment dies a man, Every moment one and one-sixteenth is born.'

"Strictly speaking this is not correct. The actual figure is a decimal so long that I cannot get it in the line, but I believe one and one-sixteenth will be sufficiently accurate for poetry."
                          —James R. Newman, *The World of Mathematics*, New York:
                                            Simon and Schuster, Inc., 1960.

Shortly thereafter, Dr. John Von Neuman of the Institute for Advanced Study at Princeton contributed the following two important principles to computer technology:

1. A number system employing only two symbols, 0 and 1, is the most efficient one upon which to build an electronic computer. This number system is called the *binary number system*. It is the most efficient system because of the two-state nature ("on" or "off") of electrical circuits.
2. Numbers in the binary number system can be used in two different ways. They can be used either as the numbers being manipulated, or they can be used as coded instructions to the computer. In other words, they can tell the computer whether to add, subtract, test the result, jump to another instruction, and so on. Since instructions are coded as numbers, they may be modified by arithmetical means during the operation of a computer to produce *new* instructions.

Digital computers rapidly went through the electro-mechanical stage and entered the electronic one. At first they used only vacuum tubes; now the vacuum tubes have been completely replaced with transistors.

Transistors have several advantages over vacuum tubes: they are much smaller; they do not generate heat as a vacuum tube does; they do not require as much electricity; they require replacement less frequently.

The latest and largest of the new digital computers cost several million dollars. They can retrieve a piece of information from memory in about a millionth of a second. Other computers had to be used to help design them.

The current models of large-scale computers are getting almost too complex for humans to program efficiently; hence, the trend is toward having computers develop the programs which computers will use. This seems paradoxical, but it is the direction events are taking.

II. APPLICATIONS OF COMPUTERS

Computers are being used in an ever increasing variety of applications. A list of the applications of computers would be outdated almost before being written down. This is perhaps the best indication of the fantastic rate at which computers are becoming a part of our everyday life. Therefore, I will list but a few and leave the creation of a more complete and up-to-date list to the student.

Applications in Mathematical Research—Probably most of the mathematical research done with computers is performed at universities, although a considerable amount is also carried on by private research organizations. Solutions of mathematical problems which require calculations to give a first approximate answer, followed up by more calculations using the first answer to get a next approximate answer, etc., lend themselves very nicely to computer solution.

Computers have added to our knowledge of number theory by supplying mathematicians with the first million prime numbers for study. Mathematicians are also experimenting with the use of computers to discover new theorems.

The following example illustrates what the change in speed of computing can do:

An Englishman named William Shanks computed π to 707 decimal places. He did this about one hundred years ago, working with pencil and paper, and spent twenty years on the task.

Later, in 1949, a computing machine known as ENIAC computed π to over 2000 places in a little over 70 hours. These modern calculations showed that Shanks made a mistake in the 528th decimal place. Still later, another computer calculated π to more than 3000 places in 13 minutes.

In 1959, a smaller machine calculated π to 10,000 places. The results were published and it was observed that the computer had made a mistake in the 7,480th decimal place. By 1962, π had been computed to 10,000 places so many times that the results are no longer novel.

This example with π is in many respects amusing. It is usually not of much value to have π to more than four or five place accuracy. For most computations 3.14159 does nicely. It does illustrate, however, that calculations which formerly took a lifetime can now be done in minutes.

Applications in Industry and Government—An important use of the computer in industry and government is in the area of data processing. Data processing concerns the filing, retrieving, sorting, and modification of large volumes of data. The data can be anything from information concerning employees and payroll to statistics received from artificial satellites.

Some computers are used in what is called a Real-Time Data Processing System. Such a system consists of a group of computer programs functioning in a manner which enables them to supply information to an activity whenever the information is demanded. In other words, it is a system which can react to its environment.

Automated Air Traffic Control would be an example of real-time data processing. Here the computer might have to supply information on a flight to the tower controller at a moment's notice upon his inquiry. The system would probably be designed to force warning displays upon the controller when potential conflicts in flight plans developed. Such a system would undoubtedly be connected with the air traffic environment by radar, communication lines, push buttons, punched cards, warning buzzers, cathode ray tubes, and other devices.

While computers offer tremendous possibilities in real-time systems, they are also used in many non-real-time applications.

The following would be an example of a non-real-time operation: Every Wednesday, a firm could feed to a computer all of the necessary inputs to compute each employee paycheck. The computer could then go to work and a few minutes later have all of the checks computed and printed. The time that the computer took or when we had it do the processing would be of little consequence as long as the checks were ready before payday. We just feed all of the information to the computer and it works at the job until it is finished. We will not interrupt it partway with a question to which we need the answer immediately.

Income tax may be computed on a national scale once a year.

Aircraft companies may simulate aircraft performance on a computer. This would eliminate expensive and perhaps dangerous real testing.

Industrial processes can be simulated without actually spending huge amounts of money in trying out the actual process. Also, a process that normally might take days to complete sometimes can be run on a computer with a reduced time scale and valuable information gained. This is somewhat analogous to the method whereby a still picture is taken of a flower every hour and the results combined into a movie whose complete run is 30 seconds.

By this method, the life of a corporation can be simulated (maybe it is 20 years) and compressed into half an hour. This life span could be run 16 times in an 8-hour day with each run giving different results for different conditions applied.

Applications in Education—A recent development has been the use of a computer to aid students in learning a particular subject. Basically, this works as follows:

The machine flashes a question to the student. The student answers to the best of his ability by pushing the appropriate button alongside a multiple choice answer, also flashed.

If the student answers correctly, a new and slightly more difficult question is presented. If the student misses the question, a new and slightly less difficult remedial question is presented. In this manner, the student progresses through the entire subject matter. Recording features can be built in, which enable an analysis to be made of the student's attempts at progressing through the course.

A student thus using this device proceeds at his own speed and never goes on to something new without understanding what went before. Teachers are not replaced, but rather they are freed for helping with individual problems. Early results of the use of these devices seem to be very promising. Experiments to determiner if machines can learn are also under way.

Applications in Medicine—Study is being carried on to see if computers can be applied to the diagnosing of ailments. They, of course, can easily maintain medical histories of patients. Use of computers in hospital billing is no problem.

Other Applications—There are numerous other uses to which computers are being put. However, enough have been stated to justify to some extent the often quoted statement that civilization has entered the second industrial revolution or the age of computers. The first industrial revolution freed man's muscles; the second is freeing his mind for more challenging pursuits.

It has been said that the only factor which could limit the computer industry is the number of applications for computers. As of now, the end of the applications is far from visible and may well be nonexistent.

Problem 1.1

Make a list of 25 specific applications of computers.

III. SOME ASPECTS OF COMPUTER PROGRAMMING

A computer program, generally speaking, is a sequence of instructions which a person (called a programmer) writes. This sequence of instructions is to be placed in the computer's memory and a button is pressed to start the computer. Needless to say, the sequence of instructions (program) is designed to perform a certain function.

A very close analogy may be drawn between computer programming and the science of deciding where to punch the holes in a player piano roll.

There are various levels of program languages. The computers with which we will be concerned will operate with a sequence of instructions in their memory in coded form. The instructions are coded in memory as a configuration of 0's and 1's because electrical devices seem to fall naturally into one of two possible states. For example; they are either on or off; they are magnetized in one direction or the other; they are conducting electricity or they are not conducting electricity. Indeed, even punched cards lend themselves readily to this 1, 0 interpretation as they have either a hole punched or not punched.

Although the computer will operate ultimately using a program coded in it in 0's and 1's, it would be very time-consuming for a person to write a program in 0's and 1's. If the program can be written in a language approaching that of English or mathematics or a combination of both, the programmer can concentrate more on programming logic and less on programming details. Thus the program should be less likely to contain errors.

The "English and mathematics" type of programming language is relatively easy to learn. Thus large groups of people can be trained to a fair degree of proficiency in a short period of time. A language which is less error prone is especially valuable as the size of the programs becomes large. It seems as if the number of errors increases at a faster rate as the size of the computer program grows.

Presently, programming involves three following major levels of programming languages:

Low level language—This is the binary (0, 1) language as found in a computer when it is operating. Frequently, a representation of the computer program is given in a more compact form. On some computers this compact representation is the *octal number system*. This is a number system with eight symbols (0 through 7). On some computers the compact representation is the *hexadecimal number system*. This is a number system with sixteen symbols (0 through 9 and A, B, C, D, E, and F). These number systems will be discussed in detail in Chapter 2.

As a rule, programmers do not write a program in the binary, octal or hexadecimal language. However, trouble-shooting a program is frequently done at this low level. Trouble-shooting a program is frequently referred to as *debugging*.

Intermediate level language—This is called a *symbolic machine language* and is much closer to English than the binary language. Each instruction is usually represented by an abbreviation. These abbreviations are called *mnemonic codes*. For example, ADD might be the mnemonic or symbolic machine code for the instruction "add," and SUB might be the mnemonic for "subtract."

There is a one-to-one correspondence between the instructions in a computer program written in this language and one in binary. That is to say, one instruction in symbolic machine language translates into one instruction in binary.

A computer program called an *assembler* will do the translation for us. A great amount of programming is carried on at this language level.

High level language—The trend in programming is toward the use of languages of this type. This is a language approaching that of English and mathematics. It is more flexible in format than the symbolic machine language. Usually one expression in a higher level language will be translated into several or many symbolic machine instructions.

Aside from being less error prone and also easier to learn, higher level languages appear to hold out the promise of being usable with different makes of computers. This would enable a group of programmers to write all of their programs in the given higher level language regardless of the make of the computer involved.

Of course, a translation will be needed which will change the higher level language to the binary format for the specific make of the computer used. Different computers have different requirements regarding their low level and intermediate level languages.

As with the symbolic machine language, a program will do the translation for us. In the case of a higher level language, however, the translating program is called a *compiler*. This distinction in names exists because an assembler translates one instruction into one instruction, whereas a compiler translates one higher level program statement into several or many computer instructions. A compiler is considerably more complicated than an assembler.

If a program were written in binary, it might look like this:

```
00001010111010101111001101
01100001001101101111000101
11011000101010001110001100
01000111101010111100111011
11010001101010000011101100
01011101011100001010011000
00011111011011010100010101
```

Here each line of 0's and 1's is a computer instruction.

If a program were written in machine symbolic code, it might appear like this:

BXTBYT	SLW	WORD
	CAL	WORD
	ANA	MASKI
DOG	LAS	BLNKCD
	TRA	*+2
	TRA	ALFMLA
	TXI	*+1, 3, 1
	TRA	BXTBYT

```
NEXTWD    CLA    FSTWRD
          TRA    DOG
```

A program written in a higher level language might appear like this:

```
FOR I = ALL(PLANES)$
  BEGIN IF JET($I$) EQ V(ABORT)$
    BEGIN CAPAC = CAPAC − 1$ TEST$ END
    FUEL = (2*REG($I$))(*3*) + 6.7$
END
```

A programmer solving a problem by means of a computer program essentially goes through the following steps:

1. Understand the problem and the data.
2. Flow diagram the logic of a solution.
3. Write the computer instructions on coding paper.
4. Punch the instructions on data processing cards to obtain a *symbolic card deck* (source deck).
5. Submit source deck to computer for translation to binary (this is assembly or compilation depending upon whether an intermediate level language or a high level language is involved). A *binary card deck* (object deck) is the result.
6. Submit the object deck to the computer for read in and operation.
7. Study the printouts, correct the program and test extensively.

Documentation of the program is completed.

A *program system* is a group of interrelated programs which will achieve a given result. A large group of programmers can develop a large system of computer programs by dividing into two smaller groups. Group A will become familiar with the present manual (non-automated) system, which is to be automated by programming it for a computer.

Group A should also be familiar with the higher level language. They will write what is called the *operational system*. The operational system is the program system which will automate the manual system.

Group B should also be familiar with the higher level language. They should know thoroughly the symbolic machine language of the computer to be used. Group B can then write the compiler program which will change the higher level language to the binary of the machine involved.

Other programs are usually written which assist in the production of programs for the automated system. These are called *utility programs*. Compilers and assemblers are examples of utility programs.

Finally, we may add that just as it takes as much effort to develop carmaking machinery as it does to develop the car, so it seems to require as much effort to develop program-writing programs as it does to develop the programs that are desired as the end result.

A system which is to be programmed generally goes through the following stages:

1. System is studied.
2. System is documented and flow diagrammed.
3. Programs are designed and written.
4. Programs are tested individually and then together on the computer.
5. System is installed and maintained.
6. The user is trained in the use of the newly automated system.

A programmer may find himself in any one of these phases—and usually does.

CHAPTER TWO

Number Systems

I. PRELIMINARIES

In this chapter, the relationship between the decimal, octal, and binary number system will be discussed. The hexadecimal number system will also be introduced as several modern computers employ its use.

Although theoretically a programmer may be able to program using entirely our ordinary every day decimal number system when writing a program, a knowledge of what is actually going on requires a knowledge of these other number systems. The programmer also frequently finds a knowledge of the octal (or hexadecimal, if applicable) and binary system indispensable in debugging his program.

Being as familiar as we are with the decimal number system, we tend to overlook its worth. However, all we have to do to recover our appreciation of it, is to work in a number system such as was used by the Mayans, Babylonians, Greeks, or Romans.

It is truly an astonishing fact that with only ten symbols (digits) of 0, 1, 2, 3, 4, 5, 6, 7, 8, 9 and the three ideas of

1.   position (or place value)
2.   . a decimal point
3. $\pm$ signs

we can represent any number, however large or small. These entities can represent a grocery bill, or they may stand for the most profound laws of the universe.

Youngsters can perform calculations with them that would have baffled the wisest men in a king's court.

We may be even more surprised to learn that using only the two symbols, 0 and 1, we can do everything that we could do using the ten symbols of the decimal system. The fact that over the centuries man has developed the ten symbols 0 through 9 probably derives from the fact that we have ten fingers. It is interesting to note that the word "digit" comes from the Latin word "digitus" meaning finger or toe.

Until about twenty years ago, no one (except for a few mathematicians) ever reflected upon other number systems or "scales of notation," as some mathematical textbooks called them. To most people reading this book, using the decimal number system is almost as natural and automatic as breathing. However, today there are many thousands of people who are becoming quite adept at working in number systems other than decimal.

A simple way for a person to convince himself that numerical quantities can be represented by 0's and 1's is to count with them. We do so in the same manner as is done in the decimal system. Therefore, let us review the counting process in decimal.

0
1
2
3
4
5
6
7
8
9

We see that going from 0 through 9 is no problem. The trick is in getting to the next higher number now that the digit in the units column is as high as it can go. Well, as you probably well know, what we do is put the units column back to 0 and add 1 to the next column on the left. In this case we would be adding 1 to the tens column. This gives us 10.

Had the tens column had a 9 in it when we tried to add 1 to it, we would have put it back to zero and added a 1 to the hundreds column. And so on and on.

The same procedure is followed for counting in binary. However, here the symbol 1 corresponds to the symbol 9 because 1 is as high as you can go in any particular column.

Thus, counting in binary we get:

0
1
10
11
100
101
110
111
1000
etc.

Problem 2.1

Count to your age in binary.

If you have skipped problem 2.1, you have made a big mistake. Most people find counting in binary extremely difficult at first. And yet a little practice counting in binary pays off handsomely in insight into working with a strange new number system. So if you haven't done problem 2.1, go back and do it. Then check your result with the answers in the back of the book.

In an octal number system, we use the same procedure except that here we have the eight symbols 0, 1, 2, 3, 4, 5, 6, 7 to use. If people were born with eight fingers instead of ten, we might have an octal system as our natural system. Counting in octal goes:

0	11
2	12
2	13
3	14
4	15
5	16
6	17
7	20
10	etc.

Problem 2.2

Answer the following questions in decimal, in octal, and in binary:

    a. How many days are there in a week?
    b. How many days are there in two weeks?
    c. How many days are there in April?

Making a further study of number systems, we note that a decimal number such as 256 is made up of two hundreds, five tens, and six ones. The number 256 is therefore a shorthand forms of notation.

This is

$$200 + 50 + 6 \text{ or}$$

$$2 \times 10^2 + 5 \times 10^1 + 6 \times 10^0.$$

Thus the column just left of the decimal point in a decimal number denotes "ones." The second column left of the decimal point denotes "tens." The next, "hundreds," then "thousands," and so on.

In the binary system, the same type of situation exists, the difference being that powers of two are involved rather than powers of ten.

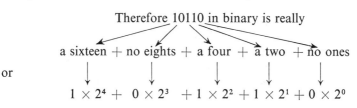

Therefore 10110 in binary is really

a sixteen + no eights + a four + a two + no ones

or

$$1 \times 2^4 + 0 \times 2^3 + 1 \times 2^2 + 1 \times 2^1 + 0 \times 2^0$$

This gives us a way of converting a binary number to its decimal equivalent. Gathering up this last expression, we get $16 + 0 + 4 + 2 + 0 = 22$. We conclude that the decimal number 22 represents the same quantity as does 10110 in binary.

Problem 2.3

How much money in decimal would a binary millionaire have?

Just as we worked left of the decimal point, so can we compare number systems right of the point. In this way 521.159 is really shorthand in decimal for:

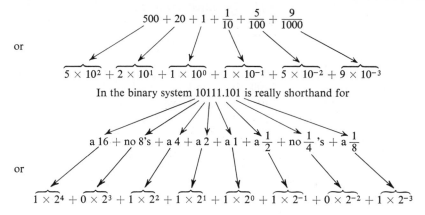

or

$$5 \times 10^2 + 2 \times 10^1 + 1 \times 10^0 + 1 \times 10^{-1} + 5 \times 10^{-2} + 9 \times 10^{-3}$$

In the binary system 10111.101 is really shorthand for

$$\text{a } 16 + \text{no 8's} + \text{a } 4 + \text{a } 2 + \text{a } 1 + \text{a } \frac{1}{2} + \text{no } \frac{1}{4}\text{'s} + \text{a } \frac{1}{8}$$

or

$$1 \times 2^4 + 0 \times 2^3 + 1 \times 2^2 + 1 \times 2^1 + 1 \times 2^0 + 1 \times 2^{-1} + 0 \times 2^{-2} + 1 \times 2^{-3}$$

Evaluating this expression in decimal we can find the decimal equivalent of our given 10111.101 which is

$$16 + 0 + 4 + 2 + 1 + \frac{1}{2} + 0 + \frac{1}{8} = 23\tfrac{5}{8} \qquad \text{or} \qquad 23.625$$

In the octal number system, a similar procedure is followed whereby each column represents a power of eight. Thus, the octal number 257.56 really stands for

$$2 \times 8^2 + 5 \times 8^1 + 7 \times 8^0 + 5 \times 8^{-1} + 6 \times 8^{-2}$$

If we are dealing with a number, say 100, and there is a question as to which number system we are working with, we would subscript the number.

Thus, 100_2 means that the 100 is a number in the binary system.

100_8 means that the 100 is a number in the octal system.

100 with no subscript generally means a number in the decimal system. However, 100_{10} is a valid expression.

Henry and Joan Bowers in their delightful book *Arithmetical Excursions* give names to the various[1] numbers in the binary system as follows:

DECIMAL SYSTEM	BINARY SYSTEM	
1	1	One
2	10	Twin
3	11	Twin One
4	100	Twindred
5	101	Twindred One
6	110	Twindred Twin
7	111	Twindred Twin One
8	1000	Twosand
9	1001	Twosand One
10	1010	Twosand Twin
11	1011	Twosand Twin One
12	1100	Twosand Twindred
13	1101	Twosand Twindred One
14	1110	Twosand Twindred Twin
15	1111	Twosand Twindred Twin One
16	10000	Twin Twosand

Problem 2.4

What wording would describe 100111_2?

The *radix* or *base* of a number system is defined as the number of different symbols in the system. This number is always given in decimal. Thus, the radix or base of the decimal system is 10. The radix or base of the octal system is 8. For the binary system it is 2.

A number system with a low base has certain advantages over a system with a high base. It also has certain disadvantages. The same is true of a number system with a high base. The lower the base, the fewer the symbols that must be memorized. Also, the lower the base, the fewer the multiplication and addition facts that must be memorized. A disadvantage of a low base, however, is that it takes many more positions to represent a number than it would with a high base.

[1]Henry and Joan E. Bowers, *Arithmetical Excursions: An Enrichment of Elementary Mathematics*, New York: Dover Publications, Inc., 1961.

This is evident when we look at $1,000,000_2$ and 64_{10}. Both represent the same magnitude, yet the former requires 7 positions and the latter, 2. We also find that a number such as $1,000,000_2$ gives us very little "feel" for the magnitude of the quantity represented. This is because we are so used to thinking in terms of decimal. The octal system provides this "feel," and numbers in it can be written almost as compactly as in the decimal system.

It is very convenient that an extremely simple technique enables us to convert between the octal and binary number systems. Just by glancing at an octal number, we will find that we can write down the binary equivalent. In fact, with a little practice, it will be easy to look at either and visualize the other without writing it down.

Because of this simple conversion, programmers usually work and think in octal (or hexadecimal) *if their computer operates in binary*. Thus, they have a system which enables numbers to be represented in almost as short a notation as decimal yet, which is practically binary for them. The conversion from decimal to octal or from octal to decimal, however, is of usual difficulty.

The *radix point* is that point, ".", which separates the fractional part of the number from its integral or whole part (for example, 25.6 or 2.56). In our conventional decimal number system, we refer to this point as the *decimal point*. By the same convention, we may call it the *octal point* when working with the octal number system, and the *binary point* if we are using the binary system. But, perhaps the most common name given to it by programmers is the *real point*. It can be called the real point regardless of the system involved.

One further point should be mentioned before a formal discussion of conversion rules for changing between systems is taken up: Digits or symbols in the binary system (i.e., 0 and 1) would ordinarily be called *binary digits*. This has been shortened to the word *bit*. Thus, a bit is a 0 or 1 in the binary system. This leads to the truism that "the only way to learn computer programming is bit by bit."

II. CONVERSION RULES

Our purpose in this section will be to convert numbers from a system of one base to a system of another base. These conversions may be done by several different methods and each programmer has his favorite. For the sake of simplicity, not all of the possible methods will be presented. Furthermore, only the rules will be given. The mathematical derivations or intuitive mathematical insights will be left for Appendix 1.

Conversions for the following will be given:

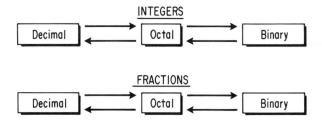

Decimal to Octal (Integers)—Successive divisions of the decimal number by 8 will give the octal number via remainders reversed.

Example: $397_{10} = \underline{\quad\quad}_8$

$$
\begin{array}{ccc}
49 & 6 & 0 \\
8\overline{)397} & 8\overline{)49} & 8\overline{)6} \\
32 & 48 & 0 \\
\overline{77} & \overline{①} & \overline{⑥} \\
72 & & \\
\overline{⑤} & &
\end{array}
$$

Thus $397_{10} = 615_8$

Note that the process ended when a quotient of zero was obtained. It should also be noted that even if a remainder is zero after a division, it is used as a digit in the final answer.

Check:

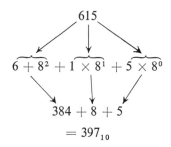

$$6 + 8^2 + 1 \times 8^1 + 5 \times 8^0$$

$$384 + 8 + 5$$

$$= 397_{10}$$

Problem 2.5

Find the octal equivalent of the following numbers:

1.	361	4. 61201
2.	1720	5. 991
3.	430	6. 4096

Octal to Decimal (Integers)—Analysis of the octal number gives the decimal equivalent.

Example: $4125_8 = \underline{\hspace{2cm}}_{10}$

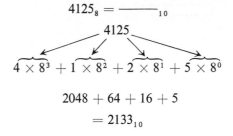

$$2048 + 64 + 16 + 5$$
$$= 2133_{10}$$

Problem 2.6

Find the decimal equivalent of the following octal numbers:

1.	162	5.	17777
2.	263	6.	7
3.	20000	7.	18 (Can this be an octal number?)
4.	1203		

Octal to Binary (Integers and Fractions)—Each octal digit is replaced by 3 binary bits. For this conversion it is necessary to memorize the following octal-binary relationship:

$$0 = 000$$
$$1 = 001$$
$$2 = 010$$
$$3 = 011$$
$$4 = 100$$
$$5 = 101$$
$$6 = 110$$
$$7 = 111$$

Example: $475.03_8 = \underline{\hspace{2cm}}_2$

4	7	5	.	0	3
↓	↓	↓	↓	↓	↓
100	111	101	.	000	011

Problem 2.7

Find the binary equivalent of the following octal numbers:

1. 74.2	5. 35550	9. 124.75	13. 44463
2. 1000	6. 67.521	10. 65741	14. 1.3460
3. 6.204	7. 22222	11. 230.04	15. 123456
4. 0.57704	8. 23	12. 77771	

Binary to Octal (Integers and Fractions)—Each group of 3 binary bits, *counting from the radix point*, is equivalent to one octal digit.

Example: $1101110.011_2 = \underline{\hspace{1cm}}_8$

$$\underbrace{1\,1\,0}\,\underbrace{1\,1\,0}.\underbrace{0\,1\,1}$$

$$\downarrow\ \ \ \downarrow\ \ \ \ \downarrow\ \ \ \downarrow$$

$$1\ \ 5\ \ \ 6\ .\ 3$$

$$= 156.3_8$$

Problem 2.8

Find the octal equivalent of the following binary numbers:

1. 011111101000.	6. 1111.00110010	11. 110011001100
2. 110.000111001	7. 10001.1100101	12. 11010100111.
3. 1000.11000010	8. 101101011010.	13. 100110110101
4. 10110001.1110	9. 11011010000.0	14. 1111011100.
5. 0.001001001001	10. 0.010010010101	15. 1010110.

Decimal to Octal (Fractions)—Multiply the decimal fractions by 8. Retain the whole number, even if zero, in the result.

A rule of thumb which supplies sufficient accuracy for our work is to carry out the computation as many times as needed in order to have one more octal digit in our answer than we have in the decimal number. Then round so that both have the same number of places. Remember that we are rounding an octal number, therefore add 1 to the next higher place if the position being eliminated contains an octal digit greater than, or equal to 4.

Example: $0.7813_{10} = \underline{\hspace{1cm}}_8$

Since our decimal number here has 4 places, we will compute 5 octal places and round off the last one.

0.7813	0.2504	0.0032	0.0256	0.2048
8	8	8	8	8
⑥.2504	②.0032	⓪.0256	⓪.2048	①.6384

$$0.7813_{10} = 0.6200_8$$

Problem 2.9

Find the octal equivalent of the following decimal numbers:

1. 0.34
2. 0.79
3. 0.50
4. 0.6741

Octal to Decimal (Fractions)—Analysis of an octal fraction gives a decimal fraction.

Example:
$$0.723_8 = \underline{\hspace{2cm}}_{10}$$

$$0.723$$

$$\overbrace{7 \times 1/8} + \overbrace{2 \times 1/64} + \overbrace{3 \times 1/512}$$

Simplifying by using the lowest common denominator.

$$\frac{7 \times 64 + 2 \times 8 + 3}{512} = \frac{448 + 16 + 3}{512} = \frac{467}{512} = 0.912$$

Problem 2.10

Find the decimal equivalent of the following octal numbers:
1. 0.46
2. 0.05
3. 0.342
4. 0.762

Mixed Numbers (Integers plus fractions)—These are handled by dealing with the integral and fractional parts separately.

Example:
$$64.5_{10} = \underline{\hspace{2cm}}_8$$

Since $64_{10} = 100_8$ and $0.5_{10} = .4_8$

we can say that $64.5_{10} = 100.4_8$

Problem 2.11

Find the octal equivalent of the following decimal numbers:
1. 27.25
2. 364.125

Decimal to Binary and Binary to Decimal—No conversion will be given for going directly from binary to decimal of from decimal to binary, as this conversion seems to be most easily done by passing through octal. If a direct conversion were desired, however, it could be done with methods similar to those discussed above or by use of a table of powers of 2. A table of powers of 2 is given in Appendix 2.

III. THE HEXADECIMAL NUMBER SYSTEM

The binary numbers that a computer employs are contained in a "computer word" as we will see in Chapter 3. If it is decided by the computer designers to employ a word consisting of multiples of three bits, then the natural shorthand representation of such binary is the *octal* number system. Thus, a group of 15 binary bits can be represented by grouping in threes to get 5 octal digits.

Thus, 101110111100001 can be represented by 56741_8.

If, however, a computer word consisting of multiples of 4 bits is chosen, then *hexadecimal* is a logical shorthand representation.

Thus, 1001001011001111 can be represented by $92CF_{16}$.

This is based upon replacement of each 4 bits by the corresponding hexadecimal digit as illustrated in the following table:

Binary		Hexadecimal
0000	=	0
0001	=	1
0010	=	2
0011	=	3
0100	=	4
0101	=	5
0110	=	6
0111	=	7
1000	=	8
1001	=	9
1010	=	A
1011	=	B
1100	=	C
1101	=	D
1110	=	E
1111	=	F

Since sixteen symbols are involved, 0 through 9 and A through F, the system is a base 16 number system. It probably should be called the sexadecimal number system. But, for some reason (perhaps sexadecimal was too racy), it is called hexadecimal.

Some present day computers have their computer words consisting of multiples of four bits (for example, a 32-bit computer word). Thus if a programmer were to work with one of this type, he would soon become adept in the use of hexadecimal.

Problem 2.12

Find the hexadecimal equivalent of the following:

    1. 1101100000111010_2 2. 01010111101111110010_2

Problem 2.13

Find the binary equivalent of the following:
    1. $29AB_{16}$ 2. $F09B6_{16}$

Problem 2.14

Find the decimal equivalent of the following:
    1. D_{16} 2. 29_{16} 3. $A3E_{16}$

Problem 2.15

Find the hexadecimal equivalent of the following:
    1. 75_{10} 2. 185_{10}

IV. MODULUS AND RANGE

Frequently, in programming, the necessity arises to talk about how many different numbers a given number of symbol positions can hold. We might ask for example, "How many different numbers can be represented using 3 decimal positions?"

The answer is 1000. Three decimal places can represent numbers from 000 through 999 and that is 1000 different numbers. We would say that the *modulus* of 3 decimal positions is 1000. The *range* of 3 decimal positions is 0 through 999 or, looking at it another way, the range is 0 through "modulus − 1."

It should be noted that the modulus depends upon both the number of positions involved and the base of the number system involved. Also, the modulus and range are expressed in the decimal system unless specifically desired in another number system. Thus, we would speak of the modulus of 3 binary positions as being 8, and the range as being 0 through 7.

To summarize:

Definition of modulus—The number of numbers which can be written in a limited number of symbol positions is called the *modulus* of that number of positions.

Modulus in the decimal number system—The modulus is 10^m where m is the number of digit positions. The range is 0 through $10^m − 1$.

Example: The modulus of 4 digit positions in the decimal system is 10^4 or 10000. The range is 0 through $10^4 − 1$ or 9999.

Modulus in the octal number system—The modulus is 8^m where m is the number of octal positions. The range is 0 through $8^m - 1$.

Example: The modulus of 3 octal positions is 8^3 or 512. The range is 0 through $8^3 - 1$ or 511.

Modulus in the binary number system—The modulus is 2^m where m is the number of binary positions. The range is 0 through $2^m - 1$.

Example: The modulus of 4 binary positions is 2^4 or 16. The range is 0 through $2^4 - 1$ or 15.

Problem 2.16

1. What is the modulus and range of 5 decimal positions?
2. What is the modulus and range of 6 binary positions?
3. How many (in decimal) different numbers can be represented by 4 octal positions? What is the range?

V. USE OF COMPLEMENT ARITHMETIC BY COMPUTERS

The word *complement* is defined as "that which completes."

In mathematics all of the numbers and their complements (negatives) "complete" the number system. The numbers of mathematics can be placed into correspondence with the points of a line. Let us only consider integers in our illustration.

number line

$$-6 \quad -5 \quad -4 \quad -3 \quad -2 \quad -1 \quad 0 \quad +1 \quad +2 \quad +3 \quad +4 \quad +5 \quad +6$$

Thus, $+3$ and -3 are complementary numbers.

Most computers perform subtraction by adding the complement of the number being subtracted. In this way, "borrowing" circuits and other circuits connected with subtraction are eliminated, and cost is reduced.

Thus, $+4$ can have $+3$ subtracted from it by having -3 added instead.

When we place a number in a computer in a limited number of bit positions, however, we introduce two forms of computer word complements.

One computer word complement is identified by the base of the number system used. When this complement is added to the number of which it is the complement, the resulting sum is the modulus of the given number of positions.

The other complement is identified by 1 less than the base of the number system used. When this complement is added to the number of which it is the complement, the resulting sum is the range of the given number of positions.

We might say that when we add a number to its complement, we get zero. This is true whether we are talking about the signed numbers of mathematics or the numbers and their computer word complements, as represented in a machine which has a computer word of a given modulus (given number of bit positions).

Before we see how number complements can be used for subtracting, let us see how to obtain them.

Complements in the Decimal Number System—The *9's complement* of a number is found by subtracting each decimal digit from 9. This generally is not used by computers or programmers, but will be used shortly in showing how complements can be used to achieve a subtraction.

Example: The 9's complement of 56709_{10} is 43290.

The *10's complement* of a number is found by first obtaining the 9's complement and then adding 1 to the result.

Example: The 10's complement of 37192_{10} is 62808.

Complements in the Octal Number System—The *7's complement* of a number is found by subtracting each digit of the octal number from 7. The 7's complement is used constantly by the programmer in his calculations and representations.

Example: The 7's complement of 34075_8 is 43702.

The *8's complement* of a number is found by first obtaining the 7's complement and then adding 1 to the result.

Example: The 8's complement of 12073_8 is 65705.

Complements in the Binary Number System—The *1's complement* of a number is found by replacing 0's with 1's and 1's with 0's.

Example: The 1's complement of 1011010_2 is 0100101.

The *2's complement* of a number is found by first obtaining the 1's complement and then adding 1 to the result.

Example: The 2's complement of 10110101_2 is 01001011.

Problem 2.17

1. What is the 1's complement of 10010011_2?
2. What is the 2's complement of 10111010_2?
3. What is the 7's complement of 427031_8?
4. What is the 8's complement of 210367_8?
5. What is the 9's complement of 5210943_{10}?
6. What is the 10's complement of 3880291_{10}?

As stated previously, complements can be used for subtraction. To see how, let us look at a mechanical counter.

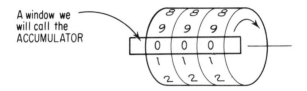

A window we
will call the
ACCUMULATOR

This mechanical device is a counter consisting of three discs, geared in such a way that if the rightmost disc makes one revolution, the disc left of it makes one-tenth of a revolution. This is just like the mileage indicator on an automobile.

We see that to add two numbers is no problem. If, for example, we wished to add 654 and 321 using this device, we see that first it could be given 654 pulses which would leave 654 in the accumulator. Then, giving it 321 more pulses would leave 975 in the accumulator. Of course, we must be careful not to exceed the capacity (3 positions) of our machine.

Suppose we wish to subtract 321 from 654. Can it be done by adding only? Assuming that we can obtain the 10's complement of 321, let's add it to 654.

10's complement of 321 is 679

$$\begin{array}{r} 679 \\ +654 \\ \hline 1333 \end{array}$$

It is seen that our device will show 333 if first we pulse it 654 times and then 679 (10's complement of 321) times. The leftmost 1 of the 1333 is lost, because our device handles only 3 positions. Yet, we see that 333 is the answer that we want.

This may give you some intuitive feel that subtraction can be done by adding. Mathematically, what we have done is this:

$$\underbrace{\text{Modulus} - 321}_{} + \underbrace{654 - \text{Modulus}}_{}$$

10's complement of 321   Modulus is subtracted here because 1000 (the modulus) was lost due to the 1 lost because of no 4th disc.

or the net result is 654 − 321 = 333.

When the 10's complement is used, subtraction comes out correctly, as we saw. Had we used the 9's complement, our answer would have been 1 short. We could handle this situation by making a rule that whenever we lose a 1 out of the left of the machine (due to its modulus), we will add a 1 to the rightmost position.

This process of adding 1 is done automatically by a computer. It is called *end-around-carry*. This process of end-around-carry is only done when a computer is designed to use 1's complement arithmetic for performing subtraction.

Let us do some of this arithmetic using an imaginary 5 bit computer. Our accumulator will look like this:

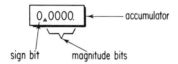

$\triangle$ is called the *machine point*. Its only purpose is to separate the sign bit from the magnitude bits. It is *not* used for separating the integral part from the fractional part.

. is called the *radix point* or *real point*. Its purpose is to separate the integral part from the fractional part.

These two points are not actually present in the machine. However, it is convenient to use them in this discussion for clarity. This "$\triangle$" convention will be used only temporarily while extreme clarity is desired. We will drop it for another convention shortly, and will return to it only occasionally when the subject warrants its use.

The value in the sign bit position may be either 1 or 0. If it is 0, the number in the accumulator is considered positive (plus). If it is 1, the number is considered negative (minus). In this 5 bit accumulator the number is contained in the rightmost 4 bits. The bits exclusive of the sign are often referred to as the *magnitude bits*.

There are two types of computer arithmetic which we will discuss eventually.

Fixed Point Arithmetic—In this type of arithmetic the *programmer* keeps track of where the real point is located.

Floating Point Arithmetic—In this type of arithmetic the *computer* keeps track of where the real point is located.

Both of these will be taken up in detail later in the text. In this chapter, we will be concerned only with fixed point arithmetic. Furthermore, for simplicity, we will consider in this chapter that the real point is located at the immediate right of the accumulator. In other words, we are only going to consider integers.

If the computer is instructed to place the value 5 in the accumulator, we can think of it as looking like this:

$$\boxed{0_\triangle 0101.}$$

Next, instructing the computer to add the value 3 to the value 5, which is currently in the accumulator, gives:

$$
\begin{array}{l}
0_\triangle 0101. = 5 \\
0_\triangle 0011. = 3 \\
\hline
0_\triangle 1000. = 8
\end{array}
$$

Were you able to add these two quantities in binary? You should be able to, as it is really very easy. The addition table in the binary number system is

$$
\begin{array}{l}
0 + 0 = 0 \\
1 + 0 = 1 \\
0 + 1 = 1 \\
1 + 1 = 10
\end{array}
$$

A more compact, but perhaps slightly confusing way of writing the table is

+	0	1
0	0	1
1	1	10

To compute $1 + 1$ using the latter table, locate the vertical column which has 1 in the top box. Then locate the horizontal row which has 1 in the left box. Where the column and row meet will be the result of $1 + 1$ which is 10.

Problem 2.18

Perform the addition of 7 and 2 in binary as a machine with a 5 bit accumulator would.

We have worked out an example as though we were the machine with the values of 5 and 3.

$$[+5]$$

The problem could have been written as $+[+3]$ where the leftmost sign specifies the operation to be performed.

Let us work out the following examples:

(a) $[+3]$ (b) $[+6]$ (c) $[-3]$ (d) $[+8]$
$\underline{-[+5]}$ $\underline{-[+6]}$ $\underline{+[+5]}$ $\underline{+[+8]}$

The results should prove to be quite interesting.

In example (a), the machine would be instructed to obtain the value 3 from its memory and place it into the accumulator. Then we would instruct the machine to subtract. We would inform it at the same time where to get the number it is to subtract.

The machine would electronically obtain this number from its electronic memory, automatically 1's complement it, and add it to the value in the accumulator.

Continuing with example (a):

$0_\wedge 0011. \longleftarrow \hspace{3cm} +3$
$\underline{1_\wedge 1010. \longleftarrow \hspace{1cm} \text{1's complement of } +5}$
$1_\wedge 1101. \longleftarrow \text{1's complement of 2, or } -2$

It is observed that our answer is negative as indicated by a 1 in the sign bit, and that is as it should be. The answer obtained by subtracting 5 from 3 should be -2. We note that in the magnitude of our answer we have the 1's complement of 2.

FACT: *In the Machine Under Consideration All Negative Numbers Will Have Their Magnitudes Represented in 1's Complement Form.*

This presents no problem whatsoever. However, the configuration of 0's and 1's that we find in the accumulator may be interpreted in essentially two different ways.

The $1_\wedge 1101$ of example (a) may represent a number, or it may represent what is called a *logically coded value*. In a logically coded value, each bit or group of bits represents something other than a number.

To illustrate a logically coded value, let us say that each bit position from left to right represents the condition of runways 1 through 5 respectively at an airfield. If the bit is a 1, it means the runway is open for traffic. If it is a 0, it means the runway is closed for traffic.

Thus our present configuration if coded logically as described above would signify:

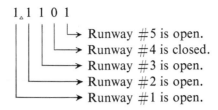

$1_\triangle 1\ 1\ 0\ 1$

→ Runway #5 is open.
→ Runway #4 is closed.
→ Runway #3 is open.
→ Runway #2 is open.
→ Runway #1 is open.

On the other hand, if $1_\triangle 1101.$ represents a number with the real point at the right, the number would be "-2."

It is seen that a negative number being in complement form is of little concern as regards logically coded values. Only if the configuration represents a number and the sign bit is 1 would we be interested in mentally complementing it to determine its magnitude. If we want the answer printed, we can write a computer program that would print $1_\triangle 1101.$ as -2.

$$[+6]$$
Performing the subtraction in example (b) of 6 from 6, or $-[+6]$ gives:

$$0_\triangle 0110.$$
$$1_\triangle 1001. \longleftarrow \text{1's complement of 6}$$
$$\overline{1_\triangle 1111}$$

Of course, 6 from 6 should be zero. Therefore, $1_\triangle 1111.$ is defined as zero. To differentiate between it and $0_\triangle 0000.$, the form with all 1's is called *Negative Zero*. The form with all 0's is called *Positive Zero*.

In mathematics, zero is not considered as either positive or negative. But with computers similar to the type we are studying, the two forms exist.

In numerical calculations positive zero and negative zero are considered equal. Each added to a number will give the number, etc.; the properties of a true zero are retained. However, it is clear that in an interpretation similar to the runway illustration negative zero and positive zero are worlds apart.

$$[-3]$$
Let us see what $+[+5]$ of example (c) will show us.

$$1_\triangle 1100. \qquad \text{representation of } -3 \text{ in computer}$$
$$0_\triangle 0101.$$
$$\overline{10_\triangle 0001.}$$

end-around-

$$\text{carry} \qquad \underline{1.}$$
$$0_\triangle 0010.$$

Note that the addition of the two numbers is done simply as if using two 5 bit numbers. Since a 1 is lost due to the modulus of the machine, the machine automatically adds 1 to the right by the process mentioned earlier called end-around-carry. It is seen that $0_\triangle 0010.$ or $+2$ is correct.

Next $\dfrac{[+8]}{+[+8]}$ of example (d) gives us:

$$0_\triangle 1000.$$
$$\underline{0_\triangle 1000.}$$
$$1_\triangle 0000.$$

It is to be observed that since there is a 1 in the sign bit, the answer is negative. But, how can adding two positive numbers result in a negative sum?

A little reflection shows that $8 + 8 = 16_{10}$ is too large for four magnitude bits.

$$16_{10} = 20_8 = 10000_2$$

Four magnitude bits of $1111_2 = 17_8 = 15_{10}$ show that 15_{10} is the largest magnitude that this 5 bit machine can handle. This condition—when the result is too large for the machine—is called *Overflow*. The machine can detect overflow automatically and notify us that it has happened by turning on an alarm. This alarm is usually just a neon light which can be tested by another computer instruction.

The computer is able to detect overflow because its circuitry can determine that the operation was addition, the two operands were positive, but the result was negative. Overflow can also result from adding two negative numbers together whose sum is too large for the machine. In this instance, the indication to the machine would be the adding to two negative numbers and getting a positive answer. No overflow can result from the addition of two numbers of opposite sign.

Problem 2.19

Consider the following as pertaining to an imaginary 5-bit accumulator:
1. What number in decimal does $0_\triangle 0101.$ represent? In octal?
2. What number in decimal does $1_\triangle 1011.$ represent? In octal?
3. What number in decimal does $0_\triangle 1110.$ represent? In octal?
4. What number in decimal does $1_\triangle 0000.$ represent? In octal?

The hypothetical machine to be studied in Chapter Five has a word length of 25 bits—one sign bit and 24 magnitude bits. Since it would be awkward to represent the word in binary, we will work with it mostly in octal.

25_{10} represented in the 25-bit machine in binary would appear as:

$$0_\triangle 0000000000000000000011001.$$

or in octal:

$$0_\triangle 00000031.$$

Notice that we have a mixture in the octal representation. The sign bit is binary and the rest is octal. This will present no problem, however.

Negative zero would be represented by $1_\triangle 77777777$.

Performing $\begin{array}{c}[-3]\\ +[+5]\end{array}$ gives:

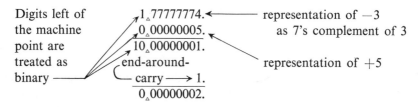

Digits left of the machine point are treated as binary

1$_\triangle$77777774. ←——— representation of -3 as 7's complement of 3

0$_\triangle$00000005. ←

10$_\triangle$00000001.

end-around-carry ——→ 1.

0$_\triangle$00000002.

representation of $+5$

Note that this is octal arithmetic and two octal numbers are being added. Thus $4_8 + 5_8 = 11_8$. A 1 is written down and 1 is carried. The carried 1 added to the 7_8 makes 10_8, etc.

I find it easiest when adding two rows of octal numbers to add the respective two digits in decimal and then if the sum of the two is 8 or greater, I add 2 to get the octal equivalent for the pair. Carries are handled normally. For example:

$$\begin{array}{r} 67_8 \\ 31_8 \\ \hline 120_8 \end{array}$$

Here 7 and 1 make 8 in decimal, hence adding 2 gives 10_8, whereby I write down the 0 and carry 1. The 6 and 3 and carry of 1 make a decimal 10, hence, adding the 2 gives 12, which is written down.

An alternate procedure would be to use the following octal addition table. Its use would be similar to that which was explained for the binary addition table.

+	0	1	2	3	4	5	6	7
0	0	1	2	3	4	5	6	7
1	1	2	3	4	5	6	7	10
2	2	3	4	5	6	7	10	11
3	3	4	5	6	7	10	11	12
4	4	5	6	7	10	11	12	13
5	5	6	7	10	11	12	13	14
6	6	7	10	11	12	13	14	15
7	7	10	11	12	13	14	15	16

Problem 2.20

1. Perform the following additions in octal:

    321750   123453
    342327   460637

2. Perform the following additions as a 25 bit machine would:

    $1_\triangle77773264.$ $1_\triangle77774072.$
    $0_\triangle00006577.$ $1_\triangle77777354.$

Up to now we have indicated the machine point by a △, but henceforth a period (.) will be used as the machine point. We will use a period except in a few isolated and obvious instances where the teaching of some concept requires a △ for clarity. However, the sole purpose of the machine point will still remain that of separating the sign bit and magnitude bits. We will not ordinarily indicate the real point (which separates integral and fractional parts).

Problem 2.21

1. Any number with an exponent of zero has a numerical value of _____.
2. A number system to the base N will contain _____ different symbols.
3. Shifting the radix point one place to the right in a number in the decimal system is equivalent to multiplying the number by _____.
4. Shifting the radix point three places to the left in a number in the decimal system is equivalent to _____ the number by _____.
5. Shifting the radix point one place to the right in a number in the binary system is equivalent to _____ the number by _____.
6. Shifting the radix point three places to the left in a number in the binary system is equivalent to _____ the number by _____.

35

7. Shifting the radix point two places to the left in a number in the octal system is equivalent to dividing the number by _____ .

8. When converting from the octal to the binary number system, there is a direct relationship between _____ digit(s) in the octal system and _____ digit(s) in the binary system.

9. What is a disadvantage of a number system with a high base? a low base?

10. Why is the binary system applicable to computers?

11. Perform the following additions in binary:

$$
\begin{array}{cc}
0010110 & 101101 \\
0101011 & 000011 \\
\hline
\end{array}
$$

_____

Problem 2.22

Miscellaneous problems dealing with theory of number systems.

1. Discuss a unitary system.

$$
\begin{array}{l}
1 \\
11 \\
111 \\
1111 \\
11111
\end{array}
$$

   (a) What would .111 equal?

   (b) How about $+1$?
   $$\underline{-1}$$

2. If state license plate numbers are represented by LLLDDD, where L stands for "letter" and D stands for "digit,"
   (a) What is the modulus?
   (b) How many more plates can be represented than by just DDDDDD?
   (c) How many plates can be represented if the 3 letter positions can vary throughout the six positions?

3. Using a literal base (the symbols run from A through Z, with A as 0 (zero), B as 1, C as 2, etc.),
   (a) What in decimal is the number CEG?
   (b) Convert 12248_{10} to a number in the literal base.

4. Change 701_8 to decimal by dividing by 12_8 using octal arithmetic.

5. A finite sequence of general form 3^0, 3^1, 3^2, 3^3, ... etc. has several of its terms missing. If the sum of the terms present is 62058, which of the powers of 3 are present?

6. In a number system to the base 15_{10}, what decimal number would the highest order symbol represent?

7. Is it necessary to have the same base in each position in a number system? Discuss the matter and give an example or two.

8. Find the integral square root of 29_r and the radix r.

9. Prove that 36_r for any integer r cannot be prime.

CHAPTER THREE

Data Representation and Organization

I. CODING OF INFORMATION ON CARDS AND TAPE

Most (or at least much) of the input to a computer, and most of the output from a computer, is through either cards or magnetic tape. Since much of the input and output is of an alphabetic nature, a method is needed for representing letters, numbers, and punctuation-like characters by configurations of 0's and 1's. This is because, as we recall, the computer will be working with 0's and 1's internally.

Alphabetic and numeric characters are frequently referred to as *alphanumeric characters*. Letters, numbers, and punctuation-like data are referred to as *hollerith characters*. The coding by 0's and 1's, which we will discuss, is called *hollerith code*.

There are two forms of this code: *12-bit hollerith code* and *6-bit hollerith code*. The former is used mainly for representation of hollerith characters on data processing cards. The latter is used mainly for representation of hollerith characters on magnetic tape or in the computer memory.

The name "12-bit hollerith code" derives from the fact that 12 bit positions are used to represent each character. The name "6-bit hollerith code" derives from the fact that 6 bits are used to represent each character. Why there are two different hollerith codes is not clear, as six bits are certainly sufficient to represent all of the necessary characters.

The history of punched cards is quite fascinating. An excellent write-up on it occurs in the Dover book on Babbage mentioned previously.

Punched-card use came into its own with the weaving industry in England. Babbage then adapted them for use in his computing machines. Later, in 1880, an employee of the United States Census Bureau named Herman Hollerith used them in census work. It is his name that was given to the coded characters.

There are methods other than the hollerith code for encoding information of alphanumeric and punctuation-like data. One is called the USA Standard Code for Information Interchange (USASCII); another is the Extended Binary Coded Decimal Interchange Code (EBCDIC). However, the 6-bit hollerith code and the 12-bit hollerith code are the two we will discuss.

The standard data processing card is a 12 by 80 array of bit positions—12 rows and 80 columns. The columns are numbered left to right—1 through 80. The rows are rather arbitrarily numbered as shown.

Columns 1 through 80

Rows 12, 11, and 0 are frequently referred to as *zones*. Thus, we might speak of the 11 zone of column 6 as being punched (containing a hole). The remaining rows (1 through 9) are referred to as *numeric* rows.

All alphabetic characters have one zone punch and one numeric punch. Numbers have the corresponding numeric row only punched. 0 (zero) has the zero zone only punched. Some punctuation marks and special characters require three punches.

The following card illustrates the coded characters:

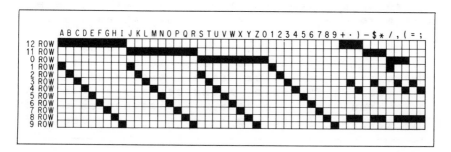

A shaded rectangle stands for a punched hole. From the illustration we see that to represent an A in a column the column requires a punch in row 12 and row 1. Cards are punched by typewriter-like machines called *key punches*.

Since it is somewhat difficult to read the punches on a card, the following chart is included for interpreting the code.

The 12 by 80 array can be partitioned by lines between groups of columns as desired and thus areas called *fields* can be created on the card. The fields can be given headings for ease of human interpretation.

A computer can obtain the information from the card (or a deck of these cards) by connecting up electrically with a machine called a *card reader*.

Problem 3.1

What message in 12-bit hollerith is contained on the following card?

Hint: The first word in the message is HELP.

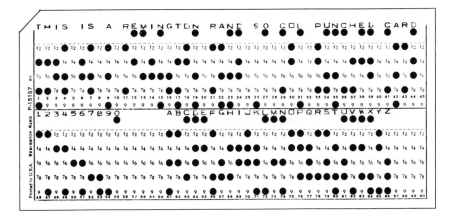

We will be interested only with 12-bit hollerith cards, but as an aside it is interesting to note that one computer manufacturer has employed punched cards using a 6-bit code and round holes.

A 6-bit hollerith code (frequently called BCI for Binary Coded Information) as was mentioned earlier, is used for storing hollerith character information on magnetic tape or in the computer memory.

Magnetic tapes are used for input and output. They may also be used to increase computer memory capacity. The magnetic tape comes on reels of 10½ inch diameter in lengths of 1200 feet or 2400 feet. This is approximately a quarter-mile and half-mile respectively.

Fourteen million characters can be written on a 2400 ft. length of tape. This is about the same quantity of information as would be contained in a stack of data processing cards over 100 feet high.

6-Bit Hollerith Code

Character	6-Bit Representation	Octal Equivalent	Character	6-Bit Representation	Octal Equivalent
0	000000	00	A	010001	21
1	000001	01	B	010010	22
2	000010	02	C	010011	23
3	000011	03	D	010100	24
4	000100	04	E	010101	25
5	000101	05	F	010110	26
6	000110	06	G	010111	27
7	000111	07	H	011000	30
8	001000	10	I	011001	31
9	001001	11	J	100001	41
=	001011	13	K	100010	42
,	111011	73	L	100011	43
$	101011	53	M	100100	44
.	011011	33	N	100101	45
+	010000	20	O	100110	46
—	100000	40	P	100111	47
*	101100	54	Q	101000	50
/	110001	61	R	101001	51
'	001100	14	S	110010	62
(	111100	74	T	110011	63
)	011100	34	U	110100	64
Blank	110000	60	V	110101	65
			W	110110	66
			X	110111	67
			Y	111000	70
			Z	111001	71

The tape itself is made of plastic and is coated with a substance containing magnetic oxide. The tape is $\frac{1}{2}$ inch wide and greatly resembles the tape found on tape recorders. The reel of tape is mounted on a machine called a *tape drive*.

As the computer obtains information from a tape or records information on a tape, the tape is wound on an empty reel on the drive. A tape may be used over and over again just as the tape on a tape recorder.

On tape the word "Rose" would appear as something like this:

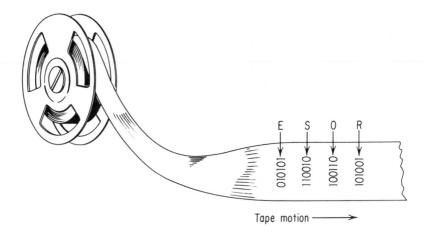

Tape motion ⟶

Each vertical column of 6 bits represents a code found in the 6-bit hollerith code table.

Here the assumption is that the tape is moving from left to right. The 1's are actually little patches of magnetic tape magnetized with the north pole of the magnetized patch pointing in one direction, while the 0's are patches which are unmagnetized. There are a few other bits associated with each vertical column on the tape which are not pictured above. They are used for control purposes.

If it were desired to represent the word "Rose" in the accumulator of a hypothetical computer of 25-bit word length, it would look like this:

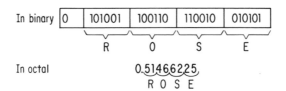

It is necessary to point out that cards and tapes can contain information which is not in hollerith coded form, but rather binary. The 25-bit word of the hypothetical computer, for example, can be stored as such on a card or tape. The binary format found on cards will be discussed in Chapter 5 in the section concerning assembler output. The binary format found on tapes will be discussed in Chapter Seven which explains tape programming for the EX-1 computer.

II. DATA ORGANIZATION IN MAGNETIC CORE STORAGE

An extremely important component in our typical computer, the EX-1, is *magnetic core storage*. Magnetic core storage is the primary memory of the computer. This is because a program must be in magnetic core storage in order to operate. Data must also be there in order to be processed. Magnetic tapes are an example of secondary or auxiliary storage. Data merely resides there until needed in magnetic core storage for processing.

Magnetic core storage is composed of small donut-shaped beads strung on thin wires. These beads are called *cores* and are made of material which is easily magnetized. The computer can magnetize a core in one direction and thus store a 1, or it can magnetize the core in the opposite direction and store a 0.

storing 1 bit   storing 0 bit

A group of these cores is connected together and given an address. Each group is called a *core memory location*. Each core memory location can hold either a computer instruction or data. The contents of a core memory location is referred to as a *core memory word*.

Magnetic core storage is often referred to as *random* access storage. This is because the contents of any core memory location can be obtained directly without being concerned with other core memory locations. This is not true of data on tape or cards. To obtain a specific piece of data from tape or cards the computer must wait for all of the data which precedes the desired data to pass by. These involve sequential access.

The EX-1 contains 777_8 core memory locations and each location consists of 25 cores or bit positions. The registers are numbered 000 through 776_8. Register 777_8 is a special type and will be explained later in the text. Although physically appearing much different than the following, the magnetic core storage for the EX-1 can be considered as logically made up as in the table on the following page.

Programmers organize the data which is to be processed into "tables, entries, and items." These have a meaning very similar to what they mean in non-computer work. For example, we all have a pretty good idea of what a table on an income tax form is.

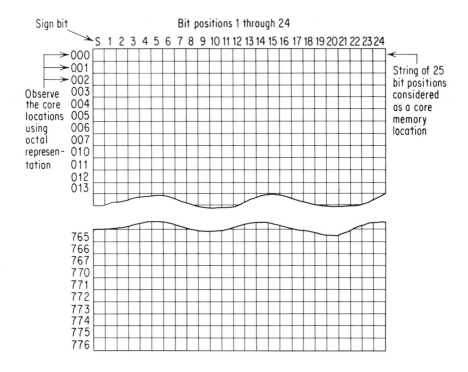

Items—An *item* is a piece of information. For the EX-1 it may be contained in a space of from 1 to 25 bit-positions, however, it may not be split between two core memory locations.

An item has a *name* with which to refer to it. It also has a *value* contained in it. For our purposes the item name will consist of 1 descriptive word in capital letters. It will be not less than 2 letters nor more than 5.

An item called AGE might have the value 16_{10} in it. (Item names and table names will be indicated by all capital letters.)

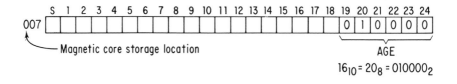

Here I have allocated 6 bits of space for the item (bit positions 19 through 24). This item would be able to contain ages only up to 77_8 or 63_{10}.

Problem 3.2

Design an item which is to represent pennies. Allow enough space to hold an amount as large as $2.00.
1. What name have you given to the item?
2. How many bit positions have you allocated to it?
3. What bit positions did you give it?

Items may be coded in several different ways. They may contain *numbers*, as was the case with item AGE; they may be coded *logically;* or they may be coded in *6-bit hollerith*. There are also other ways that they may be coded but these three are the main ones.

To code AGE logically we might decide that the 4 age groups 0–15, 16–30, 31–45, and 46–63 would be suitable for our purposes. We could logically code these 4 age groups using 2-bit positions thus:

$$00 \text{ represents } 0\text{–}15 \text{ years}$$
$$01 \text{ represents } 16\text{–}30 \text{ years}$$
$$10 \text{ represents } 31\text{–}45 \text{ years}$$
$$11 \text{ represents } 46\text{–}63 \text{ years}$$

Each of the possible conditions of a logically coded item is referred to as a *status*. Therefore, AGE as we have coded it logically has 4 statuses (0–15 years, 16–30, years, 31–45 years, and 46–63 years).

Quite often each status is given a name. For example, an item called COLOR might have the six statuses: RED, GREEN, YELLOW, PURPLE, WHITE, and BLACK.

Problem 3.3

Design a status type item which is to represent school grades from A through F.
1. What name have you given to the item?
2. How many bit positions have you allocated to it?
3. What bit positions did you give it?
4. Show the correpondence between each grade and the number you have assigned it.

To code AGE in 6-bit hollerith we might represent an age of 10_{10} as follows:

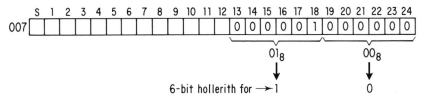

or:

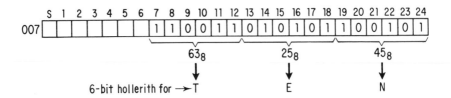

An item may occupy an entire core memory word or just a portion of a word. If several different items are small enough, we may place them all in one computer memory word, thus:

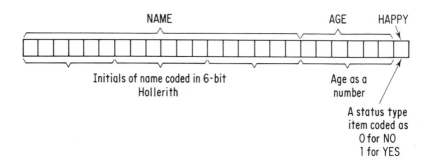

When items are compact in a core memory word as above, we say the items are *packed*. When we have only 1 item per computer memory word and it does not fill the word, we say the items are *not packed*. Packing is designed to save magnetic core storage space. However, packing makes programming more complicated—at least at the intermediate level of programming languages.

Entries—A group of items associated with one object is referred to as an *entry*. The 3 items NAME, AGE, and HAPPY could represent information about an individual and could be considered an entry. An entry can occupy 1 core memory word, or it may occupy several.

Tables—Several entries pertaining to similar objects form a *table*. A table is a collection of related entries. The entries are referred to by an entry number. These numbers start with 0. We will give each table a name. It will consist of 5 letters. The name will also represent the starting address of the table. We will use this fact later in processing tables with a computer program.

Let us summarize by describing a table called EMPLS which contains information on employees at a certain company. The information pertaining to each employee makes up an entry. Let us have 4 items to describe each employee. Let them be

NAME—The employee's initials in 6-bit hollerith in bit positions 1 through 24.

SALRY—The employee's salary coded as a number representing dollars.

AGE—The employee's age coded as a number representing years.

HAPPY—The employee's outlook coded as a status item with 0 meaning not happy and 1 meaning happy.

Our table might look as follows:

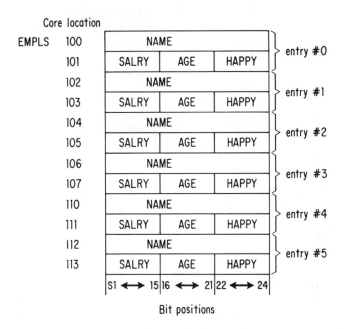

This table contains data about 6 employees. The table name EMPLS represents 100_8 which is the starting address of the table. The table contains 6 entries and each entry consists of the 4 items NAME, SALRY, AGE, and HAPPY. Each entry occupies 2 core memory locations.

When discussing an item in a particular entry we can use an index factor. An *index factor* is a number or letter which is attached as a subscript to an item name and it represents the entry number.

Thus $SALRY_3$ refers to the item SALRY in entry 3. The 3 is the index factor.

An index factor may also be a letter. When it is a letter it represents a *variable index factor;* that is, one which can take on different values.

For example, $SALRY_i$ where i takes on all values from 1 through 5 represents each item SALRY depending upon the value of i at a particular time.

Problem 3.4

Given the format for table EMPLS and that it contains the following contents in octal:

Core location	Octal contents
100	0.00212545
101	0.00300261
102	0.00664770
103	0.00325270
104	0.00412623
105	0.00275301
106	0.00506321
107	0.00360321
110	0.00306427
111	0.00470340
112	0.00417126
113	0.00524421

1. What are the initials of each employee?
2. Is HUG happy?
3. How much money is represented in $SALRY_4$?
4. What age is represented in AGE_1?
5. Which contains the larger amount, $SALRY_0$ or $SALRY_2$?
6. What age is represented in AGE_i if i is 4?
7. What would the combined salary of $SALRY_i$ and $SALRY_{i+1}$ be when i is 1? When i is 3?
8. Are more employees happy than unhappy?
9. What are the initials of the oldest employee?

We see that tables are composed of entries and that entries consist of items. All items, however, are not in tables. Sometimes it is advantageous to have a single item which is not in a table. An item which is to contain a tally or sum might be an example of a single item.

Our discussion of data organization has been far from exhaustive.

Furthermore, we have not discussed such types of auxiliary storage as magnetic drums or discs. Many computers employ these as storage devices; however, sufficient groundwork has been established for us to proceed toward our goal—to write some computer programs.

CHAPTER FOUR

Flow Diagramming

Flow diagrams are commonplace in many areas of man's endeavor. They are used in chemistry, physics, business, and in a myriad of other areas.

In computer programming the flow diagram is very important. A flow diagram serves several purposes in programming, but the primary use is for the development of the logic in the solution of a problem.

Therefore, a programmer who has a problem to solve by means of a computer program would first study the problem, make a flow diagram of a solution, and finally write the computer program using the logic evident in the flow diagram.

A good flow diagram is usually more than half the battle won. However, a good flow diagram, which can be used to program from easily, is not easy to make. For the beginner this type of diagram is especially difficult to create.

This is because, in order to make a flow diagram which can be programmed from easily, one must know some of the details and techniques of programming; yet, the techniques and a good computer program depend upon a good flow diagram. We need to break into this circle somewhere, and flow diagramming without a knowledge of programming seems to be as good a place as any.

The following illustration is of a non-computer oriented flow diagram. It demonstrates a solution by a student of how to spend a Saturday evening.

Let us now apply flow diagrams to programming problems.

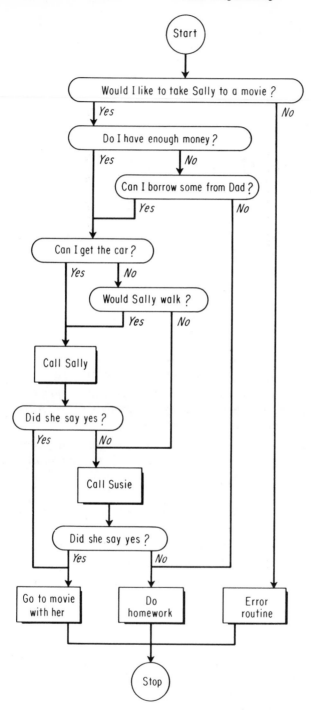

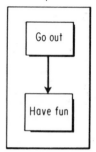

Oversimplification

Illustrative example

We wish to make a flow diagram for a program which will set an item
PRODT to the product of the contents of items MCAND and MLIER. We
will assume that items MCAND and MLIER contain positive integers or
zero. Furthermore, we will assume that the multiplication cannot be done
directly, but will need to be achieved by repeated addition. I am placing this
latter restriction in order to make the solution more educational than would
otherwise be the case.

Core memory

MCAND	2
MLIER	3
PRODT	

What we have then is a situation analogous
to the figure at the left. If, for example,
item MCAND contains 2 and item MLIER
contains 3, then our flow diagram is for a
program that should set item PRODT to 6.

By trial and error we can come up with the following possible solution:

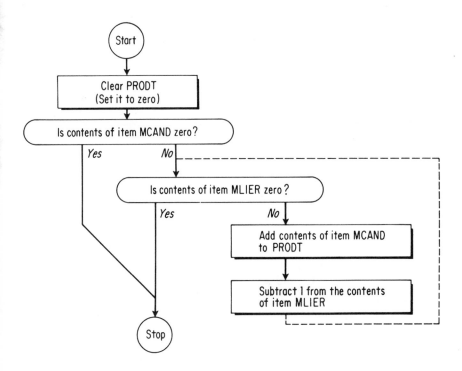

There are several points to observe. First of all, the flow could have been drawn equally well in a horizontal position as well as in the vertical one. Note that decision boxes are sausage shaped. Only one line enters each box and each line terminates with an arrowhead. If two lines go to the same box, they join first and then enter.

Questions are posed inside of decision boxes which generally require an answer of yes or no. This is not always true, as some decision boxes may have more than two exits. For example, a box might use exits of greater than, equal to, or less than.

Dash lines are used in small flows to indicate a return flow.

The flow should be done using English and mathematical symbols rather than specific machine instructions. It should be readable by someone other than the person who created it.

Next we should test out the logic of the flow diagram by running through representative input values to see if we get expected output values. Completing the following *test matrix* should help.

Input values		Expected Output	Actual Output
MCAND	MLIER	PRODT	PRODT
0	2	0	
2	0	0	
2	3	6	
4	1	4	

It is important to include unusual values such as 0 and 1 in our testing. Sometimes a solution that works with most values will fail for special values.

Let us run through the trial for 2 in MCAND and 3 in MLIER and see if the result is a 6 in PRODT.

The first box in the flow diagram sets PRODT to zero. This *initializes* PRODT so that we are assured of it containing zero. The undesirable number which may be in PRODT before initializing is referred to as *garbage* in programming jargon.

MCAND	2
MLIER	3
PRODT	0

MCAND	2
MLIER	3
PRODT	2

Since MCAND contains 2 and MLIER contains 3 the answer to the first two decision boxes is "no." Next, adding MCAND to PRODT results in a 2 in PRODT.

MCAND	2
MLIER	2̸3̸
PRODT	2

A value of 1 is subtracted from MLIER and a return along the dash line is made to ask the question again: "Is the contents of item MLIER zero?"

MCAND	2
MLIER	1̸2̸3̸
PRODT	4

The "no" answer causes us to add MCAND to PRODT again to get 4 in PRODT, and to subtract 1 from MLIER to get 1 in MLIER. A return is then made again along the dash line.

MCAND	2
MLIER	0̸1̸2̸3̸
PRODT	6

The last iteration is made and **PRODT** now has 6 in it while MLIER has been reduced to zero. This time control goes to "Stop" after asking the question "Is the contents of item MLIER zero?"

Thus, it appears that the logic of the solution as shown in the flow diagram is correct, provided it still holds up with the other test values.

Flow diagramming is perhaps the most creative aspect of computer programming: There is no "formula" that can be applied to come up with the solution logic. The flow diagram solution is arrived at by trial and error, insight, magic, and you-name-it. Creating flow diagrams is probably as much, if not more, of an art than it is a science.

To prevent you from getting discouraged, however, it should be kept in mind that experience and knowledge of program coding will make flow diagramming easier. At the present you are most likely lacking these two factors.

Getting back to our solution of the multiplication problem, there are some points to discuss. First, there is more than one way to satisfy the problem requirements. We might, for example, choose to eliminate the first decision box ("Is the contents of item MCAND zero".) The solution would still be satisfactory. Either solution might be the better and more efficient one, depending upon the probability of input item MCAND containing zero.

Secondly, our solution is destroying the original contents of item MLIER. Under some circumstances it may be disastrous to do so—for example, if another program expects to use it.

Also, a more sophisticated program might determine which was larger, MCAND or MLIER, and add up the larger number the fewer number of times. This would reduce the number of iterations through which the program would need to go. It would be more efficient to add up 1000 three times than to add up 3 a thousand times. Determining which was larger, however, would add a few more steps to our program.

The above are all considerations that a programmer might take into account. A good programmer should consider all of the alternatives and ramifications and then make a decision based on what he thinks is best.

Problem 4.1

Given a value of 7 in item ALPHA, what would result in item BETA if the logic of the flow diagram shown below is applied?

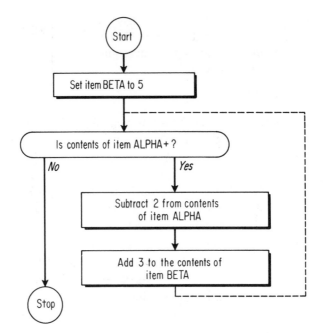

Problem 4.2

Given an item called DIVND and one called DVSOR, each of which contains a positive whole number (DIVND can be zero), and assuming a computer which possesses only the arithmetic operations of addition and subtraction (not multiplication and division), make a flow diagram of a program which will obtain the integer quotient of DIVND divided by DVSOR and place it into item QUTNT. Place the integer remainder into item REMAN.

Let me clarify terms with an example:

$$
\begin{array}{r}
5 \text{ quotient} \\
3 \overline{\smash{)}17} \text{ dividend} \\
\text{divisor } 15 \\
\hline
2 \text{ remainder}
\end{array}
$$

In other words, given 17 in item DIVND and 3 in item DVSOR, your flow diagram should result in getting 5 in item QUTNT and 2 in item REMAN.

After making your flow diagram, test it with the following text matrix.

Inputs		Expected Outputs		Actual Outputs	
DIVND	DVSOR	QUTNT	REMAN	QUTNT	REMAN
7	2	3	1		
6	3	2	0		
2	3	0	2		
0	2	0	0		
3	3	1	0		

Problem 4.3

Given a positive integer (or zero) in a single item called NUMBR, make a flow diagram for a program that will set item TYPE to EVEN if the number in NUMBR is even. Otherwise, set item TYPE to ODD.

Note: A number is even if it is divisible by 2 without a remainder. However, for this problem assume that we cannot divide. Also assume that we *cannot* ask the following questions:

Is contents of item NUMBR even?		Is contents of item NUMBR odd?	
No	*Yes*	*No*	*Yes*

Be sure to test your flow diagram. Try numbers like 0, 1, 2, 3, 4, and 5 in item NUMBR.

Next, let us apply flow diagramming to the processing of a table.

Illustrative Example

We wish to make a flow diagram for a program which will count how many positive numbers are contained in a table called TABLE. TABLE contains 4 entries and each entry contains the item NUMBR. The count will be kept in a single item called COUNT. All of the items occupy a full computer memory word.

We must be sure that COUNT initially contains zero, since adding 1 to anything which might happen to be in COUNT would result in an invalid count. This is the reason for the box containing "Clear COUNT." It means that COUNT is to be set to zero.

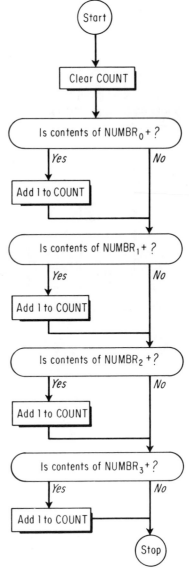

S 1 2 3 4 5 6 7 8 9 10 11 12 13 14 15 16 17 18 19 20 21 22 23 24

| $NUMBR_0$ |
| $NUMBR_1$ |
| $NUMBR_2$ |
| $NUMBR_3$ |

| COUNT |

It should be observed in the flow just made that there is much that is repeated. If we had many more entires to examine for positive numbers, our flow would be quite long.

A much better flow is the following:

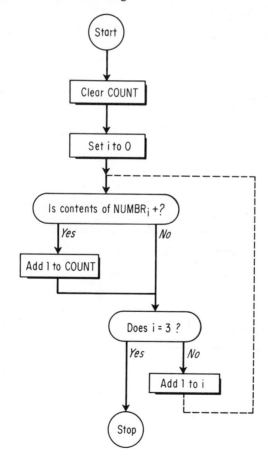

Above is the way an experienced programmer might flow the solution to the problem. Dash lines are used in small flows to indicate a return flow.

Note that on the 1st encounter of the 1st decision box i would be 0 and thus entry 0 of NUMBR would be examined. On the second encounter i would be 1 and therefore entry 1 of NUMBR would be examined. This would continue for i = 2, and i = 3.

These iterations are referred to as *looping* and each trip through the loop is called a *pass*.

The following flow solves the same problem and in some respects is more general. It will handle any number of entries:

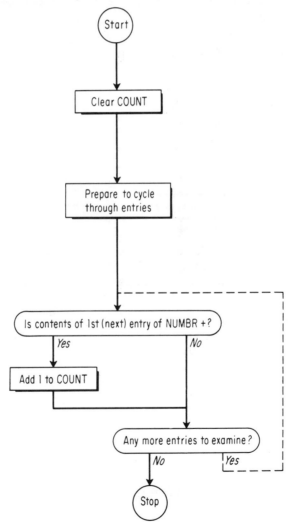

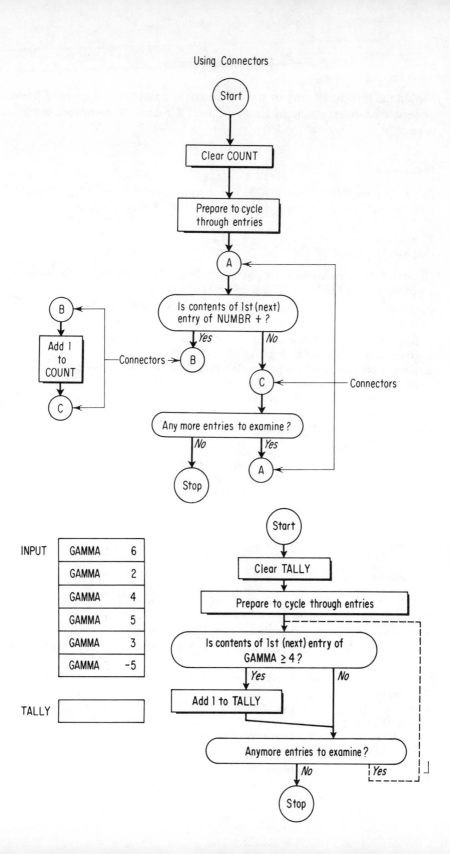

Using Connectors

Start

Clear COUNT

Prepare to cycle
through entries

A

Is contents of 1st (next)
entry of NUMBR + ?

Yes   No

B   C

B   ——Connectors——→

Add 1
to
COUNT

C

Any more entries to examine?

No   Yes

Stop   A

Connectors

INPUT

GAMMA	6
GAMMA	2
GAMMA	4
GAMMA	5
GAMMA	3
GAMMA	-5

TALLY

Start

Clear TALLY

Prepare to cycle through entries

Is contents of 1st (next) entry of
GAMMA ≥ 4 ?

Yes   No

Add 1 to TALLY

Anymore entries to examine?

No   Yes

Stop

Should the flow be lengthy or tend to be confused because of crossing lines or long dash-lines, connectors may be used for simplification. (See top of page 59.)

Problem 4.4

Given the table INPUT shown below, what will be the contents of item TALLY if the logic of the flow diagram shown is applied? (See bottom of page 59.)

Problem 4.5

Given: A table called ALPHA containing 99 entries. Each entry consists of a 1-word item called BETA. BETA is coded as a number.

Required: Make a flow diagram of a program which will examine each entry of item BETA and act as follows:

1. Keep a count in a single item called ZEROS of the number of entries which contain either positive or negative zero.
2. Keep a count in a single item called POSTV of the number of entries which contain non-zero positive numbers.
3. Keep a count in a single item called NEGTV of the number of entries which contain non-zero negative numbers.

Note: A typical decision box might be:

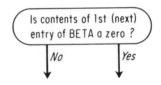

Problem 4.6

Given: A table called FIXUP containing entries of a full word item called NUMBR. NUMBR is coded as a number.

Required: Make a flow diagram for a program which will:

1. Add 1 to the contents of each entry of NUMBR which contains a number that is both even and positive.
2. Add 2 to the contents of each entry of NUMBR which contains a number that is both even and negative.
3. Add 3 to the contents of each entry of NUMBR which contains a number that is both odd and positive.
4. Add 4 to the contents of each entry of NUMBR which contains a number that is both odd and negative.

Use only the following 11 boxes in your flow:

Add 1 to contents of NUMBR	Add 2 to contents of NUMBR	Add 3 to contents of NUMBR	Add 4 to contents of NUMBR

Is contents of 1st (next) entry of NUMBR even ?

Is contents of 1st (next) entry of NUMBR + ?

Stop

Is contents of 1st (next) entry of NUMBR odd ?

Finished examining all entries ?

Start

Prepare to cycle through all entries of table FIXUP

Note: By specifying the exact boxes to use in your flow diagram for this problem, I am simplifying one aspect of the solution—namely, your wording. You will note that this restricts the order in which you use the boxes. To illustrate this, try solving the above problem in several ways, using your own wording. You will be surprised at the variety of solutions possible.

Problem 4.7

Given: A table called RANDY consisting of 20_{10} entries. Each entry consists of a full word item called NUMBR coded as a number.

Required: Make a flow diagram for a program which will search the table for the smallest number and place it in the single item WEEST. Assume that only two numbers can be compared at a time.

Problem 4.8

Given: A table called MIXUP consisting of 5 entries. Each entry consists of a full word item called NUMBR coded as a number.

Required: Make a flow diagram for a program which will arrange the table so that the numbers are in ascending order (smallest at top, next largest next, etc.).

Note: It may be of help to realize that a table is completely ordered if, and only if, the contents of each adjacent pair of entries satisfies the pertinent ordering relationship.

Problem 4.9

Given: A table called RNDOM consisting of entries of item NUMBR. NUMBR is a full word item and is coded as a number. It will always contain a non-zero positive number.

Required: Make a flow diagram of a program which will keep a count of how many of the numbers in RNDOM are prime. Keep the count in single item COUNT.

Note: A prime number is a positive integer (other than 1) which is divisible only by 1 and itself without a remainder. Some examples of primes are 2, 3, 5, 7, 11, 13, 17, 19, 23, etc. In this problem we cannot simply ask "Is the number prime?" in a decision box. Rather, assume a given register called ONE which contains the value 1 and divide the number being examined by 1, 2, 3, etc., checking the remainder each time.

Problem 4.10

(This problem may take a little time to understand but it is an excellent exercise in flow diagramming.)

Assume the existence of two tables, one called EORWT (for east or west) and the other called NORST (for north or south). The item in EORWT is called EWDIS (for east or west distance). The item in NORST is called NSDIS (for north or south distance). Each item is coded as a signed number.

EWDIS contains the distance in miles that an aircraft is east or west of a given airport. If EWDIS contains a positive number, the aircraft is east of the airport. If EDWIS contains a negative number, the aircraft is west of the airport. The magnitude of the number tells the distance in miles east or west.

The *corresponding entry* of item NSDIS contains the distance in miles north or south that the *same* aircraft is from the airport. If NSDIS contains a positive number, the aircraft is north of the airport. If NSDIS contains a negative number, the aircraft is south of the airport. The magnitude of the number tells the distance in miles north or south.

To illustrate this further, let us look at the following specific situation:

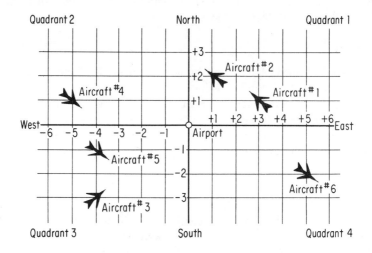

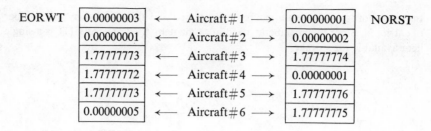

The problem is to make a flow diagram for a program which will keep the following 4 counts but only for aircraft which are within or on a 10-mile square whose center is at the airport:

1. Single item QUADA is to contain a count of the number of aircraft which are in the 1st quadrant. (east and north)
2. Single item QUADB is to contain a count of the number of aircraft which are in the 2nd quadrant. (west and north)
3. Single item QUADC is to contain a count of the number of aircraft which are in the 3rd quadrant. (west and south)
4. Single item QUADD is to contain a count of the number of aircraft which are in the 4th quadrant. (east and south)

Note: Assume only one item at a time can be examined in a decision box. For example, two decision boxes might be like those shown below:

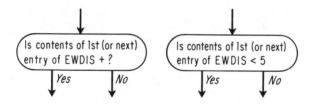

It should be made clear that the specific example given for 6 aircraft was for illustration purposes only. The required flow diagram does not know which quadrant any of the aircraft are in. It should be able to handle tables EORWT and NORST of any size.

Problem 4.11

The accompanying flow diagram is supposed to solve the problem below. Does it do the job? If not, why not?

Compute the arithmetic mean (average) of the numbers stored in entries of item NUMBR of table TABLE. Exclude from consideration those entries in which item NUMBR contains zero. If the contents of every item NUMBR is zero, indicate this in single item ALZER. The possibility that the sum of any pair of numbers in the table may exceed the capacity of the accumulator must be taken into account.

In other words, a total sum cannot be obtained and this divided by the number of entries N. Store the arithmetic mean in single item AVRAG. ZRCNT is a single item available for storage.

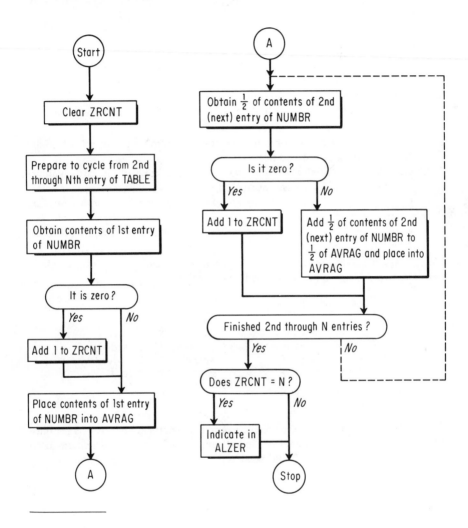

Problem 4.12

Make your own flow diagram for Problem 4.11 and test the solution with a sample table.

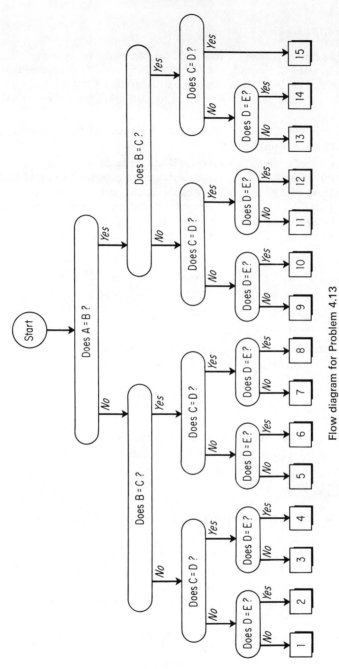

Flow diagram for Problem 4.13

Problem 4.13

A man has five cards (from a deck of 52 playing cards) symbolically labelled Card A, Card B, Card C, Card D, and Card E. His five cards are ordered from low to high; that is, Card A is the lowest of the five cards and Card E is the highest of the five cards. Adjacent cards may be equal to each other and the suit of the card is immaterial.

Complete the flow diagram on page 65 by placing one of the six possible symbolic values into boxes 1 through 15:

4KND (Four of a Kind). . . . . .Four cards are the same
FHSE (Full-house). . . . . .Three cards are the same and two cards are the same
3KND (Three of a Kind). . . .Three cards are the same
2PAR (Two pair). . . . . .Two cards are the same and two others also
1PAR (One pair) . . . . .Two cards are the same
NONE (Nothing). . . . . .None of the above conditions exist

Illustrative example

The flow diagram on page 67 illustrates formula calculation for all possible permutations of the variables.

A, B, C, and D are variables which contain integer values which may range from 0 to 5. Calculate

$$X = \frac{A - 2B}{3D + C + 1}$$

for all possible permutations of the variables. Store each possible value of X into item XNUMB in successive entries of table ALPHA.

Problem 4.14

Make a flow diagram for a program which will compute each value of X where

$$X = \frac{2A + 3B}{5C + D + E + 1}$$

A, B, C, and D can each represent the values 0, 2, 4, 6, and 8. E can vary in integer values from 1 to 3 inclusive. Store each value computed into item XNUMB in successive entries of table ALPHA.

One box in your solution may read: $XNUMB_i = \dfrac{2A + 3B}{5C + D + E + 1}$

The purpose of this problem is to test your ability to vary A, B, C, D, and E in an ordered manner so that all values of X are computed.

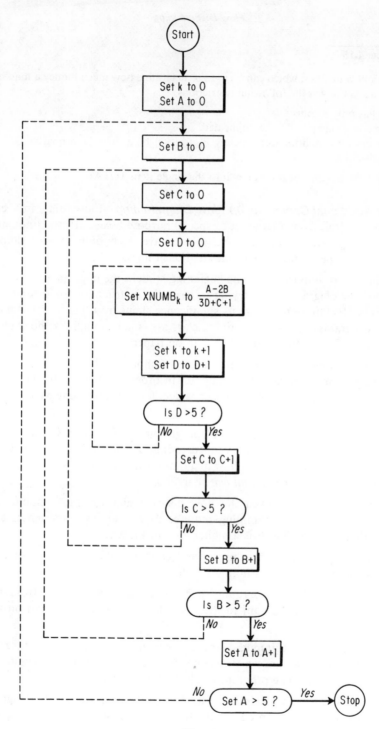

Problem 4.15

Make a flow diagram which can be used to determine how much money a man has in his pocket, given the following restrictions:

1. He has only 3 coins.
2. The coins may possibly be duplicated.
3. The coin possibilities are: a penny P, a nickel N, a dime D, a quarter Q, and a half-dollar H.

Set the total amount of his money into the single item TOTAL.

Some Additional Comments on Flow Diagramming—Flow diagrams can employ symbols from a large set of special purpose boxes, arrows, lines, and other configurations. For simplicity, we have used only sausage-shaped boxes, rectangles, circles, solid lines and dash lines.

It is difficult to impress upon the beginning student the importance of drawing the flow diagram before trying to write the instructions for a computer program. His failure to realize its significance stems from the fact that most of the programs written in a training class are small enough for the student to have the flow in his head rather than on paper.

When the problem to program becomes complex and large, the student finds that he must make a flow diagram in order to proceed. In the initial stages of learning he almost always considers flow diagramming as an added encumbrance.

It is possible to define two levels of programming. One level is called programming, and the other level is called coding. *Programming* involves defining the problem and making a flow diagram for the solution—*a flow diagram from which a computer program can be written.*

Coding involves being given the flow diagram and writing computer instructions from it. Programming requires more training, experience, and ability than does coding. It is a higher level of the art.

A distinction between programmers and coders may exist in some organizations and companies, but in many it does not.

At many installations programmers carry a problem through from the creation of the flow diagram to the final checkout of the program on the machine.

It was stated at the beginning of this chapter that the principle purpose for making the flow diagram was to create the logic that a program would use to solve a problem. The program would then be written.

The flow diagram is also helpful for describing the operation of the program to persons other than the program creator. It is an important part of program documentation. The flow diagram is an excellent means for conveying the structure of a program.

Going over someone else's flow diagram can be, and usually is, an extremely worthwhile endeavor. If you have been asked to debug (to find errors in the program), modify, rewrite, or maintain someone else's program, there is nothing more valuable than his flow diagram when it has been accurately maintained. Even if it has not been maintained, it usually serves as a starting point which gives an insight into the approach used in writing the program.

CHAPTER FIVE

The EX-1 Computer

Our purpose in this and the next four chapters will be to develop enough programming skill to write short programs for a make-believe computer. The name of this computer will be EX-1 (for EXperimental model #1).

Although this machine is a hypothetical one, it has many of the basic features of current computers. It is, of course, simplified to a large extent.

I. GENERAL CHARACTERISTICS OF A COMPUTER

A complete computer configuration is generally divided into five parts:

1. Input Unit—one or more devices for getting information into the central computer.
2. Storage Unit—one or more devices for retaining information and partial results within the central computer.
3. Arithmetic Unit—a part of the central computer which performs the computer manipulations.
4. Output Unit—one or more devices for getting information out of the central computer.
5. Control Unit—the "nerve center" for coordinating all of the above activities.

In many respects, a computer is a more highly automated desk calculator in that the individual instructions, as well as the data, are fed in prior to the machine's starting. This can perhaps be best illustrated by a drawing.

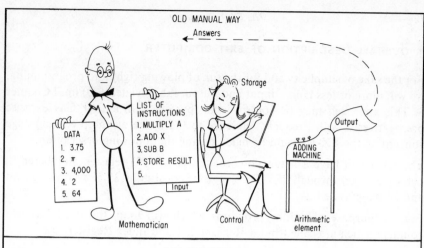

OLD MANUAL WAY

Answers

LIST OF
INSTRUCTIONS
1. MULTIPLY A
2. ADD X
3. SUB B
4. STORE RESULT
5.

DATA
1. 3.75
2. π
3. 4,000
4. 2
5. 64

Storage

Output

ADDING
MACHINE

Input

Mathematician

Control

Arithmetic
element

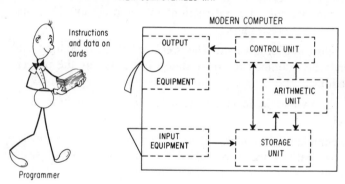

NEW COMPUTERIZED WAY

MODERN COMPUTER

Instructions
and data on
cards

OUTPUT

EQUIPMENT

CONTROL UNIT

ARITHMETIC
UNIT

INPUT
EQUIPMENT

STORAGE
UNIT

Programmer

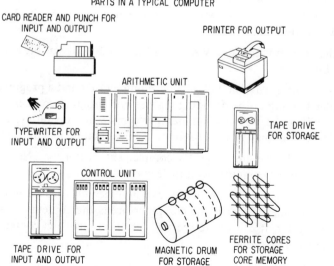

**SOME OF THE BASIC
PARTS IN A TYPICAL COMPUTER**

CARD READER AND PUNCH FOR
INPUT AND OUTPUT

PRINTER FOR OUTPUT

ARITHMETIC UNIT

TYPEWRITER FOR
INPUT AND OUTPUT

TAPE DRIVE
FOR STORAGE

CONTROL UNIT

TAPE DRIVE FOR
INPUT AND OUTPUT

MAGNETIC DRUM
FOR STORAGE

FERRITE CORES
FOR STORAGE
CORE MEMORY

II. OVERALL DESCRIPTION OF EX-1 COMPUTER

For the sake of simplicity and for the fun of plowing right into programming, we will more or less ignore input and output (abbreviated I-O) until Chapter 8. This approach may be controversial, but since an author may exercise prerogatives, I will. Frequent reference to the figure on the preceding page concerning the EX-1 should be made during the following description.

The EX-1 will have a magnetic core storage of 777_8 registers numbered in octal from 000 through 776. Each register consists of 25 bits—one sign bit and 24 magnitude bits.

For the purpose of writing programs which will loop, the EX-1 has two counters which are called Index Register #1 and Index Register #2.

There are three devices on the console that we can cause to operate by using the appropriate computer instructions in our program. They are: a bell, a red light, and a green light.

There is also an overflow light. The overflow light, the red light, and the green light may be examined for their state (on or off) by the proper computer instructions.

There are two main machine registers: the Accumulator and the Mask Register.

The Accumulator, you might say, is the computer's workbench. The numbers and other entities to be processed are brought into the Accumulator—worked on—and put back into core storage.

The Mask Register plays the role of a kind of sieve. It enables a group of bits in a computer word to be processed, thus eliminating others from consideration. The Mask Register is also used as an extension of the Accumulator in multiplication and division.

Both the Accumulator and Mask Register contain a sign bit and 24 magnitude bits.

We will, in our discussion, talk of a decoding register and a program counter. An understanding of the decoding register and program counter is basic for understanding the way a computer performs when operating a program. Console switches may be used for inserting information in a limited manner.

The EX-1 will operate using 1's complement arithmetic. Negative numbers will be in the computer with their magnitudes in 1's complement form.

Magnetic core storage access time is two milliseconds (two-thousandths of a second). This means that if the computer needs the contents of some core memory register, it can locate the register and obtain the contents in two-thousandths of a second.

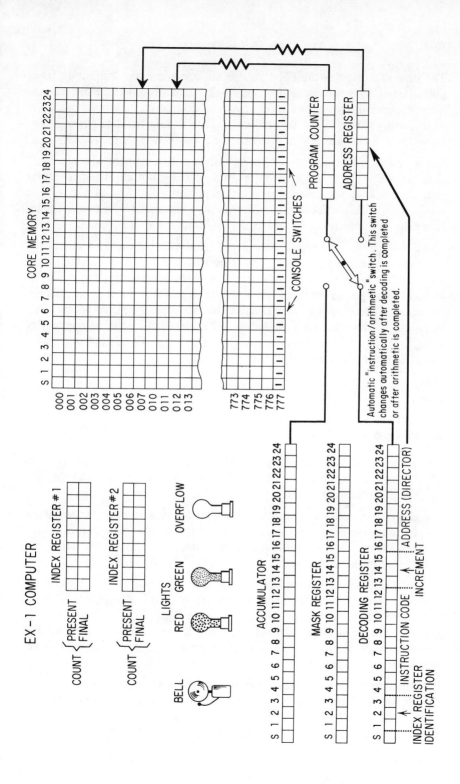

EX-1 COMPUTER

CORE MEMORY

CONSOLE SWITCHES

PROGRAM COUNTER

ADDRESS REGISTER

Automatic "instruction/arithmetic" switch. This switch changes automatically after decoding is completed or after arithmetic is completed.

INDEX REGISTER #1
COUNT { PRESENT / FINAL

INDEX REGISTER #2
COUNT { PRESENT / FINAL

LIGHTS
BELL   RED   GREEN   OVERFLOW

ACCUMULATOR

MASK REGISTER

DECODING REGISTER

INDEX REGISTER IDENTIFICATION   INSTRUCTION CODE   INCREMENT   ADDRESS (DIRECTOR)

The time that it takes the EX-1 to operate one computer instruction is six milliseconds. This is because it takes two milliseconds to get the instructions from its core memory, one millisecond to decode or determine what the instruction wants it to do, two milliseconds to obtain the data (from a core memory register), and one millisecond for it to operate on the data.

Some computer instructions do not need data and some need to make more than one reference to magnetic core storage. Thus, not all of the computer instructions take six milliseconds to be performed. Most of the EX-1's instructions take six milliseconds, however. This means that the computer is capable of performing $1000 \div 6$, or $166\frac{2}{3}$ additions per second.

The EX-1 is a *stored program* computer. This means that the instructions of a program will be placed into magnetic core storage along with the data. Control will then be given to the first instruction in the program and the computer will work along at its own very fast speed. It is clear that the computer cannot be fed one instruction at a time because the machine could then operate only as fast as the instructions were fed to it. The instructions in the memory of the EX-1 will operate in sequence unless a sequence-interfering instruction like JIX (to be explained later) is encountered.

III. GETTING UNDER WAY

Let us try to follow the operation of a small program in the EX-1. A series of cartoon drawings can illustrate the process. You might say that this is a simplified explanation of the operation of the simplified computer.

Imagine core memory as a flexible board with two nails in each slot (location). The nails are used for hanging on program instructions. Note that each core memory location has a fixed location and a location number. We will represent the location number in octal.

On the wall is a timer which Mr. Control can use in order to set his working pace. Below the timer is a program counter. With this device, Mr. Control can tell which instruction to take next. To the right of the program counter is the arithmetic element—a blackboard which Mr. Control can use to perform calculations. Below the arithmetic element is Mr. Control's workbench—the Accumulator.

Imagine that in some manner a program becomes stored in core memory on cards hanging on the nails. In these illustrations, we will use symbolic instructions as shown. The programmer will actually write his program in this symbolic manner. Observe the five instructions and three data words.

EX-1 COMPUTER

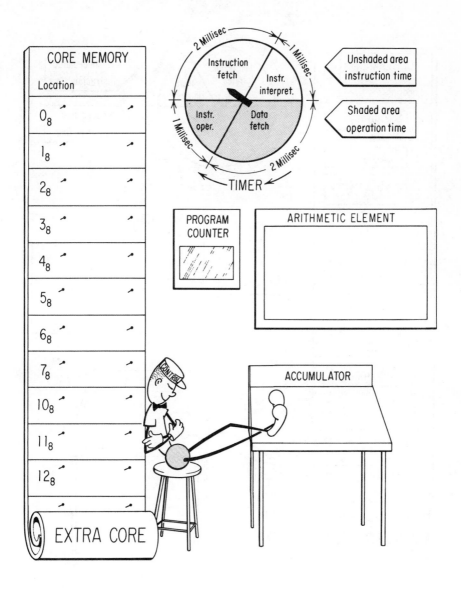

EX-1 COMPUTER

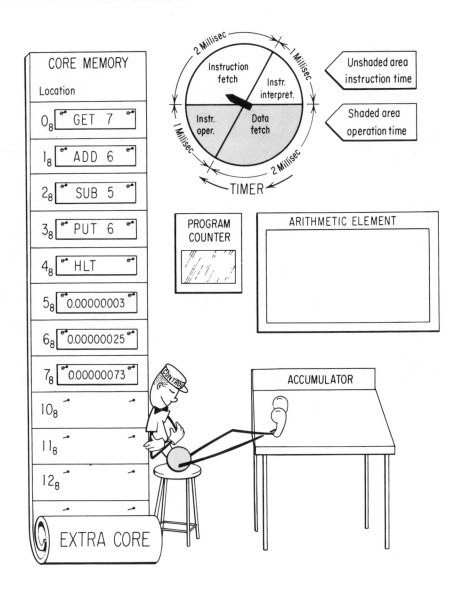

We should keep in mind, however, that within the computer the instructions are 0's and 1's as shown here—even though we will use the symbolic notation in our illustrations. Notice that instructions and data look exactly alike. We see that now Mr. Control has been awakened; the program counter has been initially set to 0 in some mysterious manner; and the timer arm is starting at "instruction fetch time." The timer arm will continue rotating in the clockwise direction and Mr. Control will keep pace (page 78).

As soon as Mr. Control removes from memory the instruction indicated by the program counter, the program counter automatically increases by 1 and now has the value 1 in it. Mr. Control places the instruction in the *decoding register* (shown on page 73) and discovers that the message to him says GET 7. Observe that he is keeping pace with the timer. GET means the following to Mr. Control: *Clear the accumulator and bring the contents of the core memory location specified by the director, into the accumulator. Do not change the contents of the core memory location* (page 79).

We see that the timer is now on data fetch and, thus Mr. Control has a copy of the contents of location 7 in his hands (page 80). Because of what GET means to Mr. Control—or rather because of what the binary code of 100000010 means as he perceives it in bits 4 through 12 of his decoding register—Mr. Control clears the junk from his accumulator and slaps down a copy of the contents of location 7. He does this during instruction operation time (page 81).

The instruction cycle repeats. Mr. Control, aware of the fact that he was entering "instruction fetch time," looked at the program counter to determine which instruction to work on next. The program counter had a 1 in it, so he took down the instruction at location 1. As soon as he removed the instruction from the nails, the program counter automatically increased by 1 to its present value of 2 (page 82).

Having interpreted the ADD instruction and having obtained a copy of the contents of location 6, we find that Mr. Control has just finished making the calculation and is placing the result in the accumulator. The ADD instructions is described as follows:

Add to the contents of the accumulator, the contents of the core memory location specified by the director. Leave the results in the accumulator. Do not change the contents of the core memory location (page 83).

One complete instruction cycle later, Mr. Control has just about finished with the operation of the SUB instruction at core location 2. We observe that in order to subtract, he automatically complemented (in actuality 1's complement, however, 7's complement in illustration) a copy of the contents of location 5. On adding the two numbers, a bit was lost because of the modulus of the machine. This resulted in automatic end-around-carry. This type of arithmetic was described fully in Chapter Two (page 84).

EX-1 COMPUTER

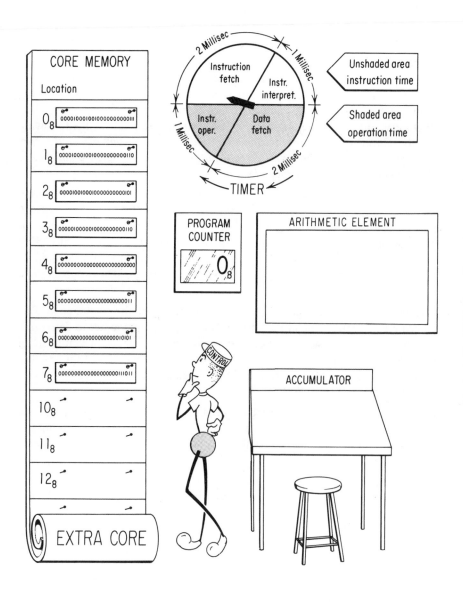

CORE MEMORY

Location

0_8 0000100010010000000000111

1_8 0000100010010000000000110

2_8 0000100010010000000000101

3_8 0000010000010000000000110

4_8 0000000000000000000000000

5_8 0000000000000000000000011

6_8 0000000000000000000010101

7_8 0000000000000000000111011

10_8

11_8

12_8

EXTRA CORE

2 Millisec — Instruction fetch — 1 Millisec

Instr. interpret.

Instr. oper.

Data fetch

1 Millisec — 2 Millisec

TIMER

Unshaded area instruction time

Shaded area operation time

PROGRAM COUNTER

0_8

ARITHMETIC ELEMENT

CONTROL

ACCUMULATOR

EX-1 COMPUTER

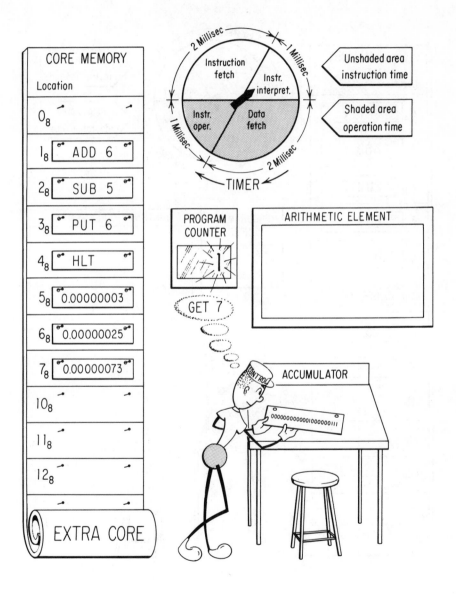

EX-1 COMPUTER

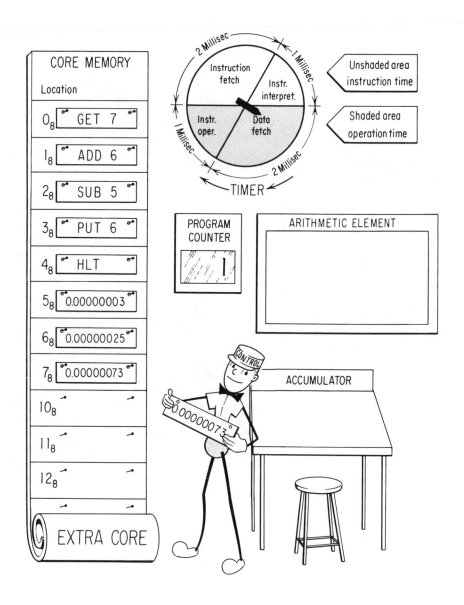

CORE MEMORY

Location

0_8	GET 7
1_8	ADD 6
2_8	SUB 5
3_8	PUT 6
4_8	HLT
5_8	0.00000003
6_8	0.00000025
7_8	0.00000073
10_8	
11_8	
12_8	

EXTRA CORE

2 Millisec — Instruction fetch
1 Millisec — Instr. interpret.
1 Millisec — Instr. oper.
2 Millisec — Data fetch

TIMER

Unshaded area instruction time

Shaded area operation time

PROGRAM COUNTER

1

ARITHMETIC ELEMENT

CONTROL C

0.00000073

ACCUMULATOR

EX-1 COMPUTER

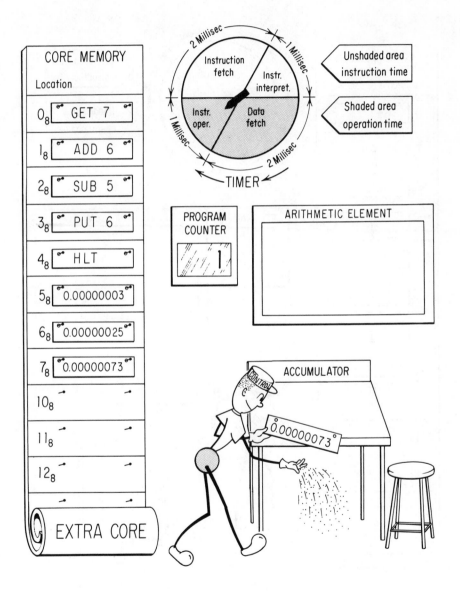

EX-1 COMPUTER

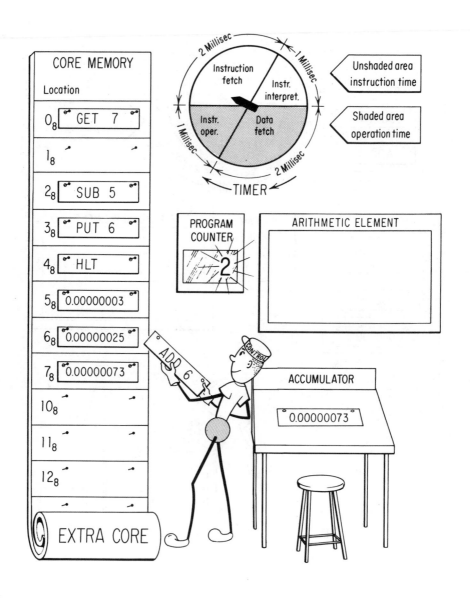

EX-1 COMPUTER

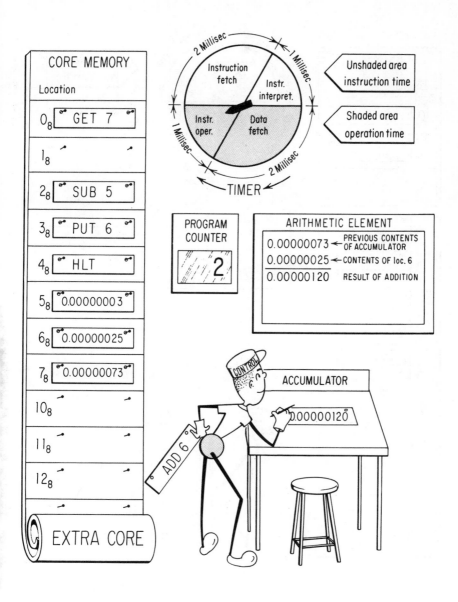

EX-1 COMPUTER

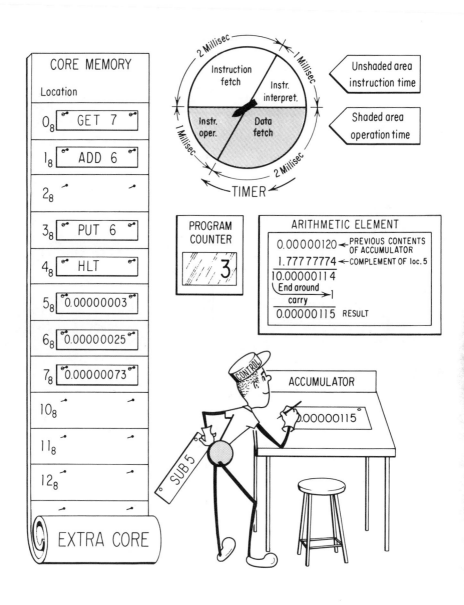

CORE MEMORY

Location

0_8 GET 7

1_8 ADD 6

2_8

3_8 PUT 6

4_8 HLT

5_8 0.00000003

6_8 0.00000025

7_8 0.00000073

10_8

11_8

12_8

EXTRA CORE

2 Millisec — Instruction fetch — 1 Millisec

Instr. interpret.

Instr. oper. — 1 Millisec

Data fetch — 2 Millisec

TIMER

Unshaded area instruction time

Shaded area operation time

PROGRAM COUNTER

3

ARITHMETIC ELEMENT

0.00000120 ← PREVIOUS CONTENTS OF ACCUMULATOR

1.77777774 ← COMPLEMENT OF loc. 5

10.00000114

End around carry → 1

0.00000115 RESULT

ACCUMULATOR

0.00000115

CONTROL

SUB 5

One complete instruction cycle later, Mr. Control is completing the operation of the PUT instruction. The PUT instruction is described as follows:

Replace the contents of the core memory location specified by the director, with the contents of the accumulator. Do not change the contents of the accumulator. Destroy the previous contents of the core memory location (page 86).

Having interpreted the HLT instruction, Mr. Control is very happy to comply. The HLT instruction is described as follows:

Stop the machine. Program counter will then be one more than location of this instruction. Accumulator is not affected (page 87).

Before leaving this series of illustrations, I would like to emphasize a few points.

Our program could have been written to start at core memory location 100_8 or any other desired core location rather than location 0 as was used here. The program would be placed in that core location by what is called a "read-in" program. Once our program was in core memory, the read-in program would transfer computer control to the first dynamic step of our program. This transferring of control by the read-in program is what initially sets the program counter to the first dynamic step of our program.

In our illustration, it may appear as if the data were written with the program. This is very seldom the case. Generally, a program would read the data into a working area of core from some peripheral equipment (perhaps a card reading machine or magnetic tape) and then start to process it.

Attention must be called to the very important fact that *there is an address (or location) OF an instruction and an address WITHIN an instruction.* This fact is very frequently overlooked by the beginner and if not clearly understood, can lead to much confusion as we go on. The information which I have called the address within an instruction is not always an address as will be seen later. Hence, a more general name for this field within the machine instruction word is "director field" (see the decoding register configuration found on page 73). The address of an instruction was the address painted on the core memory board in our illustrations. The address within an instruction (director) would, for example, be the 7 in GET 7—the first instruction in our illustration.

Frequently, in computer literature, one finds a complete revolution of the timer arm (as used in our illustration) referred to as an *instruction cycle.* The top half and bottom half of our timer revolution would generally each be called a *machine cycle.* Thus, two machine cycles generally make an instruction cycle.

EX-1 COMPUTER

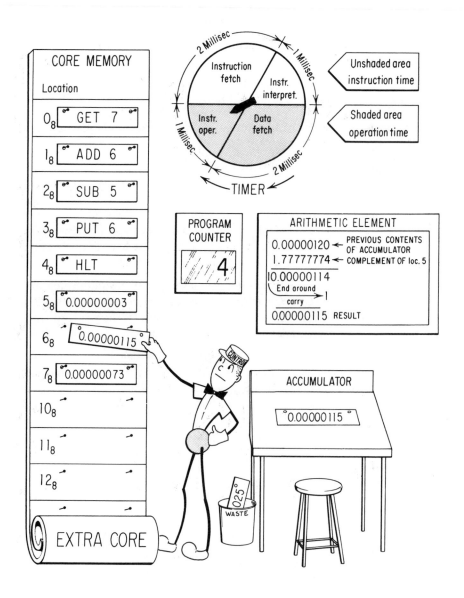

EX-1 COMPUTER

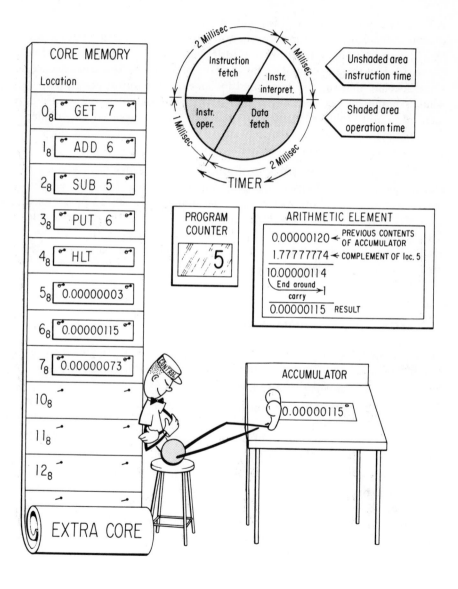

The portion of a revolution dealing with instruction fetch time is usually known as a *memory cycle*. Therefore, we have memory cycles, machine cycles, and instruction cycles. The specific details connected with the cycles—their associations, variations, subdivisions, and overlappings—are extremely involved.

A word of caution is due at this point. It hardly needs mentioning that in a computer there is no core memory board with nails, nor accumulator work bench, nor rotating timer arm, nor little stick man named Mr. Control. Clearly, I used these as analogies for the sake of learning. As a consequence, I must declare that rigor suffered, and for an exactly rigorous description of what is going on electronically within a working computer, the reader is referred to other sources. I trust I do not insult the intelligence of the reader by making this confession. I merely do so to still the anticipated jibes of colleagues into whose hands this manuscript may fall.

It is hoped that with this series of illustrations, the reader has obtained a knowledge of the functions of the program counter, the decoding register, the instruction cycle, core memory, the accumulator, a stored program, a sequential machine, and 1's complement arithmetic. Also, the reader should now be familiar with the EX-1 instructions of GET, ADD, SUB, PUT, and HLT. These some very vital concepts for understanding basic computer operation. Are they clear?

IV. GETTING THE PROGRAM WRITTEN AND IN THE COMPUTER

Let us follow the development of the program from the writing of it to the running of it on the EX-1. We would have coded our recently discussed program on coding paper (top of page 89).

Some conventions must be followed when writing a program on coding paper. Observe that I have slashed all zeros, but not the letter O. This is so that the keypunch operator will not confuse the two. The letter O has different punches than the symbol 0 (zero).

The letter I and the number 1 must also be clearly differentiated on coding paper. Some organizations use the convention of slashing the letter O rather than zero. The choice of which convention is used is purely arbitrary. In this book we will use the slashing of the zero. Therefore, anytime we write a program on coding paper, we will slash the zeros and make sure the letter I is differentiated from the number 1.

The 2 headings, INDEX, and INCRMT as found on the programming paper will be described later when we discuss indexing. The remaining 4

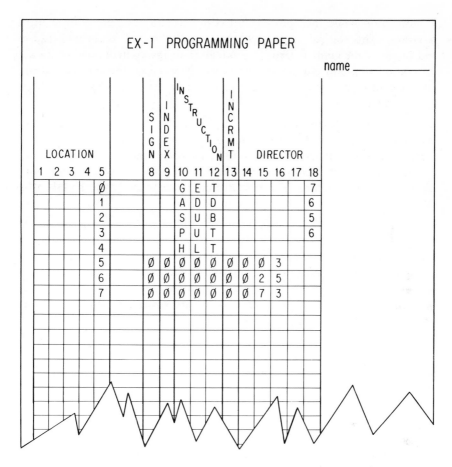

headings, LOCATION, SIGN, INSTRUCTION, and DIRECTOR are self-explanatory.

This coding sheet would have been sent to the keypunching department and each line punched on one card. The numbers at the top of the coding sheet refer to the card columns of a data processing card. Thus, we see that the G of GET would have been punched in column 10 of a card in 12-bit hollerith code. When the deck of eight cards was returned from keypunching, it would have been sent next to the computer with a "request" card. The request card would ask that the deck be assembled; that is to say, used to produce a deck containing binary machine words.

The computer operator would place a control card on the top of our deck, tip the whole deck over, and place it in a card reader. The card reader is accessible electrically to the computer.

The operator would then push a button to call in a "master utility control program." This control program would "select" the card reader and read-in and interpret the control card. Interpretation of the control card would tell the control program that an assembly is to be done on the following deck. So, the control program would then call in the assembler program (perhaps from magnetic tape).

The assembler program, now in core memory after having been brought in from tape, would read the information on the cards of our program into core one at a time and change the hollerith to binary machine words. These binary machine words *are then* punched by the computer on cards—11 binary machine words to a card. The exact format of these cards will be taken up later.

The assembly complete, the programmer would receive his original symbolic deck, the new binary deck, and a listing indicating errors and other information. The programmer would then add a control card to his binary deck—assuming there were no errors—and send it back to the computer for read-in and operation. The program is read into core memory by a utility read-in program, and control is transferred to the first operating instruction of the program in question (called the object program).

The object program operates and perhaps printouts are obtained of the tables worked upon by the object program. This, in essence, is the procedure a program goes through. In summary, we have:

1. Problem and data studied.
2. Flow diagram created.
3. Program written on coding paper.
4. Symbolic deck keypunched from coding paper.
5. Binary deck obtained from symbolic deck by process called assembly.
6. Read-in of binary deck information and program operation.
7. Printouts obtained of program and/or data. Program corrected, extensively tested, and documented.

V. EX-1 INSTRUCTIONS

A complete list of instructions for the EX-1 computer will be given in Appendix 3. The computer is electronically designed to respond to these instructions in the described manner. Individual uses will be taken up as we go along. At this point let us summarize the five instructions which we have discussed:

Mnemonic	Octal Code	Interpretation	Function
GET	402	G̲E̲T̲	Clears the accumulator and brings contents of core memory register specified by the director into accumulator. Does not change the core memory register.
ADD	422	A̲D̲D̲	Adds to contents of accumulator, the contents of core memory register specified by director. Leaves the results in the accumulator. Does not change the contents of the core memory register.
SUB	442	S̲U̲B̲TRACT	Subtracts from the contents of the accumulator, the contents of the core memory register specified by the director. Leaves results in accumulator. Does not change the specified core memory register.
PUT	202	P̲U̲T̲	Replaces the contents of the core memory register specified by director with the contents of the accumulator. Does not change contents of accumulator. Destroys previous contents of core memory register.
HLT	000	H̲A̲L̲T̲	Stops the machine. Program counter will then be one more than location of this instruction. Accumulator not affected.

Problem 5.1

What (in octal) are the contents of the accumulator when the following program halts?

LOCATION 1	2	3	4	5		SIGN 8	INDEX 9	INSTRUCTION 10	11	12	INCRMT 13	DIRECTOR 14	15	16	17	18
		1	0	0				G	E	T				1	0	5
		1	0	1				A	D	D				1	0	6
		1	0	2				S	U	B				1	0	7
		1	0	3				P	U	T				1	1	0
		1	0	4				H	L	T						
		1	0	5		0	0	0	0	0	1	2	3	4		
		1	0	6		0	6	2	0	0	1	7	0	2		
		1	0	7		0	3	0	0	0	3	2	1	4		
		1	1	0		0	0	0	0	0	0	0	0	0		

The program of Problem 5.1 may be represented in octal. Usually the assembly listing (printout) will show the symbolic instructions (intermediate level language) and also in octal (law level language). Also, if a core memory printout is obtained of the program as it resides in memory, the printout program will print at the low level.

The various fields on the coding paper translate into binary and octal as shown.

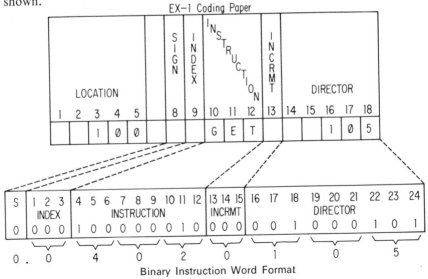

Binary Instruction Word Format

Thus, GET 105 becomes 0.04020105 as an EX-1 computer word consisting of a sign bit and 8 octal digits.

Problem 5.2

Write the complete program of problem 5.1 in octal where *each instruction* and *data word* consists of a sign bit and 8 octal digits.

Problem 5.3

What (in octal) are the contents of the accumulator when the following program halts? (NOTE: We will omit the coding paper format in the rest of this document unless some special emphasis requires its use in an illustration.)

200	GET	204
201	SUB	205
202	PUT	206
203	HLT	
204	1.73210000	
205	0.30003214	
206	0.00000000	

Problem 5.4

Write a program on EX-1 coding paper starting at core location 30_8 which will make a copy of the contents of core locations 5 and 6. Have your program place this copy into locations 12_8 and 13_8 respectively.

Problem 5.5

Write a program on EX-1 coding paper which will add the contents of locations 301_8 and 302_8 and place the result in location 407_8. Have your program start at location 500_8.

Problem 5.6

Write a program on EX-1 coding paper which will add the value 1 to the contents of locations 100 and 101. Have your program start at location 10.

VI. TWO DECISION-MAKING INSTRUCTIONS AND THE JUMP INSTRUCTION

Thus far, we have been somewhat limited in what we could do in the way of programming by a lack of decision-making instructions. Let us add to our repertoire the two instructions JZE and JPO.

JZE performs as follows:

> If the accumulator is positive or negative zero, jump to operate the instruction at the location specified by the director.

> If the accumulator is not zero, do not jump, but continue on with the next instruction in sequence.

> If a jump occurs, save the instruction location of what would have been the next instruction (had the jump not occurred) in the mask register.

Whether or not a jump occurs, the contents of the accumulator are not affected.

JPO performs as follows:

> If the accumulator sign is 0, jump to operate the instruction at the location specified by the director.

> If the accumulator sign is 1, do not jump, but continue on with the next instruction in sequence.

> If a jump occurs, save the instruction location (current contents of program counter) of what would have been the next instruction (had the jump not occurred) in the mask register.

> Whether or not a jump occurs, the contents of the accumulator are not affected.

JMP performs as follows:

> Control transfers to the address specified in the director field. Save the instruction location (current contents of program counter) of what would have been the next instruction (had the jump not occurred) in the mask register. Do not disturb contents of the accumulator.

The jump instructions (if a jump occurs) first replace the contents of the mask register with the current contents of the program counter. This latter has in it the core location of the next instruction immediately following the jump.

Then the transfer of control is caused by the contents of the program counter being replaced by the value of the director field in the jump instruction.

This saving of the contents of the program counter will be very useful when we discuss subroutines in Chapter Seven.

Using two of these new instructions, JZE and JMP, we are now in a position to code the illustrative example that we flow diagrammed in Chapter Four.

Let us arbitrarily state that MCAND, MLIER, and PRODT are memory locations 200, 201, and 202 respectively, and that we want our program to start at location 100.

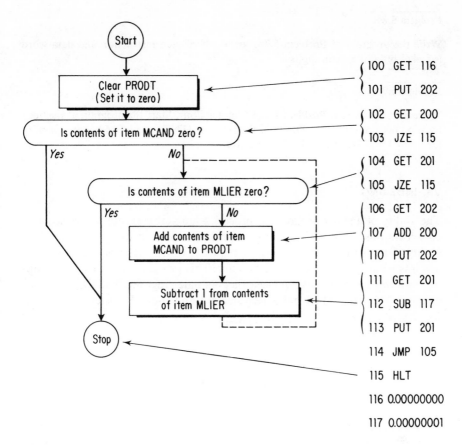

	100	GET	116
	101	PUT	202
	102	GET	200
	103	JZE	115
	104	GET	201
	105	JZE	115
	106	GET	202
	107	ADD	200
	110	PUT	202
	111	GET	201
	112	SUB	117
	113	PUT	201
	114	JMP	105
	115	HLT	
	116	0.00000000	
	117	0.00000001	

Problem 5.7

What are the contents of the accumulator (as a sign bit and 8 octal digits) when the
following program halts?

400	GET	412
401	SUB	413
402	PUT	412
403	JPO	406
404	GET	414
405	HLT	
406	GET	414
407	ADD	413
410	PUT	414
411	JMP	400
412	0.00000007	
413	0.00000002	
414	0.00000006	

Problem 5.8

Write the program of Problem 5.7 in octal where each instruction and data word is a sign bit and 8 octal digits.

Problem 5.9

Write the program for Problem 4.2 of Chapter Four. Start the program at memory location 600. Assume that DIVND, DVSOR, QUTNT, and REMAN are memory locations 150, 151, 152, and 153 respectively.

VII. INDEXING

The ability of a short program to process a long table (group of consecutive core locations) is one of the most important aspects of programming. This ability to perform an instruction, or sequence of instructions over and over again is what gives power to a computer. This process—usually called looping—utilizes a counter-like device called an index register. The EX-1 has two of these. They are called Index Register #1 and Index Register #2.

We can think of an index register appearing like this:

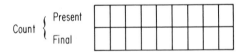

We observe that the index register is 9 bits long. This is the same length as the address field within an instruction. This is so because the present count of an index register will generally be used to modify the address field.

This modification will take place automatically and internally within the computer at the moment the address within the instruction being interpreted is used to reference core for the data. Thus, the instruction within the program is itself really never changed even though it has an index register associated with it.

Let us illustrate the use of an index register with an example.

Given: A 3 entry table starting at location 100_8. Each location in the table contains numerical data.

Required: Write a program which will compute the sum of the contents of the table. Have this sum placed into location 200_8. Start the program at location 0.

There are two general solutions to the problem, but let us analyze the following one first:

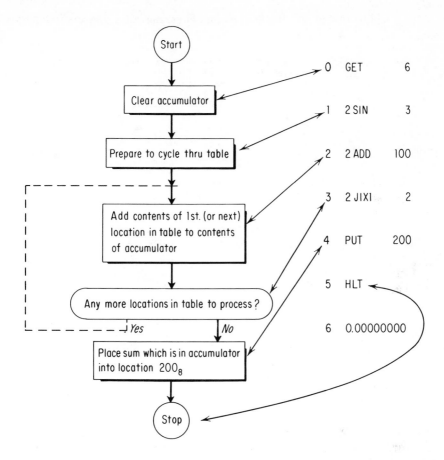

It works out that in this solution there is a one-to-one correspondence (except for START) between each box in the flow diagram and each instruction in the program. This usually will not be the situation. It is convenient in this illustration however. Let us assume the table in question looks like this:

100	4
101	1
−102	−2

It is easy to see that GET 6 clears the accumulator.

When 2SIN 3 is encountered by the computer, it causes Index Register #2 to be set. The present count of Index Register #2 will be cleared to 0 and the value 3 will be placed into the final count. Thus, the index appears in binary as:

Present Count	0	0	0	0	0	0	0	0	0
Final Count	0	0	0	0	0	0	0	1	1

or symbolically in octal as:

Present	0
Final	3

I chose to set the index register with the value 3 because I want the program to perform three passes of the loop. This is because there are three memory locations in the table.

The instruction at core location 2 will be encountered next.

2ADD   100

During the interpretation of this instruction, the computer will form an "effective address" in order to reference memory for the data. This effective address will consist of the sum of the value of the address part of the instruction (which is 100_8 in this case) and the contents of the index register specified (Index Register #2 is specified with this instruction and the present count in the index register is 0).

Therefore, the effective address is $100 + 0$ or 100 on this first pass. Thus, operation of this instruction at memory location 2 has resulted in the contents memory location 100 being added to the accumulator contents.

The computer next encounters the JIX instruction. This instruction is the most complicated one that we will meet in our study of the EX-1. It is also one of the most powerful.

The computer will behave as follows when it meets the 2JIX1 2 in this specific example:

First, add the increment (which is 1 as found to the right of the JIX) to the present count of Index Register #2 (Index Register #2 as is indicated by the 2 just left of the JIX).

Second, compare the present count and final count.

If the present count of the specified index is less than the final count, transfer control to the instruction whose location is given in the address field of the JIX instruction.

Otherwise (if present count is greater than or equal to final count), do not jump, but continue with next instruction after the JIX instruction.

Clearly, a jump will occur at this encounter, because at this first test instituted by the JIX, the computer will find 1 in the present count and 3 in the final count.

Thus, the computer finds itself at the 2ADD 100 instruction again. Now, the effective address is 100 + 1 or 101. Therefore, the contents of memory location 101 is added to the accumulator contents.

Arriving at the JIX instruction, the contents of Index Register #2 is increased by 1 (the increment) giving a present count of 2. The test by the JIX indicates a jump, so the computer finds itself back at memory location 2.

This results in the contents of memory location 102 being added to the contents of the accumulator. This is so because this third arrival at the 2ADD 100 instruction has resulted in an effective address of 100 + 2 or 102.

Back at JIX again, the incrementing gives 3 as a present count resulting in no jump (called "fall through" by programmers). The instruction PUT 200 achieves the placing of the accumulated sum as found in the accumulator into memory location 200.

Then HLT operates.

This program would be written on coding paper as follows:

LOCATION					SIGN	INDEX	INSTRUCTION			INCRMT	DIRECTOR				
1	2	3	4	5	8	9	10	11	12	13	14	15	16	17	18
				Ø			G	E	T						6
				1		2	S	I	N						3
				2		2	A	D	D				1	Ø	Ø
				3		2	J	I	X	1					2
				4			P	U	T				2	Ø	Ø
				5			H	L	T						
				6	Ø	Ø	Ø	Ø	Ø	Ø	Ø	Ø	Ø		

We talked of an alternate solution earlier. It would take this form:

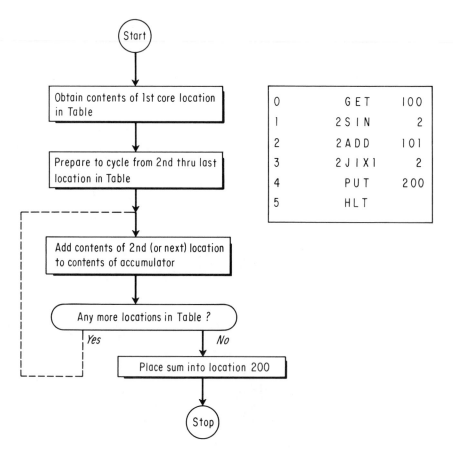

This second method appears to require one less location for the program. We can, however, shorten our first solution as follows:

0	G E T	5
1	2 S I N	3
2	2 A D D	100
3	2 J I X1	2
4	P U T	200
5	H L T	

This is possible because the octal equivalent of the HLT mnemonic is 000. Hence, when the assembly program changes the instruction at location 5 of our program to the binary necessary for machine operation, the 25 bits of memory location 5 will be all zeros.

Observe that although the first instruction GET 5 causes what amounts to HLT to come into the accumulator, the computer does not stop. This emphasizes the fact that *an instruction is not operated by its being in the accumulator*. To operate an instruction, the computer must, so-to-speak, run into an instruction via the program counter. It must be in the decoding register.

Since the table being summed in the problem was so short, using an index register was not shorter than merely adding without looping. But, it is easy to see that with an increase in table size, say 100_{10} registers, the use of an index register to achieve looping "has it all over" a program which does not loop. To write a program to process this larger table, we simply set the index to the higher value.

We observe that the index had two applications; one use was address modification; the other use was looping. The former application we see in the 2ADD 100 instruction; the latter application we see in the 2JIX1 2 instruction.

Also, notice that the PUT 200 instruction did not have an index register associated with it (there is no 2 to the left of PUT). We did not want to associate an index register with this instruction in the program because the PUT was concerned with only one memory location; namely, 200. It was not concerned with a table as the ADD instruction above it was; hence, the 2ADD 100. The student should keep this idea in mind and be able to distinguish where and where not to specify an index register.

A few final details before leaving this formal discussion of indexing:

The SIN instruction takes a *decimal* director on the EX-1 coding sheet. This is more convenient for the programmer as the number of locations in a table is usually expressed in decimals in a problem. (Thus, the assembler program can have the built-in capability to make a decimal to binary conversion of the director whenever it encounters SIN.)

An octal *increment* may be specified with the SIN instruction. An increment of 1 through 6 causes the SIN instruction to set the present count to the increment value and the final count to the director value. An increment of 7 causes the SIN instruction to set both the present and final count of the specified index register to the value of the director.

For example, 2SIN5 29 causes the present count of index register 2 to be set to 5 and the final count to be set to 29. The instruction 2SIN7 29 causes both the present count and final count of index register #2 to be set to 29.

This capability will be very valuable later in Chapter Seven.

Finally, the increment as specified by the digit following JIX may be any octal digit 0 through 7.

Problem 5.10

Describe what happens if the instruction 1 SIN 9 is operated by the computer.

Problem 5.11

1. Describe what happens if the instruction 2SIN3 17 is operated by the computer.
2. Describe what happens if the instruction 2SIN7 19 is operated by the computer.

Problem 5.12

What (in octal) is in accumulator when the following program halts?

0	2 S I N	2
1	G E T	5
2	2 A D D	6
3	2 J I X 1	2
4	H L T	
5	1.07777654	
6	0.04445555	
7	0.76543210	

Problem 5.13

Write a program which will make a copy of the contents of the 9 memory locations found at location 60_8 and following. Have this copy placed into memory location 120_8 and following. Start your program at location 20_8.

Problem 5.14

Write a program starting at location 200_8 which will add the value 3 to the contents of every location in a 15_{10} entry table. The table starts at memory location 300_8.

Problem 5.15

Write a program starting at location 300_8 which will obtain in the accumulator the contents of the 9th location within a 50_{10} entry table. The 1st location in the table is at location 100_8.

Problem 5.16

Write a program starting at location 400_8 which will move the contents of each memory location in an 18 entry table one location up in the table. Have the contents of the first location placed into the last location. The table starts at memory location 600_8.

Problem 5.17

Write a program starting at location 400_8 which will move the contents of each memory location in an 18 entry table one location down in the table. Have the contents of the lost location placed into the first location. The table starts at location 600_8.

Problem 5.18

Write a program which will start at location 50_8 and which will count the number of positive and negative zeros contained in the 99 entries at locations 200_8 and following. Have your program keep the count in memory location 40_8.

Problem 5.19

Write a program starting at location 150_8 which will replace all negative values in a 29 entry table with the value $+0$. The table starts at location 300_8.

VIII. SYMBOLIC LOCATIONS AND ADDRESSES

You may have noticed a certain awkwardness when writing a program. This may have been the case when you wanted to add the value 1 to the contents of the accumulator. You needed to use the ADD instruction, and to have in the director the address of a memory location containing a 1. The problem was that it was difficult to know what address to use until you had finished the program and placed a constant in a memory location at the end of the program; or, you may have wanted to JMP somewhere, but couldn't determine the address to use until you had worked out the intervening steps.

Also, you may have had your program written and found you needed to insert or delete an instruction somewhere within the program. Generally, this insertion or deletion played havoc with the addresses already used—in effect, necessitating rewriting the program. All of these problems can be eliminated by using symbolic locations and addresses. Let us solve the following problem using this concept.

Illustrative example

Write a program starting at location 200_8 which will count the number of positive numbers (let us include $+0$ as a positive number) contained in a table of 15 entries. The table starts at location 300_8. Keep the count in location 50_8.

1	2	3	4	5		S I G N 8	I N D E X 9	10	11	12	I N C R M T 13	14	15	16	17	18
								B	E	G				3	0	0
							2	S	I	N					2	8
A	G	A	I	N			2	G	E	T				6	0	0
								J	P	0		A	D	T	R	E
A	N	Y	M	0			2	J	I	X	1	A	G	A	I	N
								H	L	T						
A	D	T	R	E				A	D	D		T	H	R	E	E
							2	P	U	T				6	0	0
								J	M	P		A	N	Y	M	0
T	H	R	E	E		0	0	0	0	0	0	0	0	3		
								E	N	D						

The column group headers above are: **LOCATION** (columns 1–5), **SIGN** (8), **INDEX** (9), **INSTRUCTION** (10–12), **INCRMT** (13), **DIRECTOR** (14–18).

Here we introduce a new instruction BEG which may be interpreted as "begin." The EX-1 was not electrically designed to handle this instruction. Thus, it has no octal equivalent. Rather, this instruction is what is referred to in programming language as a *pseudo instruction*. This is because it is an instruction *to the assembler program* rather than to the machine. In the director field we place the memory address for which we want our program assembled.

Next, I used the instruction GET ZERO. ZERO is the symbolic name which I arbitrarily gave to a memory location which I will later attach to the end of my program. It will have zero in it. Notice that I can completely write this GET ZERO instruction at this time even though I would not, at this 2nd step in the writing of the program, know which location will ultimately be the one with zero in it. I could not do this were I using absolute locations and addresses.

Observe, also, that I chose the name ZERO as it is somewhat descriptive of the way I want to use the register.

Next we write

$$\text{P U T} \quad 5 \ 0$$
$$\text{2 S I N} \quad 1 \ 5$$

so that thus far we have:

```
BEG        2 0 0
GET     Z E R O
PUT          5 0
2 S I N       1 5
```

Next, I would obtain the contents of the first (or next) location in the table and examine it to see if it is positive. This gives us:

```
BEG        2 0 0
GET     Z E R O
PUT          5 0
2 S I N       1 5
2 G E T     3 0 0
J PO    TALLY
```

Notice that thus far I have not attached a symbolic location symbol to the 2GET 300 instruction as we saw existed in our finished version previously. This is because there has been no need for one so far. I picked TALLY as the symbolic address within the JPO instruction because it is descriptive of what I intent to do if a jump occurs at JPO.

If a number is not positive (if we fall through JPO), we wish to do nothing special, merely see if there are any more to examine; and if there are, go back and get the next one. If there are no more, we want to stop. So, presently our program stands thus:

```
BEG        2 0 0
GET     Z E R O
PUT          5 0
2 S I N       1 5
2 G E T     3 0 0
J PO     TALLY
2 J I X 1 M O R E
HL T
```

Now we feel a need to attach the symbol MORE to the 2GET 300 instruction. Hence, we have:

```
            BEG        2 0 0
            GET     Z E R O
            PUT          5 0
            2 S I N       1 5
MORE    2 G E T     3 0 0
            J PO    TALLY
            2 J I X 1 M O R E
            HL T
```

Next, writing the tally routine gives:

```
              BEG       2 0 0
              GET    Z E R O
              PUT         5 0
              2 S I N     1 5
MORE          2 G E T     3 0 0
              J PO    TALLY
              2 J I X 1 M O R E
              HLT
TALLY         GET         5 0
              ADD     ONE
              PUT         5 0
              JMP     ANYMO
```

This makes us feel a need to attach the symbolic label ANYMO to the 2JIX1MORE instruction, where we check to see if there are any more locations to examine. Also, we must attach the two registers containing 0 and 1 which we respectively call ZERO and ONE. Finally, we include the pseudo instruction END in our program to tell the assembler program that this is all of our program. This completes the final program.

```
              BEG       2 0 0
              GET    Z E R O
              PUT         5 0
              2 S I N     1 5
MORE          2 G E T     3 0 0
              J PO    TALLY
ANYMO         2 J I X 1 M O R E
              HLT
TALLY         GET         5 0
              ADD     ONE
              PUT         5 0
              JMP     ANYMO
ZERO          0 0 0 0 0 0 0 0 0
ONE           0 0 0 0 0 0 0 0 1
              END
```

Let us emphasize the fact that whenever we employed a symbolic address in the director field of an instruction, we had to have a symbolic location corresponding to it in the location field of some instruction. In other words, if you tell the computer to JPO to TALLY, you must have a TALLY to to which it can go.

Similarly, you cannot have two or more locations in a program which have the same symbolic name.

If there were two different instructions in a program whose locations were symbolically given as TALLY, a JPO to TALLY would result in the assembler not knowing which TALLY was meant. Had the programmer mistakenly done this, the assembler program would print out an error message upon assembly.

In the director field, the symbolic address TALLY could appear more than once. This simply means that you can jump to TALLY from one or more different places.

Summarizing this particular aspect, we might say: (1) For each symbolic label in the director field there must be one and only one instruction with the same label in the location field. (2) Symbolics in the director field need not be unique.

Another convention to be stated for our EX-1 programming will be that symbolics in the location and director fields will be written on the coding paper starting at the left within the field; whereas absolute locations and directors will be as far right as possible within the respective fields.

When data or symbols are placed to the left within a field, we say that the content is *left justified*. The field would then contain trailing blanks (or in some situations, zeros).

When the data or symbols are placed to the right within a field we say that the content is *right justified*. The field would then contain leading blanks (or, in some situations, zeros). Thus, we can say that symbolic directors and labels are left justified, whereas absolute locations and directors are right justified.

Attaching the symbolic labels used in this last program to the flow diagram may be helpful. (See top of page 108.)

We observe that we can easily insert or delete instructions in our program without rewriting the program. If we wanted to insert an instruction ADD ONE in between our present ADD ONE and PUT 50 instructions it would cause no problem.

Also, we see that if it were decided by some authority that our program should begin at 400_8 rather than 200_8, all that would need to be done would be to change the BEG card. Then, we would assemble over again with the new BEG card. Clearly, it would not have been so simple to change the starting location had the program been written using absolute locations and addresses.

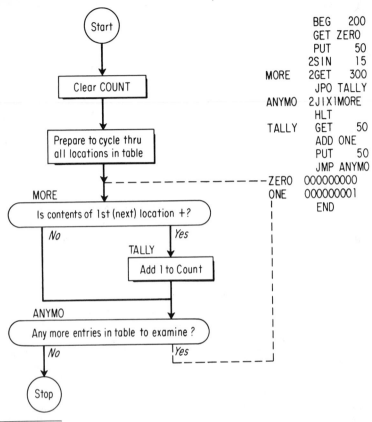

```
                                        BEG    200
                                        GET  ZERO
                                        PUT     50
                                        2SIN    15
                              MORE      2GET   300
                                        JPO  TALLY
                              ANYMO     2JIX1MORE
                                        HLT
                              TALLY     GET     50
                                        ADD  ONE
                                        PUT     50
                                        JMP  ANYMO
                              ZERO   000000000
                              ONE    000000001
                                        END
```

Problem 5.20

Write a program starting at location 300_8 which will add the value 3 to each positive number (include $+0$ as a positive number) contained in a table of 28 entries. The table starts at location 600_8. Use symbolic locations and addresses where possible.

Problem 5.21

Given the program developed in the last illustrative example (page 00), write each instruction and data word as a sign bit and 8 octal digits. [Note: The BEG 200 pseudo instruction specifies that the 1st instruction in the program (in this case GET ZERO) is contained in memory location 200.]

Problem 5.22

Write a program starting at location 50_8 which will replace each number in a 9 entry table with its complement. The table starts at location 150_8. Use symbolic locations and addresses where possible.

IX. THE COMPOOL

We would like to get our programming even more symbolic than we now have it; the less coded in absolute, the better. The necessity for more complete symbolic programming becomes greater as the size of the system being programmed increases.

If we could use symbolic quantities for table starting-locations, table lengths, and individual system memory locations, we would be most pleased. This can easily be done by the creation of a table to which the assembler program will have access. This table will function like a dictionary in that the assembler program will use it to define terms which it encounters in our program and which are not defined in our program. This will occur during assembly.

The table will be called a *compool*. The name is derived from "Communication Tag Pool." This is because it is used essentially to define memory locations used for communication between programs. Thus, if program A wants to give information to program B, A can use a symbolic name, say ALPHA, and PUT ALPHA. Program B can obtain the information by GET ALPHA. Neither need know that location ALPHA is location 200_8. But the compiler program can refer to the compool at the time of complilation and find that ALPHA is really location 200_8. Therefore, it can replace ALPHA with 200_8 in each program.

If, later on, system design authorities decide that ALPHA should be location 300_8 rather than 200_8, all that needs to be done is change the compool. The many programs using ALPHA do not need to be rewritten as would be the case if absolute rather than symbolic reference to ALPHA had been employed. The many programs will have to be reassembled, however, using the new compool.

You have probably already observed that ALPHA is really what we have defined in Chapter Three as an item consisting of 1 memory location. Thus, we can say that the compool defines items. It is possible to develop program systems which employ compool defined items that require less than a full memory location. As you may recall, we called these packed items. However, as the explanations involved in using items which are compool defined and require less than a full memory location would be quite lengthy, we will confine our discussion to full word items.

Since communication between programs is done via tables as well as single items, tables will be defined in the compool also.

Let us do the illustrative example of section VIII using the compool concept. We will rewrite the problem as follows:

Write a program, starting at location 200_8, which counts the number of positive numbers (let us include +0 as a positive number) contained in table RANDY. Keep the count in location COUNT.

Here it is inferred that table RANDY and location COUNT are defined in the compool. So, we would write:

```
                    BEG      200
                    GET    ZERO
                    PUT    COUNT
                   2SIN    RANDY
MORE               2GET    RANDY
                    JPO    TALLY
ANYMO           2JIX1MORE
                    HLT
TALLY              GET    COUNT
                    ADD    ONE
                    PUT    COUNT
                    JMP    ANYMO
ZERO        000000000
ONE         000000001
                    END
```

This will be as symbolic as we will want it to be. It can be seen that given this symbolic program, the assembler program can change it completely to binary. It has all the required information to do so. You can verify this fact by seeing how you would do it manually. Let us now do this.

On a first pass you would assign a memory location to each line of the program.

```
200                    GET    ZERO
201                    PUT    COUNT
202                   2SIN    RANDY
203   MORE            2GET    RANDY
204                    JPO    TALLY
205   ANYMO        2JIX1MORE
206                    HLT
207   TALLY          GET    COUNT
210                    ADD    ONE
211                    PUT    COUNT
212                    JMP    ANYMO
213   ZERO      000000000
214   ONE       000000001
```

A second pass could replace the symbolic addresses in the director field with the correct absolute addresses.

```
2 0 0        G E T        2 1 3
2 0 1        P U T      C O U N T
2 0 2      2 S I N      R A N D Y
2 0 3      2 G E T      R A N D Y
2 0 4        J P O        2 0 7
2 0 5      2 J I X 1      2 0 3
2 0 6        H L T
2 0 7        G E T      C O U N T
2 1 0        A D D        2 1 4
2 1 1        P U T      C O U N T
2 1 2        J M P        2 0 5
2 1 3    0 0 0 0 0 0 0 0 0
2 1 4    0 0 0 0 0 0 0 0 1
```

On a third pass (if you were the assembler program), you could, upon consulting the compool, decide to replace COUNT with the absolute location 50_8. You would likewise replace RANDY in the instruction at location 203 with the absolute address 300_8 (the first core location in the table called RANDY)

You would know that whenever the SIN instruction was encountered, you would replace the symbolic in the director field with, not an address, but a number of entries. Therefore, consulting the compool, you would find that RANDY should be replaced by 15_{10} in the SIN instruction. This now gives:

```
2 0 0        G E T        2 1 3
2 0 1        P U T          5 0
2 0 2      2 S I N          1 5
2 0 3      2 G E T          3 0 0
2 0 4        J P O        2 0 7
2 0 5      2 J I X 1      2 0 3
2 0 6        H L T
2 0 7        G E T          5 0
2 1 0        A D D        2 1 4
2 1 1        P U T          5 0
2 1 2        J M P        2 0 5
2 1 3    0 0 0 0 0 0 0 0 0
2 1 4    0 0 0 0 0 0 0 0 1
```

Actually, the assembler would do all this in a total of two passes. What we have done manually in the 2nd and 3rd passes would have been done by the assembler in the second pass. In the first pass, it would also have replaced each mnemonic with the octal equivalent as determined from some table internal to the assembler. Of course, all this replacement is being done in core memory in binary.

Problem 5.23

Write this last illustrative program where each instruction and data word are represented by a sign bit and 8 octal digits.

Problem 5.24

Make a flow diagram and write a program which will count the number of *positive zeros only* contained in the entries of table TBETA. Keep the count in location COUNT. Start your program at location 30_8. Consider TBETA and COUNT as being compool defined.

Problem 5.25

Given that the compool defines table TBETA of problem 5.24 above as consisting of 28 entries starting at location 100 and that COUNT is 1 word at location 250, show the octal representation of your program (where each instruction and data word consists of a sign bit and 8 octal digits).

Problem 5.26

Write a program which will examine each entry of table GAMMA, and add the value 6 to each memory location which contains the value 9. Replace the contents of all other locations in the table with the value 5. Have your program start at location 125_8.

Problem 5.27

Given: Two compool defined tables of the same length called RADXX and RADYY. RADXX contains the x-coordinate of a radar return in each memory location, and RADYY contains the y-coordinate of the return in the corresponding memory location. Also given are 4 compool defined items called QUADA, QUADB, QUADC, and QUADD, which are to contain the counts of how many returns are in quadrants 1, 2, 3, and 4 respectively.

Required: Make a flow diagram for a program which will make the above-mentioned counts. Code the program on EX-1 coding paper. Have your program start at core location 250_8. [NOTE: Consider $(+0, +0)$ returns, $(+0, +X)$ returns, $(+X, +0)$ returns as being in quadrant 1: $(-0, +0)$ returns, $(-X, +0)$ returns, $(-0, +X)$ returns as being in quadrant 2; etc.]

Problem 5.28

Given a table called TNUMB which contains positive and negative numbers, write a program which will replace each number with its absolute value. Have your program start at location 77_8.

Problem 5.29

Given a 5 entry table called **MIXED** containing positive and negative numbers (some may be equal to each other, but none are zero), write a program which will sort them into ascending order; i.e., smaller numbers at the top of the table and larger ones toward the bottom. Have your program assemble for location 200_8.

Problem 5.30

Given a table called **RANDY**, write a program starting at location 35_8 which will place the sum of the positive numbers into memory location **POSUM** and the sum of the negative numbers into location **NGSUM**.

X. THE ASSEMBLER OUTPUT

It should be remembered that if the assembler reads in a card from the card reader stating 2JIX1 50, it must convert it as follows:

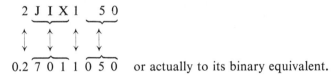

or actually to its binary equivalent.

What is the format of the binary cards produced by the assembler from the symbolic program deck?

EX-1 BINARY CARD FORMAT

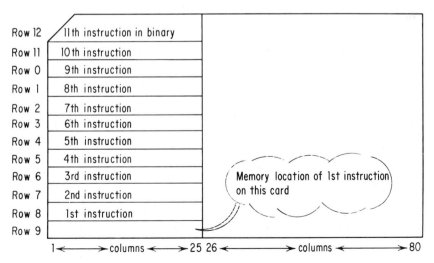

In this simple computer, we are placing only 11 program instructions on a binary format card. It is probably quite clear that on an 80-column card we could get more than three times as many—or in actuality 35(3 × 12 = 36 minus the memory location space = 35 spaces for instructions). However, we will use only the first 25 columns on a card for the sake of simplicity.

Let us take a specific example. Suppose our symbolic program appears thus:

```
              BEG        50
              GET      ZERO
              PUT      COUNT
            1 SIN      NUMBO
AGAIN       1 GET      NUMBO
              JZE      TALLY
CHECK       1 JIX 1 AGAIN
              HLT
TALLY         GET      COUNT
              ADD      ONE
              PUT      COUNT
              JMP      CHECK
ONE         0 0 0 0 0 0 0 0 1
ZERO        0 0 0 0 0 0 0 0 0
              END
```

We will say that COUNT and NUMBO are defined in the compool, to which the assembler has access.

COMPOOL

ENTITY	ADDRESS	LENGTH
NUMBO	200	99
COUNT	40	1

The first three symbolic cards in the input deck look like this.

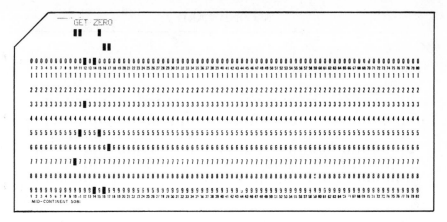

The assembler output for this given program would consist of two cards and appear like this:

FIRST CARD

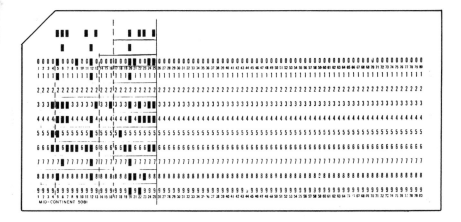

SECOND CARD

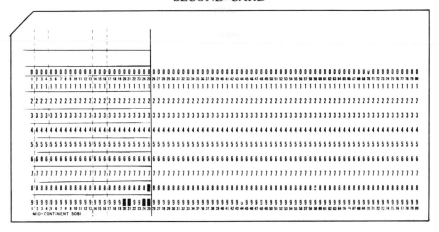

The student should be able to decipher these binary cards by referring to pages 113 and 114 in order to convince himself that it compares instruction by instruction with the original symbolic program.

CHAPTER SIX

EX-1 Arithmetic Operations

I. INTRODUCTION

In making computations by means of a digital computer, the following must be known about each quantity used:

1. The digits that express the quantity (for example, the digits 7852).
2. The position of the radix point (for example, 78.52 or 7.852).
3. The units in which the quantity is expressed (for example, knots, seconds, dollars).

All three of these must be known for the quantity to be completely expressed.

Digital computers do not keep a record of the units associated with the numbers that they process. The task of keeping a record of this information is the responsibility of the programmer. He must include it in his documentation and write his program using the information. For example, if the units of two items are miles and hours respectively, he must realize that dividing the two will result in a quantity which has units of miles-per-hour.

Some digital computers are built to keep an automatic record of the position of the real point in every number taking part in the computation. In such a computer, the point will automatically assume a position that depends upon the result of the computation. A computer that does this is called a *floating point computer.*

A computer that does not keep a record of the position of the point with respect to the digits is called a *fixed point computer*.

The EX-1 computer is *both* a fixed point and a floating point computer.

When performing arithmetic computations the EX-1 can work in either of two modes.

Fixed Point Mode	Floating Point Mode
The way to employ this mode, is to write the computer program using *Fixed Point* instructions.	The way to employ this mode is to write the computer program using *Floating Point* instructions.

The whole problem can be summed up in the question, "Where is the real point?"

In floating point arithmetic the computer keeps track of the real point.

In fixed point arithmetic the programmer keeps track of the real point.

It is undoubtedly more convenient for the programmer to use floating point arithmetic, but a disadvantage of this type of arithmetic is that certain bits in the computer word are required to keep track of the point. Therefore, fewer positions are left for the significant bits of the number.

Generally, if the range through which the values of the variables in a computation vary is relatively small, and if the range is definitely known, fixed point arithmetic is used. Floating point arithmetic is used when the range of numbers which is anticipated during a calculation is either large or unpredictable. Then it may be extremely difficult to program using fixed point instructions.

Floating point instructions are used perhaps more frequently in scientific calculations, whereas, data processing relies heavily upon fixed point instructions.

A program can be written using fixed point instructions by employing logical reasoning, or, in other words, common sense. However, a more advanced method of keeping track of the real point is available. The more advanced method is called *scaling* and employs an algebraic notation called *scaling equations*.

In this chapter we will use only the common sense method to write programs that use fixed point arithmetic. We will take up the advanced method which uses scaling equations in Chapter Nine.

II. FIXED POINT ARITHMETIC

We wish to be able to compute with numbers which may be either integers, fractions, or mixed; whereas, heretofore we have considered all of our numbers as integers. This was for the sake of simplicity.

Suppose we want to represent the number 6.5_{10} in a memory location. We could do it in many ways, some of which are the following:

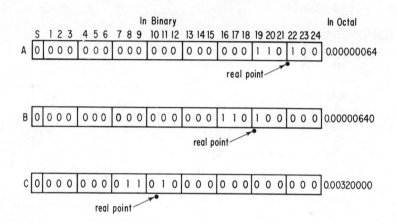

If an individual examined each of the above memory locations he would not know that the number contained therein was supposed to be 6.5_{10}. We need something to state where the real point is intended to be.

The notation that we will use is Bn, where B signifies binary point and n is the number of the bit position preceding the point.

Thus, we would say that the number in momory location A is scaled B21; the number in register B is scaled B18; the number in location C is scaled B10.

The n in Bn may be greater than 24 for our machine, or it may be negative. Thus, we can represent a binary point outside of the machine either to the left or to the right.

Do not consider the sign bit position in counting. A simple way is to think of the sign bit as a little above the rest of the word and removed from consideration.

☐ Sign bit

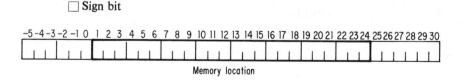

Memory location

Problem 6.1

1. Given the following, find the number (in octal) which is being represented:

Computer word	Bn	Number (in octal)
0.37426000	B12	_____
0.00015400	B14	_____
0.64000000	B-3	_____
1.77540000	B12	_____
0.00000376	B26	_____

2. Given the following, find Bn:

Computer Word	Number (in octal)	Bn
0.42750000	427.5	_____
0.00375200	.03752	_____
1.24677777	−5.31	_____
0.30000000	.003	_____
1.57277777	−4.12	_____

3. Given the following, what does the computer word look like?

Number (in octal)	Bn	Computer Word
256.4	B12	_____
.0075	B-6	_____
−423577770.0	B27	_____
.653	BO	_____
.15	B-2	_____

Let us write a program which will solve a simple addition problem.

Illustrative example

Given: Memory location ALPHA contains a number A scaled B3. ALPHA 0.60000000 A is 6.0 in this particular case.
Memory location OMEGA contains a number B scaled B6. OMEGA 0.77500000 B is 77.5_8 in this particular case.

Required: Write a program which will add A and B together, and place the result C into memory location GAMMA. Store the answer in maximum precision (this means to store the answer with as many fractional places as possible).

Let us solve this by using just common sense.

We see that to add we must line up the real points just as we would in adding a column of numbers on paper. So, our program might be:

```
G E T   A L P H A   Obtain A
S A R             3   Move A right 3 binary places
A D D   O M E G A   Add B to A
P U T   G A M M A   Store answer
H L T
```

We have not used SAR before. It is described as follows:

Mnemonic	Octal Code	Interpretation	Function
S A R	1 0 3	SHIFT ACCUMULATOR RIGHT	All bits in the accumulator with the exception of the sign bit are moved as many places to the right as is specified by the director. Bits leaving the rightmost bit position are lost.[1] Vacancies caused by bits moving right out of bit position 1 are filled with duplicates of the sign bit. The sign bit is not affected. The director is specified in decimal on EX-1 coding paper.

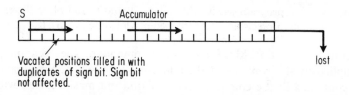

S   Accumulator

Vacated positions filled in with
duplicates of sign bit. Sign bit
not affected.   lost

The instruction SAL, Shift Accumulator Left, operates in a similar manner and is described in Appendix 3.

Let us continue with the illustrative example and make the addition as the machine would.

```
0.06000000   After the shift 3 places right
0.77500000
─────────
1.05500000
```

---

[1]The lost bits fall into a container called a bit bucket. They are emptied periodically and the collected bits are used for confetti at weddings, parties, and other festive occasions.

But this is clearly overflow—adding two positive numbers and getting a negative answer. We should have expected this because $77.5_8 + 6.0_8 = 105.5_8$, which indicates that we need seven places for the whole number part of our answer. This is so because $105_8 = 1000101_2$. Since we allowed only six places in our answer, we had problems. Our coding should have been:

```
        GET    ALPHA    Obtain A.
        SAR        4    Move A right 4 binary places.
        PUT    TEMPA    Store A temporarily.
        GET    OMEGA    Obtain B.
        SAR        1    Move B right 1 binary place.
        ADD    TEMPA    Add B to A.
        PUT    GAMMA    Store answer scaled B7.
        HLT
TEMPA  0.0 0 0 0 0 0 0 0
```

Problem 6.2

Given: Memory location NUMBA contains a positive number A scaled B5. The number A may be as large as the value 31_{10}.

Memory location NUMBB contains a positive number B scalad B4. The number B may be as large as the value 15_{10}.

Memory location NUMBC contains a positive number C scaled B6. The number C may be as large as the value 63_{10}.

Required: Write a program which will add A, B, and C and place the result in maximum precision into core memory location ANSER.

The multiply instruction MUL causes the contents of the accumulator to be multiplied by the contents of the addressed location. The resultant product is contained in the combined accumulator and mask register with the most significant part of the product in the accumulator and the least significant part in the mask register.

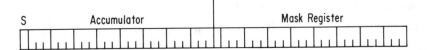

The sign bit position of the mask register does not contain a true sign bit when obtained as a result of the multiply instruction. It contains a magnitude bit just as is found in other magnitude bit positions of the mask register.

The last bit in the mask register is meaningless because multiplication in the EX-1 of two 24 bit registers will result in a 48-bit product plus a sign bit. This makes a total of 49 bits and the 2 registers consist of 50 bits.

If either the multiplier or the multiplicand is "zero," then the resultant product will be $+$ or $-$ zero, depending upon the algebraic sign of the product.

Illustrative example

Given: Memory location NUMBA contains a number A scaled B24.

NUMBA   0.00000005.

Memory location NUMBB contains a number B scaled B9.

NUMBB   0.013.60000

Required: Write a program which will multiply A by B and place the result into memory location ANSER scaled B21. What, in octal, would be the contents of the accumulator?

Solution: GET   NUMBA   Obtain A scaled B24.
MUL   NUMBB   Multiply by B scaled B9. Product is now scaled B33.
SBL   1 2   Shift left 12 to change B33 scaling to B21.
PUT   ANSER   Store result.
HLT

The EX-1 multiplies as if both factors were fractions with the real point located at the machine point. We recall that in ordinary arithmetic, the number of fractional places in a product is the sum of the fractional places in each of the factors. For example, multiplying .09 by .1 results in a product of .009. This is why multiplying A scaled B24 by B scaled B9 resulted in a product scaled B24 $+$ B9 or B33. The easiest way to find the octal contents of the accumulator after the program halts is to multiply in decimal and convert to octal.

$$\text{NUMBA} \qquad 0.00000005. = 5_{10}$$
$$\text{NUMBB} \qquad 0.013.60000 = 11.75_{10}$$
$$11.75_{10} \times 5_{10} = 58.75_{10}$$
$$= 72.6_{8}$$

Therefore, the combined accumulator-mask register after the MUL instruction and before the SBL would be

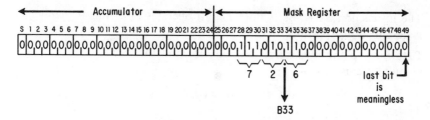

Thus the steps to follow when trying to determine the octal contents of the accumulator are:

1. Convert the two factors to decimal.
2. Multiply them and place the decimal point in the product.
3. Convert the product to octal.
4. Place the real point in the empty combined accumulator-mask register.
5. Place the octal product in binary into the combined accumulator-mask register so that the real point from step 4 and the point in the product are in the same position.

The instruction S B L is described as follows:

Mnemonic	Octal Code	Interpretation	Function
S B L	021	SHIFT BOTH LEFT	All bits in the combined accumulator and mask register with the exception of the accumulator sign bit are moved as many places to the left as is specified by the director. Bits leaving bit position 1 are lost. Vacancies caused by bits moving left out of the rightmost position of the mask register are filled in with duplicates of the accumulator sign bit. The director is specified in decimal on EX-1 coding paper.

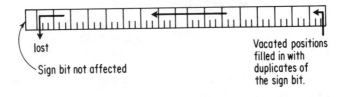

lost

Sign bit not affected

Vacated positions filled in with duplicates of the sign bit.

The instruction S B R, Shift Both Right, operates in a similar manner and is described in Appendix 3.

Returning to the illustrative example, we find that S B L 12 results in accumulator contents of:

$$0.00000726$$

Problem 6.3

Given: Memory location NUMBA contains a number A scaled B9.
Memory location NUMBB contains a number B scaled B18.

Required: Write a program which will multiply A by B and place the product into memory location ANSER scaled B21. If A and B are 47.5_{10} and 429.0_{10} respectively in a particular situation, what would be the contents in octal of the accumulator when the program halts?

The divide instruction, DIV, causes the contents of the combined accumulator and mask register to be divided by the contents of the addressed location. Thus this operation uses a 49 bit dividend—a sign bit and 49 magnitude bits. If the division has been carried out immediately following a multiplication, we would have a good accurate dividend of 48 magnitude bits. The rightmost bit in the mask register is questionable as we learned earlier (for the case of no shift after multiplying).

The quotient will be contained in the accumulator. When the DIV instruction is executed, the absolute magnitude (uncomplemented value) of the divisor must be greater than the absolute magnitude (uncomplemented value) of the dividend. Otherwise a meaningless quotient will result. In order to have a correct quotient, all division performed must yield a fractional result—as far as the machine is concerned. The machine divides as if the real points and machine points coincide in the dividend, divisor, and quotient.

Illustrative example

Given: A number X in XNUMB scaled B10. The magnitude of X is always less than 1604_8 and greater than 144_8.
A number Y in YNUMB scaled B6. The magnitude of Y is always less than 60_8 and greater than 11_8.

Required: Write a program which will divide X by Y and store the result Z into ZNUMB.

Solution: We want to insure that X is always less than Y as far as the machine is concerned. This will insure that Z is fractional. Therefore, we must examine the ranges of X and Y. To make certain that Z is fractional, X must be scaled before dividing by Y in such a manner that the *largest* value of X will be smaller than the *smallest* value of Y.

The smallest value of Y is greater than 11_8 (given) and scaled B6. The number 11_8 would appear like this:

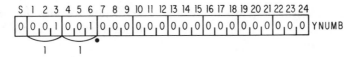

The largest value of X is less than 1604_8 (given) and scaled B10. The number 1604_8 would appear like this:

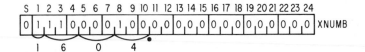

To insure that the contents of XNUMB is smaller than the contents of YNUMB means that the 1st significant bit in XNUMB must start in bit position 4 since the 1st significant bit in YNUMB is in bit position 3.

Therefore, before dividing, the contents of XNUMB must be shifted right 3 bit positions. This will cause X to be scaled B13.

Since X is now scaled B13 and Y is scaled B6, the quotient Z obtained by dividing X by Y will be scaled B13 — B6 or B7. Therefore, the program can be written as follows:

```
START    GET    XNUMB
         SBR        3
         DIV    YNUMB
         PUT    ZNUMB
         HLT
```

Problem 6.4

Given: A number X in XNUMB scaled B12. The magnitude of X is always less than 7605_8 and greater than 127_8.
A number Y in YNUMB scaled B7. The magnitude of Y is always less than 175_8 and greater than 13_8

Required: Write a program which will divide X by Y and store the result Z into ZNUMB. How is the answer scaled?

III. FLOATING POINT ARITHMETIC

When using floating point instructions, the data being manipulated (added, subtracted, multiplied, etc.) are construed by the computer to be of the following format:

The characteristic describes the scaling. The fraction contains the significant bits of the number. The sign bit still determines whether the number is positive or negative.

Since 9 bits are allocated for the characteristic, its value can vary from 000_8 to 777_8. It is desirable to be able to scale numbers so that Bn can have a negative n. Therefore, the EX-1 considers a characteristic of 400 to correspond to scaling of B0.

The following relationship exists for the EX-1.

Octal Characteristic	Decimal Characteristic	Bn
777	511	B255
. . .	. . .	. . .
. . .	. . .	. . .
. . .	. . .	. . .
401	257	B1
400	256	B0
377	255	B-1
. . .	. . .	. . .
. . .	. . .	. . .
. . .	. . .	. . .
000	000	B-256

Let us see how the number $\frac{1}{2}$ would appear in the computer word in floating point format.

$$\frac{1}{2} = .1_2, \text{ therefore,}$$

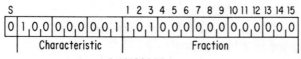

or 0.40040000 in octal

The number is scaled B0 in the above case.

The number $1\frac{1}{4}$ would appear this way since $1\frac{1}{4} = 1.01_2$.

or 0.40150000 in octal

The number is scaled B1 in the above case.

The number $\frac{3}{8}$ would appear this way since $\frac{3}{8} = .011_2$.

or 0.37760000 in octal

The number is scaled B-1 in the above case.

Observe that a significant bit is always in position 1. In other words, the fraction is always shoved as far left as is possible without losing anything.

When the fraction is shoved as far left as is possible (and this occurs automatically in the EX-1), we say that the fraction is *normalized*.

For negative numbers the entire computer word is 1's complemented.

Thus, -3.75_{10} would appear as:

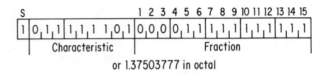

or 1.37503777 in octal

Problem 6.5

Write the octal machine representation of the following decimal numbers. Assume that they are in the machine in floating point form.

1. 9.5
2. 68.125
3. .0055
4. −9.25
5. −.00005

We must have a convenient way of getting floating point constants or numbers into the EX-1. We will do this by the use of a pseudo instruction.

By placing the letters FLO (for FLOATING POINT) in the instruction field on EX-1 coding paper and the decimal number (it must contain a decimal point) in the director field, the assembler will set up the computer word in floating point form.

Illustrative example

Given: memory location ALPHA contains a number in floating point format, write a program to add the number 9.875 to it. Place the result back into ALPHA.

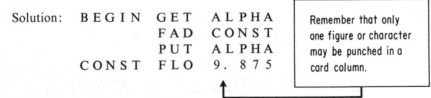

Solution: BEGIN   GET   ALPHA
                    FAD   CONST
                    PUT   ALPHA
            CONST   FLO   9. 875

Remember that only one figure or character may be punched in a card column.

If we desire a floating point number that is larger or smaller than the pseudo instruction FLO can get for us, we will have to manually convert the number to floating point form as was done in Problem 6.5 and put it in the program as an octal constant.

The 4 floating point instructions are FAD, FSB, FMU, and FDV. They are described in Appendix 3.

Problem 6.6

Given: X in memory location XNUMB in floating point form.
        Y in memory location YNUMB in floating point form.
        Z in memory location ZNUMB in floating point form (Z is not zero).
Required: Write a program which will compute

$$W = \frac{XY + 9.675}{Z} \text{ using floating point instructions.}$$

Store the result W into WNUMB.

CHAPTER SEVEN

Programming Techniques

I. TABLE SEARCH AND TABLE LOOK-UP

When we must examine each entry of a table to obtain desired information, we call the process *table search*. When we need not examine each entry of a table to acquire the needed information, but can go directly to the location of the information, we call the process *table look-up*.

Let us illustrate the table search method.

Illustrative example

Given: A compool defined table called EMPLY. Each entry is composed of items EMPSL and EMPNO. EMPSL contains the monthly salary in dollars of an employee. EMPNO contains the employee's number. The entries are sorted so that employee numbers are consecutive from low to high, starting with 0.

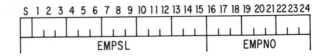

Required: Write a program which will count the number of employees whose monthly salary is more than $600. Place this count into compool defined item RICH. RICH occupies an entire core memory location.

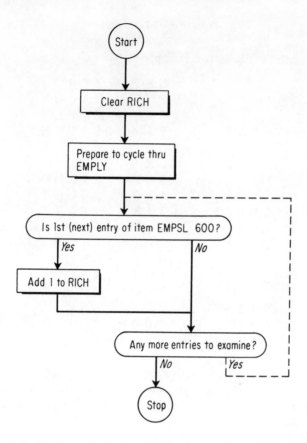

Solution:

This is the first time that we have attempted to program using packed items. In order to isolate EMPSL we will need the following two instructions:

Mnemonic	Octal Code	Interpretation	Function
PIM	767	PUT IN MASK	Clears the mask register and brings the contents of the core memory register specified by the director into the mask register. Does not affect specified core memory register or accumulator.
EXT	533	EXTRACT	Takes no director. For each bit position in the mask register which contains a zero replaces the corresponding bit position of the accumulator with a zero. Does not affect other bit positions. Does not affect mask register.

Continuing with the illustrative example:

```
              GET    ZERO
              PUT    RICH
            1 SIN    EMPLY
NEXT          PIM    SIEVE
            1 GET    EMPLY
              EXT
              SUB    SIXHD
              JPO    COUNT
CHECK       1 JIX1   NEXT
ZERO          HLT
COUNT         GET    RICH
              ADD    ONE
              PUT    RICH
              JMP    CHECK
SIEVE     1 . 7 7 7 7 7 0 0 0
ONE       0 . 0 0 0 0 0 0 0 1
SIXHD     0 . 0 1 1 3 0 0 0 0
```

It should be recalled that any active jump instruction will alter the contents of the Mask Register. The core location of what would be the next instruction, if the jump didn't occur, replaces the contents of the Mask Register. This fact will be valuable when we discuss subroutines.

Right now, however, JPO JIX and JMP in the above program may all change the mask in the Mask Register; so we will want to be sure to set it each time we extract with EXT.

Problem 7.1

Using the given information of the above illustrated example, write a program which will give a $50.00 raise to every employee whose salary is greater than $600.00 but less than $850.00. Place the payroll increase that this will cause into compool defined register INCSE.

Let us illustrate the table look-up method.

There are two ways in which table look-up may be performed. We may use an index register, or we may use the accumulator as an index. We will try an index register first.

We can use the following new instruction:

Mnemonic	Octal Code	Interpretation	Function
PAD	766	PUT ADDRESS	Takes contents of bits 16–24 (director field) from mask register and places these contents in bits 16–24 of the core memory location specified by director. Does not affect accumulator or mask register. Does not affect contents of bits S–15 of core memory location specified by director.

Illustrative example

Given: Table EMPLY described in the previous illustrative example and a single 1-word item called WHICH that contains an employee number right justified.

Required: Write a program which will obtain the monthly salary of the employee whose number is in item WHICH. Place the entire entry (EMPSL and EMPNO) into compool defined item ANSER. ANSER occupies an entire core memory register.

Solution:

```
        P I M   WH I C H   Place employee number into mask
                           register.
        P A D   I N D E X   Places employee number into 2SIN
                           instruction.
I N D E X 2 S I N 7         Director left blank. Modified by above
                           instruction.
        2 G E T   E M P L Y   Obtain correct entry in table.
        P U T   A N S E R   Store result.
        H L T
```

You will recall from Chapter Five that specifying an increment of 7 with the SIN instruction causes both the present and final count of the specified index register to be set to the value of the director.

Note that table look-up is possible in this problem only because the entries of table EMPLY are ordered consecutively by employee number EMPNO.

An alternate solution may be written using the deposit instruction DEP.

Mnemonic	Octal Code	Interpretation	Function
DEP	534	DEPosit	For each bit position in the mask register which contains a 1, replaces the contents of the corresponding bit position of the memory location specified by the director with the contents of the corresponding bit position of the accumulator. Does not affect the other bit positions in the memory location. Does not affect contents of the accumulator or mask register.

Alternate solution:

	GET	WHICH	Place employee number into accumulator.
	PIM	SIEVE	Place a deposit mask into the mask register.
	DEP	INDEX	Deposit employee number into director of 2SIN.
INDEX	2SIN7	0	Director left blank. Modified by above instruction.
	2GET	EMPLY	Obtain correct entry in table.
	PUT	ANSER	Store result.
	HLT		
SIEVE	0.00000777		

The second method which we can use for table look-up involves using the accumulator as an index register. As such, it is designated by a 3 in the index field on the EX-1 coding paper. It cannot be set with the SIN instruction or tested or incremented with the JIX instruction. It can be used for address modification however, and this is what we need in table look-up. Bits 16–24 of the accumulator are used to modify the director when 3 is specified as the index register.

Using the above example and employing the accumulator as index register number 3, we get

```
        GET   WHICH
       3GET   EMPLY
        PUT   ANSER
        HLT
```

Problem 7.2

Given: A compool defined, 1-word item, called NMBER which contains an integer N from 0 to 100 scaled B24.

A compool defined, 1-word item, called SQRUT which is to contain the square root of the number scaled B4.

A compool defined table ROOTS built on the following plan:

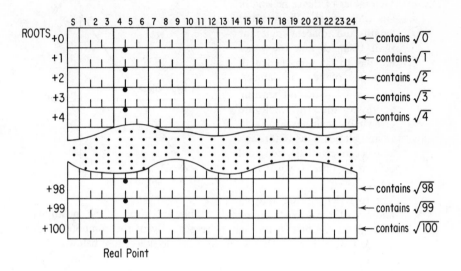

Real Point

Square roots are what is in table ROOTS. For example, in register ROOTS +4 we find the square root of the number 4. In register ROOTS +100 we find the square root of 100. Since the biggest square root encountered will be $10_{10} = 12_8 = 1010_2$, four places must be allotted for the integral parts in this table. Hence, the square roots are scaled B4 in this table.

I have tried to illustrate this in the drawing above. The symbolic representations $\sqrt{0}, \sqrt{1}, \sqrt{2}, \sqrt{3}$, etc., are merely representations in the drawing and are in actuality 0's and 1's. In register ROOTS +4, for example, we would have the $\sqrt{4}$ represented as

S	1	2	3	4	5	6	7	8	9	10	11	12	13	14	15	16	17	18	19	20	21	22	23	24
0	0	0	1	0	0	0	0	0	0	0	0	0	0	0	0	0	0	0	0	0	0	0	0	0

Real Point

or 0.10000000 in octal

Required : Write a program which will place the square root of the number found in NMBER into item SQRUT.

Problem 7.3

Given the information in problem 7.2, write a program to compute $N + 2\sqrt{N} + 29$ and place the result into 1-word item ANSER scaled to take care of the largest N.

Problem 7.4

Given: Two tables of the same length. One table contains hypotenuse lengths and adjacent angles for right triangles and the other table is to contain the length of the legs of the right triangles.

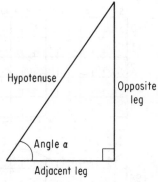

The total length and starting address of the "leg" table are given in bit positions 4 through 12 and bit positions 16 through 24 respectively of the compool defined, single, 1-word item RECOR.

The total length and starting address of the "hypotenuse-angle" table are given in bit positions 4 through 12 and bits 16 through 24 respectively of the compool defined, single, 1-word item POLAR. These tables look as those below.

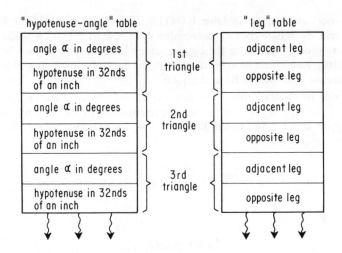

Also given are two compool defined tables called SINES and COSNS which are designed as follows:

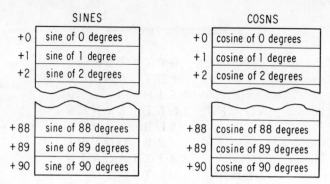

SINES		COSNS	
+0	sine of 0 degrees	+0	cosine of 0 degrees
+1	sine of 1 degree	+1	cosine of 1 degree
+2	sine of 2 degrees	+2	cosine of 2 degrees
+88	sine of 88 degrees	+88	cosine of 88 degrees
+89	sine of 89 degrees	+89	cosine of 89 degrees
+90	sine of 90 degrees	+90	cosine of 90 degrees

The scaling on the sines and cosines is B0. Trigonometric functions which have a value of 1 are thus represented by .111—in binary.

The transformation equations to use are:

$$\text{adjacent leg} = (\text{hypotenuse}) \times (\text{cosine } \alpha)$$

$$\text{opposite leg} = (\text{hypotenuse}) \times (\text{sine } \alpha)$$

Required: Write a program which, using the "hypotenuse-angle" table as input, will create the "leg" table, and have the adjacent and opposite legs in quarter inches.

We might try a slightly different approach to table processing.

Illustrative example

Given: The table SINES of problem 7.4 and compool defined, single, 1-word item UKNON which contains the sine of an angle scaled in the same manner as the SINES table.

Required: Write a program which will place the angle whose sine is in UKNON into compool defined, single, 1-word item ANGLE. Consider the angle to be in increments of degrees—that is, scaled B24.

Solution: We will require a new instruction called Add Index to Director, AXD.

Mnemonic	Octal Code	Interpretation	Function
AXD	563	ADD INDEX TO DIRECTOR	Adds the contents of the specified index register (present count) to the director (not contents of the location specified by the director) and place the result in mask register. The accumulator is not affected.

137

```
              GET   ZERO
              PUT   ANGLE
             2 SIN         90
AGAIN        2 GET   SINES
              SUB   UKNON
              JZE   GOTIT
             2 JIX 1 AGAIN
ZERO          HLT
GOTIT        2 AXD          0
              PAD   ANGLE
              HLT
```

Problem 7.5

Given: A compool defined table called ALPHA which contains 1-word items
          THETA.

Required: Write a program which will compare each entry of THETA with
          the contents of a compool defined, single, 1-word item GAMMA.
          When a match occurs replace the value in GAMMA with the relative
          position in the table of the entry that matched. Only one entry will
          match.

Problem 7.6

Given: A compool defined table called EMPLY. Each entry of the table con-
          tains two items, EMPNO and EMPSL. EMPNO contains an employee
          number and EMPSL contains the employee monthly salary in dollars.

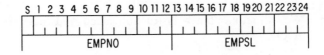

          The salary is given to the nearest dollar and the table is ordered by salary
          in ascending order; that is, low salaries at the top and large salaries at
          the bottom.

Required: Write a program which will obtain the number of the employee whose
          salary is nearest to $600 and place this number in bit positions 1
          through 12 of compool defined, single, 1-word item CLOSE. In bits
          16 through 24 of CLOSE place the relative position of the register in
          the table where the information was found.

II. A SQUARE ROOT ROUTINE

We have seen how we can obtain square roots of numbers by the means of table look-up. Table look-up requires core space, and sometimes this space might be considerable. It might be more advantageous to use a method which would compute square root.

Several mathematical routines exist which can be used to extract square roots. One method might be the usual math class method of grouping in pairs from the decimal point. One which lends itself more readily to computers is called *Newton's Method.*

Mathematically stated $\sqrt{n} \approx \dfrac{1}{2}\left(R_0 + \dfrac{n}{R_0}\right) = R_1$

Where: n is the number whose root is to be extracted.
R_0 is an approximation of the root of n.
R_1 is the improved approximation resulting from the operation.
$\approx$ is a symbol which means "is approximately equal to."

This equation represents a method for extracting a root as accurately as desired by repeating the calculation, using R_1, the result of the preceding calculation, as the approximation R_0 in the next iteration. The first approximation (the value of R_0 used in the first iteration) need not be close to the final result; almost any number will do. However, the closeness of the first approximation to the final result determines the number of iterations required to obtain the root with a given accuracy. For example, n/2 is frequently taken as R_0.

Problem 7.7

Given: A number n in floating point format. The number is to be found in the compool defined register NUMBR.

Required: Using floating point instructions, compute $\sqrt{n}$ using Newton's Method. Consider the root sufficiently accurate when $|R_0 - R_1| <$ $.0001_{10}$ and place the result into RZULT.

Problem 7.8

Given: An integer n such that $0 \leq n \leq 100$. The integer n is scaled B24 and is found in the compool defined register UNCLE.

Required: Using fixed point instructions, compute $\sqrt{n}$ using Newton's Method. Store the result into ANSER using maximum precision.

Problem 7.9

Make a flow diagram and write a program using fixed point instructions which will compute π to maximum precision and store the result into location **PYE**. Use John Wallis' Formula which is

$$\frac{\pi}{2} = \frac{2}{1} \times \frac{2}{3} \times \frac{4}{3} \times \frac{4}{5} \times \frac{6}{5} \times \frac{6}{7} \times \frac{8}{7} \times \frac{8}{9} \times \frac{10}{9} \times \cdots$$

Problem 7.10

Make a flow diagram and write a program using floating point instructions which will compute π and store the result into register PI. Use Leibnitz's Formula which is

$$\frac{\pi}{4} = 1 - \frac{1}{3} + \frac{1}{5} - \frac{1}{7} + \frac{1}{9} - \frac{1}{11} \cdots$$

A routine to compute π as is done in the above two problems is probably of little practical value. Since we know the value of π, it would best be stored in the computer as a constant. Mathematical routines, however, exist which compute the various trigonometric functions and they are valuable, just as the square root routine could be valuable.

Problem 7.11

Write a paragraph defining or describing the term "Numerical Analysis."

Problem 7.12

See if you can do some research and locate a mathematical routine which will compute the sine of an angle having been given the angle.

III. SUBROUTINES

Frequently, a mathematical routine (such as obtaining a square root) or a data processing routine (such as sorting a table) must be done at several different places in a program or program system. Depending upon the circumstances (frequency of use, core space, length of routine, etc.), the programmer may elect to insert the coding for his routine at the several places of need throughout his program, or he may create a *subroutine*.

A subroutine is a piece of code which may be branched to from any one of several places in a program. The piece of code performs its function and returns control to the point from which it originated.

Usually the subroutine must have some input information. Thus, if it were a subroutine for computing square root, the number whose root is to be obtained might be contained in the accumulator prior to branching to the subroutine. The result of the subroutine might also be contained in the accumulator upon returning to the main program. These inputs to a subroutine and outputs from a subroutine are frequently called *entrance* and *exit parameters*.

Sometimes entrance and exit parameters are contained in a location (or locations) immediately following the branch to the main program. The branch to the subroutine is termed *the call*.

PICTORIAL REPRESENTATION OF A SUBROUTINE

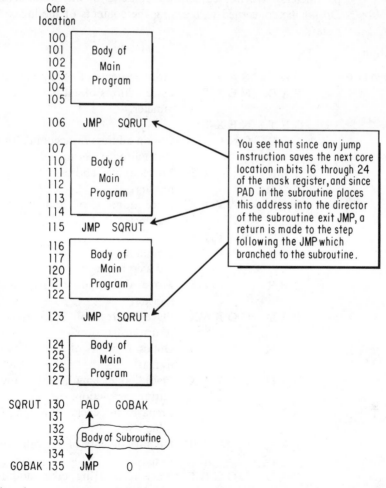

The above sequence of code was written with the plan to have the entrance and exit parameters in the accumulator. Let us look at another example.

Illustrative example

Given: A table of numbers whose starting location and length are given
         respectively in the first and second locations following the call.

Required: Write a subroutine whose first location is symbolically labeled
            ADDUP. It is to add up the numbers in the table and place the
            sum into register SUM. Assume that the scaling is such that the
            numbers may simply be added and the result stored away.
            Have the subroutine return control to the main program to the
            third location following the call (because of the two entrance
            parameters). Do not destroy the contents of the accumulator.
            Do not be concerned with saving the contents of the index re-
            gisters.

Solution:

ADDUP	PUT	SAVAC	Store contents of accumulator.
	PAD	NEXT	Place address of 1st entrance parameter.
	GET	NEXT	
	ADD	ONE	Obtain address in accumulator of 2nd entrance parameter.
	SBR	2 5	Move above address into mask register.
	PAD	SAVIX	Place address of 2nd entrance parameter.
	GET	SAVIX	
	ADD	ONE	Obtain address in accumulator of 3rd step following call.
	SBR	2 5	Move above address into mask register.
	PAD	GOBAK	Place address of 3rd step into return instruction.
SAVIX	PIM	0	Obtain contents of 2nd call word in mask.
	PAD	SETIX	Place table length into index setting instruction.
SETIX	2 SIN	0	Prepare to cycle through the table.
NEXT	PIM	0	Obtain contents of 1st call word in mask.
	PAD	GOGET	Place it (starting table address) into instruction.
	GET	ZERO	Clear accumulator.

```
GOGET     2 ADD           0    Add contents of 1st (or next)
                                register in table.

          2 JIX1 GOGET
          PUT   SUM            Store sum away.
          GET   SAVAC          Pick up contents of accumulator.
GOBAK     JMP             0    Return to main program.
ZERO    0 . 00000000
ONE     0 . 00000001
SAVAC   0 . 00000000
```

Problem 7.13

Will the solution to the above illustrative example work the second time it is entered from the main program? The third time? (Remember, we have modified instructions—or at least their addresses—in many places.)

Problem 7.14

Invent about 3 instructions that might be useful for the EX-1 to have when solving problems in subroutines.

Another common method of working with the entrance and exit parameters is shown below. Here, let us assume that we wish to add the first two entrance parameters together and place the sum into the exit parameter. This is probably not a very practical use for a subroutine, however, it illustrates what I want to show—the linkage technique.

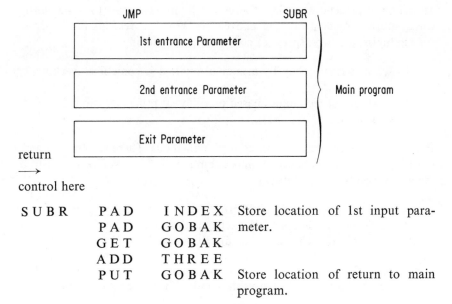

```
SUBR      PAD    INDEX    Store location of 1st input para-
          PAD    GOBAK    meter.
          GET    GOBAK
          ADD    THREE
          PUT    GOBAK    Store location of return to main
                          program.
```

```
INDEX 2 S I N 7        Ø
      2 G E T          Ø
      2 A D D          1
      2 P U T          2
GOBAK   J M P          Ø    Return to main program.
```

In the 2GET Ø, 2ADD 1, and 2PUT 2 instructions the effective addresses referred to are the 1st entrance parameter, the 2nd entrance parameter, and the exit parameter respectively. This is so because the index register #2 contains the location of the 1st entrance parameter.

Problem 7.15

Write a subroutine which will compute the factorial of a number (symbolically stated n !). The number as an entrance parameter will be in the accumulator in floating point format. Have your subroutine store the result in floating point format into the register whose address is found in the word in the main program immediately following the call. Use the symbol FACTO as the label of your first instruction. (Factorial $n = 1 \times 2 \times 3 \times \cdots (n - 1) \times n$; thus, 3 ! = $1 \times 2 \times 3 = 6$ and 7 ! = $1 \times 2 \times 3 \times 4 \times 5 \times 6 \times 7 = 5040$.)

IV. SORTING

A programmer invariably finds himself with the task of sorting a table into ascending or descending order. Therefore, the process of sorting is a worthwhile subject. Aside from the above very practical reason, the study of sorting highlights two aspects of computer programming.

1. What is done easily by a manual method is sometimes very tricky to program.
2. A variety of techniques based on different principles can achieve the same result.

In this section we will discuss three sorting methods. There are many others, but these three are probably the most common and will suffice to illustrate the above points. We will discuss

(1) The Simple Sort,
(2) The Shuttle Exchange Sort, and
(3) The Binary Radix Exchange Sort.

The Simple Sort—Let us look at the problem as a manual exercise first. Suppose we had a box with shelves in it and each shelf contained a ball with a number on it. We know that, looking at the group of balls, we could manually arrange them in ascending order. We might have to stop and think, however, if we were asked to explain our process.

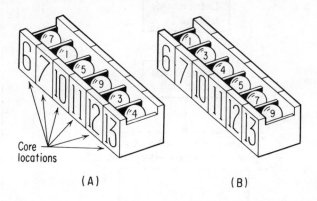

(A)   (B)

What we have in computer sorting is something analogous to the following manual arrangement.

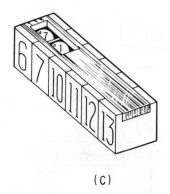

(C)

The addition in the above figure is a slidable cover to the set of shelves. The cover has a hole in it so that only two balls can be compared at a time. This is analogous to the EX-1 being able to compare only two core memory locations at a time.

The solution is relatively simple. We move the cover down one location at a time. If the two balls that we can see are out of the desired order, we exchange them. Getting the hole in the cover all the way down and having made the necessary exchanges all of the way, assures us that the largest number is in the bottom place.

If we did not have to make any exchanges, the set of balls was in order. If we had to make any, the chances are that the set of balls was not in order.

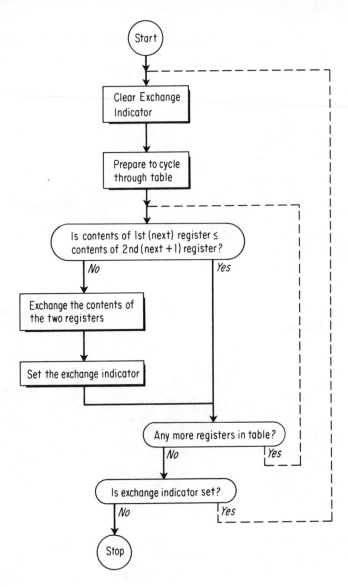

So we slide the cover to the starting location and start coming down again with it one shelf at a time, making the necessary exchanges. On this second pass we are assured of getting the next highest number into the next to last spot. In fact, we do not need to compare the last two again.

Continuing this procedure, we will arrive at a pass when no exchanges were made, and we can rest assured that the balls are in order. This method is sometimes called *the sinking sort* since each pass sinks the heaviest remaining to the bottom. It is also called *the simple sort*.

This sort is flow diagrammed on page 146.

Let us program a specific problem.

Given: A 5 entry table of numbers. The starting location of the table is at core memory location 100.

Required: Write a program which will sort the numbers into ascending order.

```
START    GET   ZERO  ⎫Clear Exchange Indicator.
         PUT   INDIC ⎭
        2SIN        4   Prepare to cycle through table.
UPPER   2GET      100
        2SUB      101
         JPO   SWITH
CHECK   2JIX1UPPER      Any more entries in table?
         GET   INDIC
         JZE   ZERO     A branch here means table is in
                        order.
         JIX   START    A branch here means that exchanges
                        were made.
ZERO     HLT
SWITH   2GET      100 ⎫
         PUT   TEMP    ⎪
        2GET      101  ⎬Exchange routine.
        2PUT      100  ⎪
         GET   TEMP    ⎪
        2PUT      101 ⎭
         GET   ONE  ⎫Set exchange indicator.
         PUT   INDIC⎭
         JIX   CHECK
INDIC   0.00000000
TEMP    0.00000000
ONE     0.00000001
```

Test the program on the previous page by acting as if you were the computer using the following table of numbers:

100	2
101	2
102	0
103	−3
104	4

Note: The farther left on the number line that a number appears, the smaller it is.

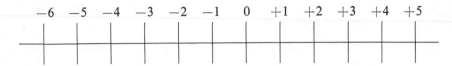

-6 -5 -4 -3 -2 -1 0 +1 +2 +3 +4 +5

Let us change the problem to use a compool defined table.

Given: Table ALPHA which contains numbers.

Required: Write a program which will arrange the numbers into ascending order.

```
START         GET   SETER
              SUB   ONE
              PUT   SETER
              GET   LOWA
              ADD   ONE
              SBR        2 5
              PAD   LOWA
              PAD   LOWB
              PAD   LOWC
BEGIN         GET   ZERO
              PUT   INDIC
SETER       2 SIN   ALPHA
UPPER       2 GET   ALPHA
LOWA        2 SUB   ALPHA
              JPO   SWITH
CHECK       2 JIX 1 UPPER
              GET   INDIC
              JZE   ZERO
              JMP   BEGIN
ZERO          HLT
SWITH       2 GET   ALPHA
              PUT   TEMP
LOWB        2 GET   ALPHA
            2 PUT   ALPHA
              GET   TEMP
LOWC        2 PUT   ALPHA
              GET   ONE
              PUT   INDIC
              JMP   CHECK
```

```
T E M P       0 . 0 0 0 0 0 0 0 0
I N D I C     0 . 0 0 0 0 0 0 0 0
O N E         0 . 0 0 0 0 0 0 0 1
```

Problem 7.16

In what way would the above sequence of code have to be modified if it were made into a subroutine?

Problem 7.17

Given: Table EMPLY whose starting address is found in the compool but whose number of entries is contained in the first location.

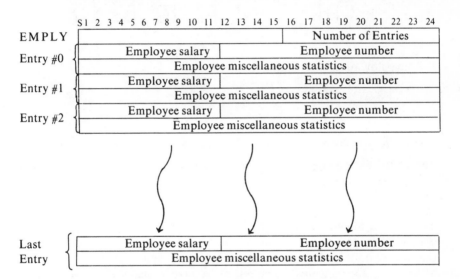

Required: Write a program which will order the entires according to employee number from low to high.

The Shuttle Exchange Sort—With this technique the table to be sorted is scanned in a manner similar to the simple sort. When the first one out of order is encountered, it is exchanged on backward (upward) until it is placed in the proper position. This routine is more complicated but faster than the simple sort.

Let us illustrate symbolically how it is going to operate.

Imagine we have the following 7 location table to sort:

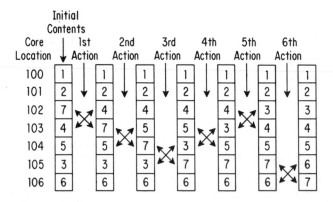

We have flow diagrammed this sort' on page 151.

Problem 7.18

Given:　A compool defined table called **NUMBR** which contains numbers.

Required:　Write a program which uses the shuttle exchange sort and will arrange
the numbers into ascending order.

The student attempting problem 7.18 above will wonder at and probably
question the statement that the shuttle sort is fast. We should remember
that we are quite limited in our EX-1 computer language in what we can do.
Much more sophisticated machines might have as many as 10 instructions
alone which work with the index registers. Then too, the size of the table to
be sorted is a factor to be considered.

The Binary Radix Exchange Sort—We will only discuss the method used in
the Binary Radix Exchange Sort. No attempt at a flow diagram or programming will be made unless it be on the student's own initiative.

Let us sort the following binary numbers using the Binary Radix Exchange
Sort. (See page 152.)

SHUTTLE EXCHANGE SORT

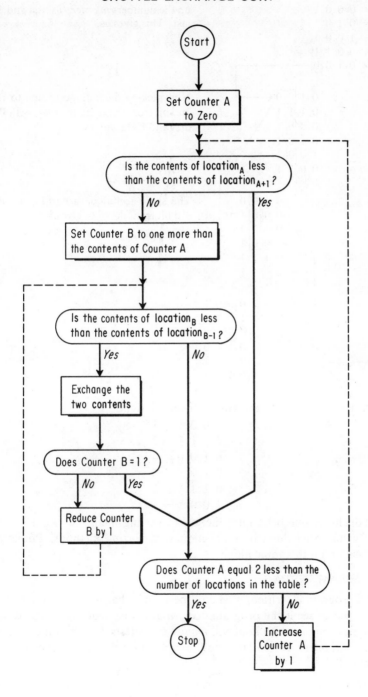

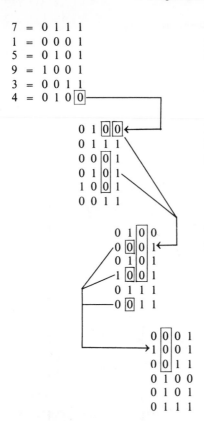

7 = 0 1 1 1
1 = 0 0 0 1
5 = 0 1 0 1
9 = 1 0 0 1
3 = 0 0 1 1
4 = 0 1 0 0

We start at the low order end and pick up the numbers *in order*, 0's first and 1's last. This gives us,

0 1 0 0
0 1 1 1
0 0 0 1
0 1 0 1
1 0 0 1
0 0 1 1

Now picking them up according to the 2nd bit from the right, *in order*, with 0's first and 1's last gives,

0 1 0 0
0 0 0 1
0 1 0 1
1 0 0 1
0 1 1 1
0 0 1 1

The same technique according to the 3rd bit from the right gives,

0 0 0 1
1 0 0 1
0 0 1 1
0 1 0 0
0 1 0 1
0 1 1 1

And lastly, according to the 4th bit from the right,

$$0\ 0\ 0\ 1 = 1$$
$$0\ 0\ 1\ 1 = 3$$
$$0\ 1\ 0\ 0 = 4$$
$$0\ 1\ 0\ 1 = 5$$
$$0\ 1\ 1\ 1 = 7$$
$$1\ 0\ 0\ 1 = 9$$

This concludes our brief introduction to sorting methods. Quite extensive research has been done in connection with sorting methods. Books have been written on this topic alone.

V. PROGRAM TESTING

After a program is written, it should be tested; that is to say, a test should be designed to see if the program does what it was logically designed to do. Sometimes complete checkout will require many tests. In fact, some programs, such as compilers, are so large and complex that they may never be "completely tested."

Testing designed to test one program is frequently called *parameter testing*.

Testing which is designed to test a system (group of programs controlled by a control program) is called *assembly testing*.

Testing should be done at the desk initially. When the programmer is satisfied that his program does what it should do by a desk check, he tries it out on the computer.

For testing at the computer many programs are usually available as tools. These test tools would consist of programs that enable easy setting of initial values, recording of results (intermediate and final), and printouts in one of perhaps several modes—English, octal, or decimal. Programs would also be available for "patching" or correcting in octal or symbolic any incorrect instructions in the object program.

In this text we will not have an opportunity for machine testing of an EX-1 program. I would, however, like to give a problem, the solution of which will give some insight into how parameter testing at the desk level might proceed.

Problem 7.19

Make a flow diagram and code a program which will examine locations ROSE and TUNIA. If ROSE contains the value 3, increase location COUNT by 1. If TUNIA contains the value 5, increase COUNT by 2. If ROSE contains the value 7 *and* TUNIA contains the value 9, increase COUNT by 4. Otherwise, reset COUNT to 0. Use fixed point arithmetic and consider ROSE, TUNIA, and COUNT as scaled B24. Then use the test matrix below to parameter test at your desk the correctness of your program.

	Value in ROSE	Value in TUNIA	COUNT should get	Your program sets COUNT to
Trial 1	3	1	+1	
Trial 2	1	5	+2	
Trial 3	3	5	+1 +2	
Trial 4	1	2	Set to 0	
Trial 5	7	9	+4	
Trial 6	7	1	Set to 0	
Trial 7	1	9	Set to 0	
Trial 8	7	5	+2	
Trial 9	3	9	+1	

↑ Expected values   ↑ Actual values

CHAPTER EIGHT

Input-Output
for the EX-1

We will provide the EX-1 with:

1. a card reader
2. a printer
3. a card punch
4. a tape drive

As these provide either input to the computer, or output from the computer, we will call these devices *Input-Output Equipment*, which is abbreviated I/O.

The process of transferring data from I/O equipment to core memory is called *reading*. Transferring data from core memory to I/O equipment is referred to as *writing*. The way to remember this is to put yourself in the place of core memory. If you were core memory you would be reading when taking in information and writing when putting out information.

This terminology—reading, writing, memory, etc.— is often misleading to the layman. It is descriptive, but, unfortunately, tends to ascribe human and living traits to an inanimate machine.

Problem 8.1

Can machines think today? If not, do you believe that they will ever be able to think? Write a paper defending either the affirmative or negative.

I. THE CARD READER

The EX-1 instruction which calls on the card reader is RCD.

Mnemonic Code	Octal Code	Interpretation	Function
RCD	130	R̲EAD A C̲AR̲D̲	Electrically selects the card reader and transfers the data (read) columns 1 through 25 of one card into magnetic core storage. Row 9 will go into core memory location 0. Row 8 will go into core memory location 1, etc.

The above is true whether or not the cards in the reader are 12-bit hollerith or binary.

Problem 8.2

What, in octal, would core locations 0 through 13 contain after an RCD was given if the following card (below right) were in the reader?

Problem 8.3

What, in octal, would core locations 0 through 13 contain after an RCD was given if the following card (below left) were in the reader?

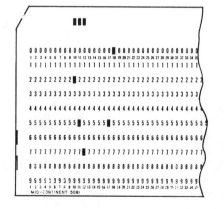

We will soon find, when we write a program to read in cards, that it will be desirable to be able to know whether or not the card reader is empty. Therefore, the EX-1 has the feature that when an RCD instruction is operated but no card was in the card reader, the red light on the computer console will come on and remain on until turned off. The instruction J R D which is the mnemonic for JUMP ON RED LIGHT can then examine the condition of the light.

Thus, to read in all the cards in the reader, one would have to give the R C D instruction, check to see if he got anything, and if he did, process it or move it.

Illustrative example

Write a program which will read all of the cards in the reader into core location 200 and following. After all of the cards are read in, branch to location START.

Solution:

	J R D	R E A D	This step insures red light is off initially.
R E A D	R C D		Read one card.
	J R D	S T A R T	Did we get anything? If not, go to S T A R T.
	2 S I N	1 2	⎫
N E X T A	2 G E T	0	⎬ Move data.
N E X T B	2 P U T	2 0 0	⎭
	2 J I X 1	N E X T A	
	G E T	N E X T B	⎫ Modify addresses into which
	A D D	S O M E	⎬ data is moved.
	P U T	N E X T B	⎭
	J M P	R E A D	
S O M E	0 . 0 0 0 0 0 0 1 4		

Problem 8.4

Write a program which will read in a binary deck of the format as comes from the assembler (Chapter 5). The cards may not be in order, hence the starting location given on each card must be used. When all the cards have been read in, branch control to the 1st step of the program which has just been read in. (Remember, the cards may be out of order, so you will have to determine the first step of the program by obtaining the lowest core memory register into which information goes.)

Problem 8.5

Write a program which will read in a symbolic program deck. Have it read the cards into core 300 and following. Have it read until an END card is reached. In compool defined COUNT, have your program keep a count of the number of core memory registers read into. Consider the BEG and END cards as the first and last cards read. Have your program branch to location CTROL when it has done this.

If you have written the program described in Problem 8.4, you have written a "read-in" program. Such a program is called a "utility" program. Utility programs help in getting object programs "on the air." But how did the read-in program get into memory? A control program undoubtedly brought it in from tape. But what if we had a brand new machine with nothing in core memory? How do we get started?— there is a push button on the computer console and it is labeled "Load From Card Reader." This button is electrically wired so that when it is pushed it causes the same result as the following two-step program:

$$RCD$$
$$JMP \quad 0$$

This will read in a card and operate the program on it. By this means, a card can "bootstrap" a whole system into the computer.

II. THE CARD PUNCH

The EX-1 instruction which punches cards is similar to RCD, the main difference being that a different area of core is used for the image. The mnemonic is PCD which comes from P̲UNCH A C̲AR̲D̲.

Mnemonic Code	Octal Code	Interpretation	Function
PCD	132	P̲UNCH A C̲AR̲D̲	Electrically selects the card punch and punches 1 card. The card will be punched in columns 1 through 25 corresponding to bit positions 1 through 25 of core memory locations 30_8 through 43_8. Row 9 will correspond to core location 30_8. Row 8 will correspond to core location 31_8, etc.

Problem 8.6

Write a program which will duplicate a deck of cards.

Duplicating cards as was done in Problem 8.6 is not a good use to which to put a computer. EAM equipment (Electronic Accounting Machines—alias card machines) can do this much more economically. Perhaps the most frequent and valuable use of a card punch connected to a computer is that of assembly.

The assembler program reads in the program punched in symbolic cards (source deck—one instruction per card) and punches out the program in binary (object deck—11 instructions per card on the EX-1).

III. THE PRINTER

The EX-1 mnemonic for printing is W R T which comes from W RITE PRINTER.

Mnemonic Code	Octal Code	Interpretation	Function
W R T	1 3 1	W RITE PRINTER	Electrically selects the printer and prints 1 line. Prints the 12-bit hollerith found column-wise in columns 1 through 25 of core memory locations 14_8 through 27_8. Row 9 will correspond to core location 14. Row 8 will correspond to core memory location 15, etc. After a W R T is executed, the paper is automatically spaced to the next line.

The EX-1 printer is built on the principle of 25 print-wheels. Each wheel contains all 47 alphanumeric characters, plus a position which is blank. Each print wheel is associated with a bit position in the core memory print area.

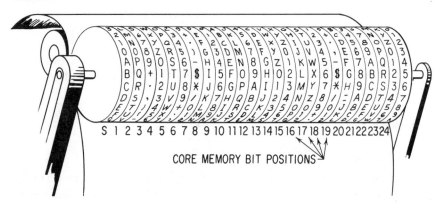

CORE MEMORY BIT POSITIONS

To illustrate, let us say that core memory locations 14_8 through 27_8 all contain 0's with the exception of the sign bit position of locations 24_8 and 27_8 which contain 1's. Pictorially this is:

Core Location	Row	S	1 2 3 4 5 6 7 8 9 10 11 12 13 14 15 16 17 18 19 20 21 22 23 24
14	9		
15	8		
16	7		
17	6		
20	5		ALL
21	4		ZEROS
22	3		ELSEWHERE
23	2		
24	1	1	
25	0		
26	11		
27	12	1	

With this in core, a WRT being executed would cause the print wheel associated with the sign position to spin to the position where an A would be in position for printing. All of the other print wheels would spin to the blank position because each column in the image other than the sign position contains 0's. Then the set of 25 wheels would be pressed against the paper for printing. Upon disengaging, the paper would move up one line and be ready for the next occurrence of the WRT command.

Problem 8.7

What kind of core memory image would be needed to print an A in the sign position followed by 24 zeros (rather than an A and 24 blanks)?

Problem 8.8

Write a program which will print out your name.

Problem 8.9

Given that core memory location ALPHA has a positive number in it scaled B24, write a program to print it out in octal.

Hint: Let us, for illustrative purposes, assume that ALPHA has in it the binary word 0.0100001111101110001011100. We would want our program to print out 20756134. A method we might use would examine the binary, 3 bits at a time, from the right. Therefore, we would want to store a 1 in position 25 of location (14_8 + 5) since the 3 rightmost bits in the binary word are 100_2 or 4. And to get a 4 in the right area we need a 1 in the correct bit position of core location 21_8 which is 14_8 + 5. The next group of 3 bits is 011_2, hence we want to store a 1 in position 24 of location (14_8 + 6). It is interesting to note that the number we are always adding to core memory location 14_8 is the 9's complement of the octal number. The following flow illustrates this:

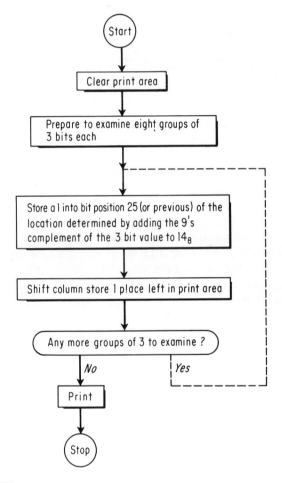

Problem 8.10

Given that core memory location ALPHA has a positive number in it scaled B24, make a flow diagram and write the coding for a program which will print it out in decimal. Do not print leading zeros. Have the number printed out as far as possible to the right on the printer.

IV. TAPES FOR THE EX-1

The EX-1 has one tape drive. The magnetic tape is similar to that used on a recording machine. However, it is about ½ inch wide and 2400 feet long.

There are three EX-1 instructions associated with tape programming. They are TAR for TAPE READ, TAW for TAPE WRITE, and TRW for TAPE REWIND.

Reading or writing a tape moves it from left to right. When rewinding, it moves from right to left. The reel on the left is the tape reel (full of tape) which is mounted on the tape drive. The reel on the right is an empty reel onto which the tape is wound as reading or writing occurs.

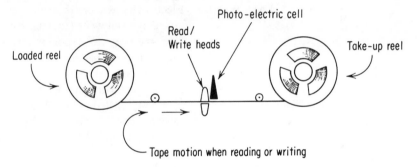

Tape motion when reading or writing

A little patch of aluminum foil is attached to the tape about 8 feet from the beginning end of the tape. This patch is called *load point* and is sensed by a photoelectric cell. A person manually puts the reel of tape on the drive and, after threading the tape through the read/write heads, he hand turns the take-up reel until the aluminum foil patch passes the electric eye. Then he pushes a button on the tape drive unit which rewinds the tape to load point. The tape is, thus, initially positioned at its beginning for reading or writing. If a program has been reading or writing on tape so that it is partially wound up on the take-up reel, the program can rewind it to load point again by executing the TRW (Tape Rewind) instruction.

When the TAW (Tape Write) instruction is given, it also specifies the number of computer words to be written on the tape. These computer words are then written and a gap of ½ inch is left on tape. The group of computer words written is called a *record*. The gap is called an *end of record gap*. The format of 2 computer words written on the tape as the first record would look as follows:

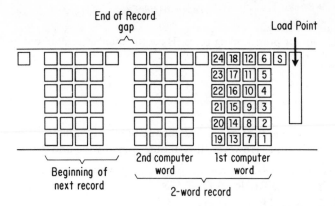

As was mentioned previously, the EX-1 instruction for writing on tape is TAW which is the mnemonic for T͟APE W͟RITE. It functions as follows:

Mnemonic Code	Octal Code	Interpretation	Function
TAW	146	T͟Aᴘᴇ W͟ʀɪᴛᴇ	Electrically select the magnetic tape drive and write (transfer from core memory to tape) as many words as are specified in the associated control word. There are two control words associated with a TAW instruction. The first control word is specified by the director of the TAW. The second control word follows the first. The first control word specifies the number of 25-bit tape words to write from core. The second control word specifies the starting core location from which to start their transfer.

Thus, in order to get the two-word record onto tape as in the illustration above, we would write the following program. This program assumes that the tape is at load point and that the two words come from core location 100_8 and following:

```
                    TAW   DATAB
              .  .     .  .  .  .
              .  .     .  .  .  .
              .  .     .  .  .  .
       DATAB  0 . 0 0 0 0 0 0 0 2
              0 . 0 0 0 0 0 1 0 0
```

Problem 8.11

Write a program which will write 25_{10} words on tape from core memory location 50_8 and following.

Problem 8.12

Write a program which will write ten records of 20_{10} words each on the tape. Take them from core memory location 300_8 and following.

The EX-1 mnemonic for reading a tape is TAR. It is described as follows:

Mnemonic Code	Octal Code	Interpretation	Function
TAR	126	TAPE READ	Electrically selects the magnetic tape drive and reads (transfer from tape to core memory) as many words as is specified in the associated control word. There are two control words associated with a TAR instruction. The first control word is specified by the director of the TAR. The second control word follows the first. The first control word specifies the number of 25-bit tape words to read into core memory. The second control word specifies the starting core memory location into which to start their transfer.

The EX-1 mnemonic for rewinding a tape is TRW. It is described as follows:

Mnemonic Code	Octal Code	Interpretation	Function
TRW	136	TAPE REWIND	Electrically selects the tape drive and rewinds it to the load point.

Problem 8.13

Given: A tape consisting of information on company employees. A tape record of 10_{10} words is associated with each employee. The first record on the tape is a one-word record which contains the number of employee records on the tape. The first word in each employee record contains the employee identification number.

Required: Write a program which will add the employee record which is found in the 10_{10} register table called HIRED. Just add it to the end of the present set of tape records. However, be sure to update the first record on the tape which contains the number of records.

Problem 8.14

Given the same tape as in Problem 8.13, write a program which will delete the record from tape whose identification number is found in core memory location QUIT. This is done by writing the records, which follow the record to be deleted, onto the tape immediately following the record preceding the record to be deleted. Be sure to update the first record on the tape.

There are two types of data that can be on a tape. The tape can contain binary EX-1 computer words, as discussed up to now, or the tape can contain 6-bit hollerith data.

The 6-bit hollerith data can be put on tape for the EX-1 by means of a card-to-tape piece of equipment. This device is not connected to the computer. A tape is mounted on the device, cards are placed in it, and a button is pushed to start the card-to-tape transfer.

Equipment which is not connected to the computer is called *off-line equipment*. Equipment which is connected to the computer is called *on-line equipment*.

Thus, 12-bit hollerith information on cards can be converted to 6-bit hollerith automatically by the card-to-tape machine and stored on tape. This is done before a program which uses the tape operates and is called *prestoring*. The purpose of prestoring is to save computer time. Information from a prestored tape can be read into core much faster than information on cards.

The format of a prestored tape for the EX-1 will appear as follows:

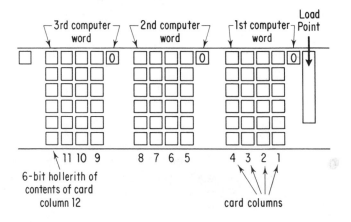

Each vertical column of 6 bits on a tape of hollerith information represents the 12-bit hollerith information found on 1 card column. Therefore, the information from each 80-column card will be prestored on tape as a 20-word record since there are 4 hollerith characters represented in each computer word. The card-to-tape machine that we are discussing will automatically set the sign bit of each word to zero on tape.

Problem 8.15

Given a prestored 6-bit hollerith tape containing records for 3 cards, write a program which will place into compool defined, single, 1-word item ALPHA the total number of card columns which contain the letter A.

V. CONSOLE SWITCHES AND THE RED LIGHT, GREEN LIGHT, AND THE BELL

By means of lights, console switches, and a bell, all of which are located at the computer operator's console, man-machine communication can be effected. The red or green lights may be turned on respectively by means of the EX-1 instruction TON with a modifier of 1 or 2 in the increment field. The bell can be rung by operating TON with an increment modifier of 3.

Thus:

TON1 turns on the red light. It stays on until a JRD instruction is operated.

TON2 turns on the green light. It stays on until a JGN instruction is operated.

TON3 turns on the bell. It stays on until the operator pushes the "bell reset" button.

The JRD and JGN instructions respectively examine the red and green light. If they are on, a jump occurs. If off, a jump does not occur. If the light is on before the JRD or JGN instruction is operated, the jump instruction turns it off.

The console switches are toggle switches. In the "on" position, a one is represented. In the "off" position, a zero is represented. Thus, an octal EX-1 word of 0.12345672, if entered in the switches, would appear physically as follows:

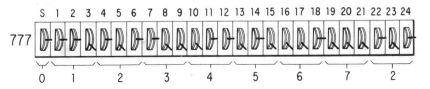

Operating the instruction GET 777 would thus bring 0.12345672 into the accumulator.

Problem 8.16

Write a program which will examine the console switches and act, if the contents are greater than 7_{10} and less than 29_{10}, to turn on the green light; if the contents are greater than 42_{10} and less than 64_{10}, turn on the red light; if the contents are greater than 75_{10} and less than 80_{10}, ring the bell. Be sure that your program initially turns off the lights.

CHAPTER NINE

Advanced Fixed Point Techniques

This chapter will discuss the use of scaling equations in fixed point arithmetic. This material may be omitted without disrupting the continuity of the text. Appendix 1 contains a review of some of the mathematical concepts required as foundation material for this chapter.

Suppose we want to represent the number 6.5_{10} in a core memory location. We could do it in many ways, some of which are the following:

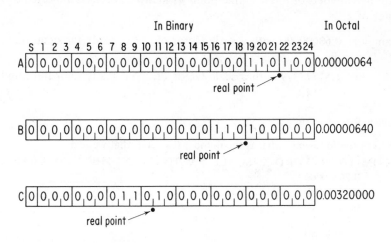

If one examined each of the above locations he would not know that the number contained therein was supposed to be 6.5_{10}. We need something to state where the real point is intended to be. This "something" we will call the *scale factor*.

The scale factor for location A is 2^{21}. This is because if we, the programmer, would multiply $+.00000064_8$ by 2^{21}, we would obtain 6.4_8 or 6.5_{10}. Remember that multiplying by 2 moves the real point one *binary* place to the right. Multiplying by 2^2 moves it two binary places to the right, etc.

The scale factor in location B is 2^{18}.

The scale factor in location C is 2^{10}.

Sometimes these scale factors are written in the literature as B21, B18, and B10 for locations A, B, and C, respectively.

Definition: The *Scale Factor* is the number (expressed as a power of 2) needed to multiply the computer word (expressed as a fraction with real point at the machine point) in order to get the actual number desired (expressed as an octal number with the real point in its correct place).

In this text we will arbitrarily take the machine point as a reference point when working with a scale factor. In this sense all computer words, when looked at as machine words and associated with scale factors, are to be considered as fractions.

The scale factor is generally documented in the documentation associated with a program or table. It would also appear in the compool if one is used in connection with the programming system employed.

The scale factor may consist of a negative power of 2, in which case the real point is really left of the machine point as many places as is indicated by the power of 2.

Example: 0.60000000 with a scale factor of 2^{-3} is really the octal number .06.

or 1.57777777 with a scale factor of 2^{-5} is really the octal number $-.004$.

Problem 9.1

1. Given the following, what is the number (in octal) that we really want?

COMPUTER WORD	SCALE FACTOR	NUMBER (IN OCTAL)
0.26540000	2^9	
0.37136000	2^5	
0.16522200	2^{-3}	
1.71760777	2^{18}	
0.62436670	2^{27}	

2. Given the following, what is the scale factor?

COMPUTER WORD	NUMBER (IN OCTAL)	SCALE FACTOR
0.24617534	246.17534	_____
0.05020000	.502	_____
1.64200077	−1.3577700	_____
0.20000000	.002	_____
0.00351000	7.22	_____

3. Given the following, what does the computer word look like?

NUMBER (IN OCTAL)	SCALE FACTOR	COMPUTER WORD
124.3	2^9	_____
.006	2^{-5}	_____
−5126777700.00	2^{30}	_____
.425	2^0	_____
.16	2^{-2}	_____

Let us use our knowledge of the scale factor in a simple addition problem.

Illustrative example

Given: Core location ALPHA contains the number A.
ALPHA 0.60000000. A is 6.0. Thus the scale factor is 2^3.
Core location BETA contains the number B.
BETA 0.77500000 B is 77.5_8. Thus the scale factor is 2^6.

Required: Write a program which will add A and B together and place the result C into core location GAMMA. Store the answer in maximum precision (this means to store the answer with as many fractional places as possible).

Let us first solve this by using just common sense. After that, we will solve it using scaling equations.

We see that to add we must line up the real points just as we would in adding a column of numbers. So, our code might be:

```
GET   ALPHA   Obtain A.
SAR       3   Move it right 3 binary places.
ADD   BETA    Add B to A.
PUT   GAMMA   Store answer.
HLT
```

Let us actually make this addition as the machine would.

```
    0.06000000    after the shift 3 places right
    0.77500000
    ----------
    1.05500000
```

But this is clearly overflow—adding two positive numbers and getting a negative answer. We should have expected this because $77.5_8 + 6.0 = 105.5_8$, which indicates we need seven places for the whole number part of our answer. This is so since $105_8 = 1000101_2$. Since we only allowed six places in our answer, we had problems. Our coding should have been:

	GET	ALPHA	Obtain A.
	SAR	4	Move A right 4 binary places.
	PUT	TEMP	Store A temporarily.
	GET	BETA	Obtain B.
	SAR	1	Move B right 1 binary place.
	ADD	TEMP	Add B to A.
	PUT	GAMMA	Store answer scale B7.
	HLT		
TEMP	0.00000000		

Let us now solve this problem, using scale factors and a scaling equation.

	TABLE OF POWERS OF 2
Scale factor for A is 2^3.	$2^9 = 512$
Scale factor for B is 2^6.	$2^8 = 256$
$A + B = 77.5 + 6.0 = 105.5_8$	$2^7 = 128$
	$2^6 = 64$

$105.5_8 = 69.5_{10} < 128$ or 2^7 which we determine by examining a table of powers of 2; hence, 7 positions are sufficient to hold the integral part of the answer.

Therefore, *the scale factor for GAMMA is 2^7.*

We would write the scaling equation as

$$2^7\bar{C} = 2^3\bar{A} + 2^6\bar{B}$$

where $\bar{C}$ (pronounced "see-bar"), $\bar{B}$ and $\bar{A}$ represent the quantities as found in the machine with the real point at the machine point.
Solving the equation for $\bar{C}$ gives

$$\bar{C} = \frac{2^3\bar{A} + 2^6\bar{B}}{2^7} = 2^{-4}\bar{A} + 2^{-1}\bar{B}$$

By this latter equation, we see that to get $\bar{C}$, or in other words, to get C scaled 2^7, we must multiply $\bar{A}$ by a factor of 2^{-4} and multiply $\bar{B}$ by 2^{-1} and then add them together. This can be done by shoving $\bar{A}$ four binary places to the right and B one binary place to the right before adding.

This, of course, is what we had discovered previously by logical reasoning.

One would soon find, however, that for problems involving multiplication, division, and complex combinations, scaling equations become almost essential (if fixed point arithmetic rather than floating point is used).

Ordinarily, before writing the program, we would not have known the specific values in ALPHA and BETA. Rather, we would have known only their range of variation.

We would probably know, for example, that

$$|A| < 8_{10} \text{ which means } |A| < 2^3$$
$$|B| < 64_{10} \text{ which means } |B| < 2^6$$

In the illustrative example we have used, we would say that C has been scaled to *maximum precision* since the answer contains as many fractional bits as is possible. If C were placed in GAMMA as 0.01055000, we would say it was scaled with a *specific precision;* namely, precision to 12 fractional places.

The type of precision simply describes the number of fractional places present. Precision, thus, is not synonymous with accuracy. Accuracy is basically involved with the correctness of digits. We will not discuss the details of accuracy, as it is very involved.

Before working some problems, let us define X and $\bar{X}$ again.

$\bar{X}$ represents the number (in uncomplemented form) as it looks in the machine with the machine point as real point.

X represents the true number with the real point in its correct place.

Example: Computer Word $0_{\triangle}0025.0000$

$$\uparrow$$
$$\llcorner \text{ real point}$$

$$\bar{X} = .0025$$
$$X = 25_8$$

Problem 9.2

1. Given that the computer word is $0_{\triangle}0000003.7$
   What is $\bar{X}$?
   What is X?

2. Given that the computer word is $1_{\triangle}777736.65$
   What is $\bar{X}$?
   What is X?

3. Give the stated absolute values.
   $|3| = \underline{\hspace{1cm}}$ $|-3| = \underline{\hspace{1cm}}$ $|9| = \underline{\hspace{1cm}}$ $|-17| = \underline{\hspace{1cm}}$

4. Given that X can have the following values, complete the statement.

$X = 1$
$X = -5.75$
$X = 4$
$X = 3$
$X = -7$
$X = 6.5$

$$|X| \leq \underline{\hspace{2cm}}$$

5. In the above example, we could have said $|X| < 8$ or $|X| < 2^3$. How many binary positions would we have to allow for the integral part to take care of the "worst" X?

6. In exercise (1), what is the scale factor?

7. Using exercises (1) and (6) above, does X = (scale factor) times $\bar{X}$?

Illustrative example

Given: X in location $XNUMB$
         Y in location $YNUMB$
         $|X| < 99$ X is scaled such that $X = 2^7\bar{X}$
         $|Y| < 35$ Y is scaled such that $Y = 2^6\bar{Y}$

Required: Compute $Z = X + Y$ and place the result into location $ZNUMB$ in maximum precision.

Solution: Now since $|X| < 99$, we see from the powers of 2 table (Appendix 2) that $99 < 128$ and since $128 = 2^7$, 7 places are sufficient for the integral portion of X; similarly for Y. Thus, we have checked to see that the scaling given us on X and Y is possible.

Since $Z = X + Y$, $|Z| < (99 + 35)$

therefore $|\bar{Z}| < 134$ or $|Z| < 2^8$

Thus $Z = 2^8\bar{Z}$ if Z is scaled to maximum precision.

A particular Z may thus not necessarily be scaled to maximum precision, but such scaling is necessary to handle the largest Z which may be encountered.

SCALING EQUATION

$2^8\bar{Z} = 2^7\bar{X} + 2^6\bar{Y}$	START GET XNUMB
hence $\bar{Z} = \dfrac{2^7\bar{X} + 2^6\bar{Y}}{2^8}$	SAR 1
	PUT TEMP
$\bar{Z} = 2^{-1}\bar{X} + 2^{-2}\bar{Y}$	GET YNUMB
	SAR 2

This final equation indi-
cates that $\bar{X}$ and $\bar{Y}$ must
be multiplied by 2^{-1} and
2^{-2}, respectively.

ADD	TEMP
PUT	ZNUMB
HLT	
TEMP	0.00000000

Problem 9.3

Given: X in XNUMB
      Y in YNUMB
      $|X| < 121$ $X = 2^7\bar{X}$
      $|Y| < 31$ $Y = 2^5\bar{Y}$

Required: Compute $Z = X + Y$ and store the answer into location ANSER in maximum precision.

Illustrative example

Given: X in XNUMB
      Y in YNUMB
      $|X| \leq 3999$
      $|Y| \leq 1999$

X is scaled in XNUMB with real point between bit positions 12 and 13.

Y is scaled in YNUMB with real point between bit positions 11 and 12.

Required: Compute $Z = X + Y$ and store Z in ANSER in 11 place precision.

Solution: Check to see if this is possible.

$X = 2^{12}\bar{X}$ $|Z| < 3999 + 1999$
$Y = 2^{11}\bar{Y}$ $|Z| < 5998$
$Z = 2^{13}\bar{Z}$ $5998 < 2^{13}$ thus 13 places are required for the integral part and thus 11 places are left for the fractional part. (Since $13 + 11 = 24$ bits, which is the number of magnitude bits in the EX-1.) So, 11 place precision is possible.

SCALING EQUATION

$2^{13}\bar{Z} = 2^{12}\bar{X} + 2^{11}\bar{Y}$

$\bar{Z} = \dfrac{2^{12}\bar{X} + 2^{11}\bar{Y}}{2^{13}}$

$\bar{Z} = 2^{-1}\bar{X} + 2^{-2}\bar{Y}$

START	GET	XNUMB
	SAR	1
	PUT	TEMP
	GET	YNUMB
	SAR	2
	ADD	TEMP
	PUT	ANSER
	HLT	
TEMP	0.00000000	

Problem 9.4

Given: X in XNUMB
       Y in YNUMB
       $|X| \leq 499$
       $|Y| \leq 199$

X is scaled in XNUMB with the real point between bit positions 14 and 15.

Y is scaled in YNUMB with the real point between bit positions 8 and 9.

Required: Compute $Z = X + Y$ and store Z in ANSER in 14 place precision.

Problem 9.5

Given: r in RSTOR
      s in SSTOR
      $|r| < 32$
      $|s| < 32$
      r is scaled B5 in RSTOR.
      s is scaled B5 in SSTOR.

Required: Compute $t = r + s$ and store t in TSTOR in maximum precision.

Note: Beware of factoring out a 2^{-1} in the final scaling equation. Why?

Problem 9.6

Given: a in ANUMB
      b in BNUMB
      c in CNUMB
      $|a| \leq 63$ $a = 2^6 \bar{a}$
      $|b| \leq 128$ $b = 2^8 \bar{b}$
      $|c| \leq 31$ $c = 2^5 \bar{c}$

Required: Compute $d = a + b - c$ and store d in RESLT in maximum precision.

Note: You can get a maximum d of 222. Why?

Problem 9.7

Given: Tables TABLX, TABLY, TABLZ, and TABLW all of the same length and defined in the compool.

    X_i is in the ith entry of TABLX.
    Y_i is in the ith entry of TABLY.
    Z_i is in the ith entry of TABLZ.
    W_i is to be placed into the ith entry of TABLW.

    $|X_i| < 700$ $X_i = 2^{11} \bar{X}_i$
    $|Y_i| < 320$ $Y_i = 2^9 \bar{Y}_i$
    $|Z_i| < 9$ $Z_i = 2^{14} \bar{Z}_i$

Required: Compute $W_i = X_i + Y_i - Z_i$ and store W_i to maximum precision in the ith entry of TABLW.

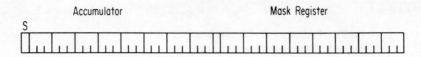

Accumulator   Mask Register

The multiply instruction MUL causes the contents of the accumulator to be multiplied by the contents of the addressed location. The resultant product is contained in the combined accumulator and mask register with the most significant part of the product in the accumulator and the least significant part in the mask register.

Illustrative example

Given: X in XNUMB in maximum precision
        Y in YNUMB in maximum precision
        $|X| < 9$
        $|Y| < 19$

Required: Compute $Z = XY$ and store Z into ZNUMB in maximum precision.

Solution: Since $Z = XY$, from the power of 2 table we see that

$$|Z| < 9 \cdot 19 \qquad\qquad X = 2^4 \bar{X}$$
$$|Z| < 171 \qquad\qquad Y = 2^5 \bar{Y}$$
$$\qquad\qquad\qquad Z = 2^8 \bar{Z}$$

The scaling equation becomes

$$2^8 \bar{Z} = 2^4 \bar{X} 2^5 \bar{Y}$$

$$\bar{Z} = \frac{2^9 \bar{X} \bar{Y}}{2^8}$$

$$\bar{Z} = 2^1 \bar{X} \bar{Y}$$

GO	GET	XNUMB
	MUL	YNUMB
	SBL	1
	PUT	ZNUMB
	HLT	

Note: Perform $\bar{X} \cdot \bar{Y}$ first. We see that since X is in maximum precision, performing $2^1 \bar{X}$ first might cause a loss.

Observe that we used the "shift combined" because the product is in both the accumulator and mask register.

Problem 9.8

Given: X in XNUMB in maximum precision
        Y in YNUMB in maximum precision
        $|X| < 66$
        $|Y| < 5$

Required: Compute $Z = XY$ and store Z into ANSER in maximum precision.

Problem 9.9

Given: a in TESTA in maximum precision
         b in TESTB in maximum precision

$|a| < 128$
$|b| < 16$

Required: Compute $c = ab$ and store in RZULT with the real point between bit positions 14 and 15.

Problem 9.10

Given: a in ANUMB scaled in maximum precision $|a| < 31$
         b in BNUMB scaled in maximum precision $|b| < 16$
         c in CNUMB scaled in maximum precision $|c| < 249$

Required: Compute $d = ab + c$ and place d into DNUMB scaled in maximum precision.

Illustrative example

Given: a in ANUMB scaled in maximum precision
         b in BNUMB scaled in maximum precision
         c in CNUMB scaled in maximum precision

$|a| < 31$
$|b| < 16$
$|c| < 7$

Required: Computed $d = ab + ac$ and store d in DNUMB in maximum precision.

The solution of this example brings up some informative points.

$a = 2^5\bar{a}$ Scaling Equation:

$b = 2^4\bar{b}$ $2^{10}\bar{d} = 2^5\bar{a}2^4\bar{b} + 2^5\bar{a}2^3\bar{c}$ GET   ANUMB

$c = 2^3\bar{c}$ $\bar{d} = 2^{-1}\bar{a}\bar{b} + 2^{-2}\bar{a}\bar{c}$ MUL   BNUMB

$d = 2^{10}\bar{d}$ SBR   1

                                                                                PUT   DNUMB

                                                                                GET   ANUMB

                                                                                MUL   CNUMB

                                                                                SBR   2

                                                                                ADD   DNUMB

                                                                                PUT   DNUMB

                                                                                HLT

Observe that this solution results in two multiplications, whereas the following solution results in only one. Since multiplication is quite a time consuming operation, the following is a much better solution. This is especially so when the terms in parentheses increase in number, i.e., $d = a(b + c + d + e + f + \cdots)$.

Factor, $d = a(b + c)$	Scaling Equation	GET	BNUMB
$a = 2^5\bar{a}$	Let $t = b + c$,	SAR	1
$b = 2^4\bar{b}$	then $\lvert t \rvert < 23$	PUT	DNUMB
$c = 2^3\bar{c}$	$\lvert t \rvert < 2^5$	GET	CNUMB
and since $\lvert d \rvert < 31 \cdot 23$	$t = 2^5\bar{t}$	SAR	2
$\lvert d \rvert < 713$	$2^5\bar{t} = 2^4\bar{b} + 2^3\bar{c}$	ADD	DNUMB
$\lvert d \rvert < 2^{10}$	$\bar{t} = 2^{-1}\bar{b} + 2^{-2}\bar{c}$	MUL	ANUMB
thus $d = 2^{10}\bar{d}$	$2^{10}\bar{d} = 2^5\bar{a}(2^4\bar{b} + 2^3\bar{c})$	PUT	DNUMB
	$2^{10}\bar{d} = 2^5\bar{a}2^5\bar{t}$	HLT	
	$\bar{d} = 2^{\overline{0}}at$		

A common pitfall, which this problem generally results in, should be discussed. Frequently, students proceed on the following basis:

$$2^{10}\bar{d} = 2^5\bar{a}(2^4\bar{b} + 2^3\bar{c})$$

$$\bar{d} = \frac{\bar{a}(2^9\bar{b} + 2^8\bar{c})}{2^{10}}$$

$$\bar{d} = \bar{a}(2^{-1}\bar{b} + 2^{-2}\bar{c}) \text{ and so why substitute } t = b + c?$$

Now the story is that this procedure of not substituting works in some cases (as in this one) but not always; hence, the problem should always be solved on the basis of making the substitutions.

The next problem is an example of a case where not making the substitution causes trouble.

Problem 9.11

Given: X in XNUMB scaled to maximum precision
Y in YNUMB scaled to maximum precision
Z in ZNUMB scaled to maximum precision
$\lvert X \rvert < 60$
$\lvert Y \rvert < 1024$
$\lvert Z \rvert < 31$
Required: Compute $W = XY - XZ$ and place W in WNUMB in maximum precision.

Let us try a problem which is somewhat turned around. Suppose we are given a program and asked about the contents (in octal) of ZNUMB after the program halts.

```
START      GET      XNUMB
           MUL      YNUMB
           PUT      ZNUMB
           HLT
XNUMB   0 . 1 5 0 0 0 0 0 0
YNUMB   0 . 1 0 2 0 0 0 0 0
ZNUMB   0 . 0 0 0 0 0 0 0 0
```

We can arbitrarily think of XNUMB as scaled 2^6 and YNUMB as 2^9; thus,

$$XNUMB \quad 0_\triangle 15.000000$$
$$YNUMB \quad 0_\triangle 102.00000$$

thus, $2^?\bar{Z} = 2^6\bar{X}2^9\bar{Y}$

$Z = \dfrac{2^{15}\bar{X}\bar{Y}}{2^?}$ and since no shifting has been done in the program, we know that $\dfrac{2^{15}}{2^?} = 2^0$—that is, $2^? = 2^{15}$, or, in other words, that the result is scaled in ZNUMB with the real point between bit positions 15 and 16,

and since $\left. \begin{aligned} X &= \ 15_8 = 13_{10} \\ Y &= 102_8 = 66_{10} \end{aligned} \right\}$ Multiplying the two gives

$13_{10} \cdot 66_{10} = 858_{10} = 1532_8$; then setting this into

ZNUMB scaled 2^{15} gives

$$ZNUMB \quad 0_\triangle 01532.000$$

It is to be observed that the multiplier we arbitrarily scaled as 2^9, and the multiplicand as 2^6, and the product turned out scaled at $2^9 \cdot 2^6 = 2^{9+6} = 2^{15}$.

In this text we will follow the convention that multiplication is done as if both the multiplier and multiplicand are fractions; that is to say, with the machine point acting as the real point. Be reminded, however, that in actuality these two points are nonexistent in the machine. We are using them merely as conventions.

Working the above problem then on this basis:

$$\left. \begin{aligned} XNUMB &= .15_8 \\ YNUMB &= .102_8 \end{aligned} \right\} \quad \text{Multiplying the two gives}$$

$$\begin{aligned} 32_8 \\ 00_8 \\ \underline{15_8} \\ .01532_8 = ZNUMB = 0.01532000 \end{aligned}$$

Problem 9.12

What (in octal) are the contents of ZNUMB after the following program halts?

```
       START    GET  XNUMB
                MUL  YNUMB
                SBL      5
                PUT  ZNUMB
                HLT
XNUMB   0 . 2 3 0 0 0 0 0 0
YNUMB   0 . 2 0 5 0 0 0 0 0
ZNUMB   0 . 0 0 0 0 0 0 0 0
```

The DIV instruction causes the contents of the combined accumulator and mask register to be divided by the contents of the addressed location. This results in a 49-bit dividend. If the division happens to be carried out immediately following a multiplication, we would have a good accurate 48-bit dividend with the rightmost bit in the mask register being questionable (for the case of no shift after multiplying).

The quotient will be contained in the accumulator.

When the DIV instruction is executed, the absolute magnitude of the divisor must be greater than the absolute magnitude of the dividend. Otherwise, a meaningless quotient will result. In order to have a correct quotient, all divisions performed must yield a fractional result—as far as the machine is concerned.

Correct use of scaling equations insures a fractional result.

Illustrative example

Given: X in XNUMB scaled in maximum precision
           Y in YNUMB scaled in maximum precision
$$100 < |X| < 900$$
$$9 < |Y| < 48$$

Required: Compute $Z = \dfrac{X}{Y}$, and store the result in ZNUMB in maximum precision.

Solution:

$$X = 2^{10}\bar{X}$$ Scaling Equation

$$Y = 2^{6}\bar{Y} \qquad 2^{7}\bar{Z} = \frac{2^{10}\bar{X}}{2^{6}\bar{Y}}$$

```
START   GET  XNUMB
        SBR      3
        DIV  YNUMB
        PUT  ZNUMB
        HLT
```

and $|Z| < \dfrac{900}{9} \qquad \bar{Z} = \dfrac{2^{10}\bar{X}}{2^{7}2^{6}\bar{Y}}$

$$|Z| < 100 \qquad \bar{Z} = \frac{2^{-3}\bar{X}}{\bar{Y}}$$

$$|Z| < 2^{7}$$
$$Z = 2^{7}\bar{Z}$$

Observe that, in computing how big Z can be, we used the lower range of Y because the quotient is largest when the divisor is smallest. However, we still must scale Y to handle the largest of its possible values.

Multiplying $\bar{X}$ by 2^{-3} (i.e., shoving it right 3 binary places) assures the numerator being smaller in absolute value than the denominator. This is because $\bar{Z}$ is by definition less than 1 and the only way this can be true is if $2^{-3}\bar{X}$ is less than $\bar{Y}$.

To convince ourselves further of this, we can examine the binary configuration for this problem.

EXAMINING THE BINARY CONFIGURATION

$$900_{10} = 1604_8 = 0_\triangle 1110000100.00 \ldots 0 \text{ is } 1604_8 \text{ scaled } 2^{10}$$
$$9_{10} = 11_8 = 0_\triangle 001001.00 \ldots 0 \text{ is } 11_8 \text{ scaled } 2^6$$

It is clearly seen in this worst case (which is with largest numerator and smallest denominator) that a shift of the numerator 3 places right will insure that the divisor is larger than the dividend machine-wise.

Is it necessary to clear the mask register when we have only 24 good bits (in the accumulator) for the dividend and yet the divide instruction uses 49 bits as the dividend? No, because garbage in the mask register is probably closer to a true 49-bit dividend than a dividend of 49 bits where the least significant 25 bits are 0.

It must be realized that some of the least significant bits of the quotient are questionable. As a matter of fact, many topics at computer conferences deal with the validity of bits with varying degrees of validity of the factors, terms, dividends, etc. Accuracy, precision, validity, and related topics are excellent subjects for a Ph. D. thesis. At any rate, they are beyond the scope of this book.

To illustrate the fact that the least significant half of a dividend can affect the quotient, let us look at the following two arithmetic examples:

Example 1	Example 2
0.50	0.52
0.40)0.2000	0.40)0.2099
200	200
	99
	80
	19
or $0.2000 \div 0.40 = 0.50$	or $0.2099 \div 0.40 = 0.52$

In the above examples, the 0.20 of the dividends are true values, whereas the 00 in Example 1 and the 99 of Example 2 are the two extremes of junk in the two least significant positions of the dividend. We see that the quotient varies from 0.50 to 0.52 depending upon the junk.

However, a common programming technique which removes any garbage from consideration is to load the dividend into the accumulator and then shift it right all the way into the mask register. This in effect expands a 25 bit dividend into a 50 bit one—the vacated bits being filled in with duplicates of the sign bit. Of course, if the dividend had been scaled B24, it is now scaled B49, and this new scaling of the dividend must be taken into account.

Problem 9.13

Given: X in XNUMB in maximum precision
Y in YNUMB in maximum precision
Z in ZNUMB in maximum precision
W in WNUMB in maximum precision

$$37 < |X| < 98$$
$$67 < |Y| < 1000$$
$$4000 < |Z| < 5000$$
$$8 \leq |W| < 1020$$

Required: Compute $V = \dfrac{X^2 + XY - Z}{W}$ and place V in VNUMB scaled to maximum precision.

Problem 9.14

Given: X in XNUMB in maximum precision
Y in YNUMB in maximum precision
Z in ZUNMB in maximum precision

$$100 < |X| \leq 256$$
$$1 < |Y| < 7500$$
$$8000 < |Z| < 10000$$

Required: Compute $W = \dfrac{8(X + Y) - 7Z + 9}{Y}$ in WNUMB in maximum precision.

Caution: Be sure to determine whether a minimum or maximum Y gives a maximum W. Also, one must take the scaling of any constants he sets up into consideration.

CHAPTER TEN

A Typical
Modern Giant Computer

I. GENERAL CHARACTERISTICS

In this chapter we will describe a machine much more sophisticated than the EX-1. It is a hypothetical computer, but typical of some of the modern giants. We will call it SMILEY.

SMILEY is a high speed, large capacity, information-processing machine. Being transistorized and containing many remarkable features, its design represents one of the most advanced levels in electronic data processing systems. The primary function of SMILEY is to aid personnel (Government, Military, Industry) in tactical, strategic, and logistic decision making. It is also used for routine data processing tasks.

SMILEY is classified as a 3rd generation computer. The 1st generation machines were vacuum tube machines; the 2nd generation machines were transistorized; the 3rd generation machines are transistorized, and the circuits are made of integrated circuits—these are minaturized circuits.

Third generation machines are faster than second generation ones. They operate in nanoseconds (billionths of a second) whereas second generation machines operate in microseconds (millionths of a second).

Third generation computers are frequently capable of *multiprocessing*. This means that several programs can operate simultaneously. In other words, the computer has several C. P. U. (Central Processing Units). SMILEY can have as many as 16 programs operating in it at the same time.

All information is stored in SMILEY in binary. Each group of 8 bits in SMILEY's memory is called a byte. Memory capacity is 16,777,216 bytes. Each byte has an address.

SMILEY's Core Memory

Byte 0	Byte 1	Byte 2	Byte 3	Byte 4	Byte 5
Byte 6	Byte 7	Byte 8	Byte 9	Byte A	Byte B
Byte C	Byte D	Byte E	Byte F	Byte 10	Byte 11
Byte 12	Byte 13	Byte 14	Byte 15	Byte 16	Byte 17
Byte 18	Byte 19	Byte 1A	Byte 1B	Byte 1C	Byte 1D

Each byte can hold a character represented either by the USA Standard Code for Information Interchange (USASCII) or the Extended Binary Coded Decimal Interchange Code (EBCDIC). Since each byte can hold 256 different numbers (modulus is 2^8), up to 256 different characters can be represented in one byte. We can have, for example, upper case letters, lower case letters, digits, special characters, punctuation marks, and many other symbols.

Since a byte consists of 8 bits in SMILEY, the contents of each byte can be represented by 2 hexadecimal digits. The hexadecimal number system was discussed in Chapter Two. You may have noticed also that the byte addresses are in hexadecimal.

II. TWO MACHINES IN ONE

SMILEY is almost two machines in one. By using the appropriate instructions it can act like a "fixed-word-length" machine. Or by using a different set of instructions it can act like a "variable-word-length" machine.

The EX-1 is a fixed-word-length machine. We can load the EX-1 accumulator by GET ALPHA. The 25 bits at core location ALPHA come into the accumulator. We can do something similar on SMILEY by writing

L   5, A L P H A

This says: "load general register #5 with the contents of memory location ALPHA." Here, general register #5 is acting similar to an accumulator. Incidentally, SMILEY has 16 of these general registers. They are 48 bits in length, and may be used for accumulators, index registers, mask registers and for a few other purposes.

When we write L 5,ALPHA, we are using SMILEY like a fixed-word-length computer, and what comes into general register #5 is the byte called ALPHA and the following 5 bytes (or 48 bits). When we use a fixed-word-length instruction such as L, the operand address of ALPHA must be "full word aligned"; that is, it must be a byte whose address is divisible by 6.

Any of these bytes would be legal for ALPHA since they are full-word aligned (address is divisible by 6).

Byte 0					
Byte 6					
Byte C					
Byte 12					
Byte 18					

If we desire to use SMILEY as a variable-word-length, machine we may use an instruction like

M V C   R H O ,   B E T A

This instruction says: "move the characters from the BETA field into the RHO field." Let us assume for illustrative purposes that each field consists of 7 bytes. We will say that the BETA field consists of bytes 9 through F and that the RHO field consists of bytes 14 through 1A. Notice that the fields RHO and BETA are not, in this instance, full word (48 bits) or full-word aligned. Hence, we are using SMILEY as a character machine (variable-word-length machine).

A little enlightenment on the rationale for the two types of operation is perhaps in order here.

If a minimum of input-output is involved in a computer system, yet a great deal of central computer processing of an arithmetic nature is involved, it is advantageous to use a fixed-word-length binary machine. The information is read into the computer in EBCDIC or USASCII, and converted into binary. Since the numbers are in pure binary they require less space in storage than if left in the EBCDIC or USASCII form. The lengthy calculations are made and, since the data is in pure binary, the arithmetic operations are performed faster. This type of operation, fixed-word-length, is usually employed in calculations of a scientific nature.

The other type of operation, variable-word-length, where the data remains coded as characters, is typical of business or commercial type programming. In this type of processing the input-output traffic is considerable, whereas the numerical calculations are minimal.

Since numerical calculations are minimal, SMILEY has a small set of instructions called the *Decimal Feature Instructions* which enable it to perform some arithmetic operations with the data in the coded form (EBCDIC or USASCII) rather than requiring a conversion to pure binary.

Summarizing this "two-machine-in-one" aspect of SMILEY, we have:

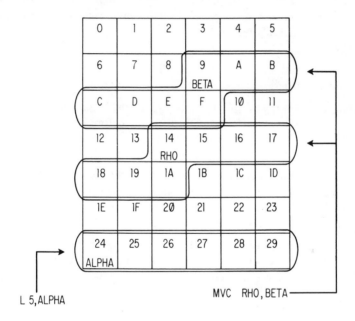

Treats machine as a fixed-word-length machine. (Data in memory must be full-word and first of 6 bytes must be on a full word boundary.)

Treats machine as a variable-word-length machine. (Data in memory need not be full words nor does data need to start on a full word boundary.)

Some of SMILEY's instructions may be indexed. Thus, if ALPHA were the starting location of a table, we might write

L   5, A L P H A (6)

Here, the address ALPHA is modified by the contents of general resister #6 (acting as an index register) in order to obtain an effective address.

III. RELOCATABLE PROGRAMS

Another interesting feature of SMILEY programs is that they are relocatable in memory at time of read-in. When we wrote EX-1 programs and had them assembled, the assembler replaced all of our symbolic addresses with absolute core locations. Hence, if our program was assembled for core location 3∅∅, the program had to be read in there. The only way to get it to go into memory elsewhere is to assemble it again with a new BEG card.

Not so with SMILEY. By using a concept called "base registers," a SMILEY program can be read into core memory wherever the master control program decides that there is room for it. I won't try to explain the detailed workings of the base register concept since it is rather complex and we are only making a survey of SMILEY's features.

We recall that the EX-1 had a binary instruction format that was the same for all instructions. SMILEY has five different instruction formats depending upon which instruction is involved.

The computer is a stored program sequential machine. This means that the program is placed completely in core memory before operation of the program begins; and also, that once it begins, the instructions work in sequence unless this sequence is changed by "branch" instructions.

SMILEY is a one's complement machine with negative numbers being represented within the computer in one's complement form. It has fixed point and floating point instructions and, therefore, can be used for scientific computation as well as for data processing tasks.

In addition to the ordinary arithmetic type of computer instructions, SMILEY has a set of instructions for performing arithmetic operations of a special type called *Boolean algebra*. These are called the *logical class of instructions*.

IV. INSTRUCTION REPERTOIRE

A listing of some of SMILEY's instructions follow; however, no attempt at explaining them will be made.

Standard Instruction Set

Mnemonic	Descriptive Name
A	Add
AH	Add Halfword
AL	Add Logical
N	And

BAL	Branch and Link
BC	Branch on Condition
BCTR	Branch on Count
BXH	Branch on Index High
BXLE	Branch on Index Low or Equal
C	Compare
CH	Compare Halfword
CL	Compare Logical
CVB	Convert to Binary
CVD	Convert to Decimal
D	Divide
X	Exclusive OR
EX	Execute
HIO	Halt I/O
IC	Insert Character
L	Load
LA	Load Address
LTR	Load and Test
LCR	Load Complement
LH	Load Halfword
LM	Load Multiple
LNR	Load Negative
LPR	Load Positive
LPSW	Load PSW
MVC	Move
M	Multiply
MH	Multiply Halfword
O	OR
PACK	Pack
SPM	Set Program Mask
SSM	Set System Mask
SLDA	Shift Left Double
SLA	Shift Left Single
SLDL	Shift Left Double Logical
SLL	Shift Left Single Logical
SRDA	Shift Right Double
SRA	Shift Right Single
SRDL	Shift Right Double Logical
SRL	Shift Right Single Logical
SIO	Start I/O
ST	Store
STC	Store Character

STH	Store Halfword
STM	Store Multiple
S	Subtract
SH	Subract Halfword
SL	Subtract Logical
SVC	Supervisor Call
TS	Test and Set
TCH	Test Channel
TIO	Test I/O
TM	Test Under Mask
TR	Translate
TRT	Translate and Test
UNPK	Unpack

Decimal Feature Instructions

AP	Add Decimal
CP	Compare Decimal
DP	Divide Decimal
EP	Edit
EDMK	Edit and Mark
MP	Multiply Decimal
SP	Subtract Decimal
ZAP	Zero and Add

Floating-Point Feature Instructions

AD	Add Normalized (Long)
AE	Add Normalized (Short)
CD	Compare (Long)
CE	Compare (Short)
DD	Divide (Long)
DE	Divide (Short)
HDR	Halve (Long)
HER	Halve (Short)
LD	Load (Long)
LE	Load (Short)
MD	Multiply (Long)
ME	Multiply (Short)
STD	Store (Long)
STE	Store (Short)
SD	Subtract Normalized (Long)
SE	Subtract Normalized (Short)

Extended Mnemonic Instruction Codes

General

| B | Branch Unconditionally |
| NOP | No Operation |

After Compare Instructions

BH	Branch on A High
BL	Branch on A Low
BE	Branch on A Equal B
BNH	Branch on A Not High
BNL	Branch on A Not Low
BNE	Branch on A Not Equal B

After Arithmetic Instructions

BO	Branch on Overflow
BP	Branch on Plus
BM	Branch on Minus
BZ	Branch on Zero
BNP	Branch on Not Plus
BNM	Branch on Not Minus
BNZ	Branch on Not Zero

After Test Under Mask Instructions

BO	Branch if Ones
BM	Branch if Mixed
BZ	Branch if Zeros
BNO	Branch if Not Ones

From this list you can get an idea of the variety of instructions. It is interesting to note a comparison between some of the EX-1 instructions and some of SMILEY's. The following are similar in operation:

EX-1	SMILEY
GET	L
ADD	A
SUB	S
PUT	ST
JIX	B
JZE	BZ

V. SIMULTANEOUS PROGRAM OPERATION AND I/O TRANSFERS

Early computers (and many recent ones) required that the program in the computer "hold up" or cease in its operation while input or output transfers were made. Input transfers, as we recall, are transfers of information from some source of peripheral equipment (card reader, tapes, drums, etc.) to core memory. Output transfers are in the reverse direction; i.e., from core memory to some piece of peripheral equipment (card punch, tape, drum, printer, etc.).

SMILEY, however, is quite sophisticated for the state of the art and can have a program operating and transfers going on simultaneously. There are certain conditions which must be adhered to by the programmer to utilize this feature. He must allocate his program and transfers in certain ways among SMILEY's four core memory banks.

The core memory of SMILEY consists of four parts called *banks*. As far as a program is concerned, however, the four banks are just one memory; i.e., the totality of registers are contignous. To illustrate the simultaneous program operation and I/O transfers, for example, a program can be operated in core bank A at the same time that information is being transferred from a tape into core bank B, from a card reader into core bank C, and from core bank D to drums.

SMILEY also has a feature called *bi-level decoding* (alias the *overlap feature*). This means SMILEY can be in the operation phase of one computer instruction, and, at the same time, be obtaining and interpreting what it believes will be the next instruction to operate. Active branch instructions will fool the computer in its look-ahead attempt, but, over the long run, its efforts pay off handsomely in program operating time. Again, to obtain this advantage, the programmer must adhere to a condition. He must write his program so that the operating program is in one bank and the data which the program is to process is in another bank.

VI. THE INTERRUPT SYSTEM

The Interrupt System is a machine feature which enables an operating program to be immediately interrupted if certain events occur. Suppose, for example, we have a program system operating which consists of a control program and sub-programs which the control program controls.

If a sub-program is operating and a flash message comes into the computer system from an "Input Keyboard Console," the sub-program will be automatically stopped and electronic control transferred to core memory location 30_8 where the control program is setting. The control program is thus jarred into action. The control program would then probably call on a particular sub-program to process the flash message. After it had been taken care of, the control program would return control to the interrupted program.

The control program in a program system is generally in charge of initiating and controlling input-output transfers. This eliminates haphazard I/O transfers and helps prevent potential areas of gross error due to improper program or data assignments. The Interrupt System is valuable in aiding the transfer process because interrupts signaling the completion of an I/O transfer will enable the control program to immediately initiate another I/O transfer, thus keeping I/O transfers occurring almost continuously. This is important because transfers of information into and out of core memory, to and from peripheral equipment, are extremely slow compared to the processing speed of the central computer.

Another type of interrupt is one which signals that something has gone wrong electrically with the machine. With this type of interrupt, control is subsequently given to a maintenance program. This program will locate the trouble and its nature, and communicate it to a maintenance man and the control program. If the trouble is such that the program system can operate by staying clear of the malfunctioning area, the control program will modify the system to continue using the good parts of the computer while the repairs are going on.

Thus, there are many different kinds of interrupts. There are communication registers involved in the Interrupt System whereby the computer can communicate to the program the nature of the interrupt. There are manually controlled switches associated with the Interrupt System. These switches in different positions can cause various actions to occur in the event of an interrupt. Thus, real time operation is promoted. Real time operation was discussed in Chapter One.

VII. CONCLUSION

SMILEY stands high on the evolutionary ladder of computing machinery. It would take many programmers years to program it and fully capitalize on its sophistication.

CHAPTER ELEVEN

TRIVIAL—
A Higher Level Language

I. RATIONALE

TRIVIAL is a higher level language. The name derives from Trusty, Reliable, Ingenius Version of the International Algebraic Language. It is a hypothetical programming language as was the symbolic machine language for SMILEY. However, many real-life versions of higher level languages do exist.

The reason for having a higher level language is so that programs may be written in a language approaching English and mathematics. It is intended to be flexible in format—at least as compared to symbolic machine language —and thus, is designed to free the programmer from details so that he can concentrate on the logic of the problem.

It is called a higher level language because it is removed one more step from the machine binary than the machine symbolic language. A program called a "compiler" will change the higher level language to the symbolic machine language and then to binary.

TRIVIAL is easier to learn than is a symbolic machine language. It is not machine oriented. In other words, it should be possible to write a program in TRIVIAL regardless of which machine is ultimately used. This, of course, requires that different compilers be employed to get TRIVIAL to the particular machine languages.

Let us examine a very simple problem solved in EX-1 language and then in TRIVIAL.

Illustrative example

Given an item called ALPHA in bits 6 through 10 of core location 60 and an item called B ET A in bits 6 through 10 of core location 61, write a program which will place their sum, called GAMMA, into bits 11 through 15 of core location 62.

<table>
<tr><td colspan="2" align="center">E X-1 SOLUTION</td><td align="center">TRIVIAL SOLUTION</td></tr>
<tr><td>P I M</td><td>M A S K A</td><td>GAMMA = A L PHA</td></tr>
<tr><td>G E T</td><td>6 0</td><td>+ B E T A$</td></tr>
<tr><td>E X T</td><td></td><td></td></tr>
<tr><td>P U T</td><td>T E M P</td><td></td></tr>
<tr><td>G E T</td><td>6 1</td><td></td></tr>
<tr><td>E X T</td><td></td><td></td></tr>
<tr><td>A D D</td><td>T E M P</td><td></td></tr>
<tr><td>S A R</td><td>5</td><td></td></tr>
<tr><td>P I M</td><td>M A S K B</td><td></td></tr>
<tr><td>D E P</td><td>6 2</td><td></td></tr>
<tr><td>H L T</td><td></td><td></td></tr>
</table>

```
MASKA    0 . 0 1 7 4 0 0 0 0
MASKB    0 . 0 0 0 3 7 0 0 0
TEMP     0 . 0 0 0 0 0 0 0 0
```

Thus, we see that the programmer's job is much simpler in the TRIVIAL solution. The "=" in the TRIVIAL statement should be interpreted as "set equal to." The "$" signifies the end of a TRIVIAL statement. It is somewhat analogous to the period at the end of a sentence. However, the period is reserved for another use in this language.

A "TRIVIAL to EX-1" compiler, therefore, would take the above programming statement *and with information from the compool* would develop the EX-1 coding and finally the binary.

II. VARIABLES

We recall in our study of the EX-1 that our problems were described in such a way that we were working with the contents of core locations. Frequently we worked with groups of consecutive bits of a core location. Sometimes, these were bytes and other times they were not. Blocks of consecutive core locations were called tables.

Core locations, bytes, and groups of bits in a location all imply machine hardware. Since TRIVIAL is to be a non-machine oriented language, we must work with entities other than the contents of locations. These entities in TRIVIAL are called *variables*. More specifically, these variables are called items, as was previously described. A collection of related items forms an entry in the table. An illustration will perhaps best show this structure.

The name of this table is AUTOS. It contains three entries. Each entry consists of three items. The names of these items are MAKE, COLOR, and QUANTY. (We are limited to six places in an item name.) The values contained in the three items of entry #0 are respectively FORD, BLACK and 9. An item like MAKE which may have a value in it of FORD, CHEV, PLYM, etc., is called a *status item*.

The pictorial description of table AUTOS which I have given here is an abstract representation of the table. We will say nothing as to how this table actually appears in the machine's core memory. We will let the compiler program worry about that. This abstract representation of the table will be basically sufficient for us to program using it.

Before the programmer writes a program using this table, he must make sure it (including its items) is "defined" so that the compiler program will be able to translate all into machine binary. This definition can be accomplished in one of two ways. The definition can be contained in the compool or dictionary-like table to which the compiler has access—or it can be defined by the programmer at the beginning of his program. Let us look at this latter method. The programmer writes on coding paper:

TRIVIAL CODING PAPER

```
 5 6 7 8 9 10 11 12 13 14 15 16 17 18 19 20 21 22 23 24 25 26 27 28 29 30 31 32 33 34 35 36 37 38 39 40 41 42 43 44 45 46 47 48 49 50
T A B L E   A U T O S   R   3   $
  B E G I N
    I T E M   M A K E   S   V ( F O R D )   V ( C H E V )   V ( P L Y M )   V ( D O D G E ) $
      I T E M   C O L O R   S   V ( R E D )   V ( B L A C K )   V ( B L U E )   $
        I T E M   Q U A N T Y   F   $
      E N D
```

The programmer first writes the word T A B L E. This means that he is going to define a table; that is to say, T A B L E is a special code word to the compiler. Next, he writes the name of the table A U T O S. The R means that this table is to have a fixed number of entries. The 3 is the number of entries. The $ denotes the end of a T R I V I A L statement.

If we had desired to make this table variable in number of entries, we would have coded a V instead of an R. Then the compiler would have set up a control item called N E N T (for number of entries) at the beginning of the table. The programmer would then have had to keep N E N T current. That is to say, he would have had to have his program modify it as entries were added to or deleted from the table.

On the second line (this corresponds to the second data processing card), the B E G I N means that the definition of the items in the table is going to begin. I T E M means that the definition of an item is about to be made. The name of the item is M A K E. The S means that it is a status type item. There are several different types of items which may be defined in the T R I V I A L language. The possible statuses of item M A K E are then listed as F O R D, C H E V, P L Y M, and D O D G E. The V( ) is symbology which denotes to the compiler that these are the various statuses. The $ denotes the end of the statement. Similarly for item C O L O R. The item Q U A N T Y is being defined as a floating point type of item which is the reason for the F. The E N D signifies the end of the definitions of the items in the preceding table.

It should be pointed out that several T R I V I A L statements may be made on one line, and also that a statement can extend for several lines. The words such as T A B L E, F O R D, and so forth, may be written so as to fall in any column. The only restriction upon card columns is that the code should not extend past column 66 on any one line.

As might be anticipated, there are several different types of items which may be defined. There are, for example, fractional-type items, integer-type items, and hollerith-type items, in addition to the S and F type of items which may be defined.

III. SETTING VARIABLES

The definition of the variables simply applies to the empty vehicles. Much of programming consists of placing values into these items, taking values from the items, and examining the contents of items for certain values. Placing a value into an item is termed "setting the item."

Suppose, for example, that we wished to set item M A K E of entry #0 to a status of F O R D. The programmer would write the statement in his program as:

$$MAKE(\$0\$) = V(FORD)\$$$

The symbology ($ $) following the item name signifies that the item is "subscripted." In this specific case, a 0 is contained in the ($ $) meaning that we are concerned with entry 0. As was previously stated, the = should be interpreted as "set equal to." The = is what is called in programmer dialect the assignment operator. It causes a value to be assigned to an item. The V( ) is the symbology which means that the item is going to be set to a status. The particular status, FORD, is enclosed in the V( ). The $ denotes the end of the statement.

If we wished to set the entire table AUTOS as we have indicated in the abstract representation given earlier, we could write the following program:

TRIVIAL CODING PAPER

```
MAKE($0$) = V(FORD)$    COLOR($0$) = V(BLACK)$
QUANTY($0$) = 9.$
MAKE($1$) = V(CHEV)$    COLOR($1$) = V(RED)$
QUANTY($1$) = 12.$
MAKE($2$) = V(PLYM)$    COLOR($2$) = V(BLUE)$
QUANTY($2$) = 3.$
```

IV. LOOPING

The value of any program language or system is severely limited in value if no provision is available for performing program iterations. Thus, one fully expects to have such a provision in TRIVIAL. Let us see how a programmer would provide for looping in his program. Suppose we wished to write a program which would set each item QUANTY to the value 9 in our given AUTOS table. Assuming that the table and items are defined:

$$FOR \quad I = 0, 1, 2\$$$
$$QUANTY(\$I\$) = 9\$$$

This small program would do the job. The first statement in this specific program is called a FOR statement. It, in effect, will cause a counter to be set up which will have 0 in it initially and be increased on each pass by 1 until a pass has been made where the counter has had the value 2. Thus, the form of the FOR statement is:

$$FOR \quad I = A, B, C\$$$

where   A is the initial value of the indexing factor.

B is the amount of increment (or decrement).

C is the final value of the indexing factor.

The name of the counter has been arbitrarily given as I. Any letter could have been used. These counters are not called index registers in the TRIVIAL language. Rather, they are called *subscripts*.

The FOR statement applies only to the statement immediately following it. In this case, it applies only to QUANTY(I) = 9$. The FOR statement in the specific example says to "perform the following statement as many times as is necessary to go through the complete range of having I contain 0 on the first pass, 1 on the second, and 2 on the last." Thus, the item QUANTY in each entry will be set to the value 9.

Another method of writing the FOR statement in the above example is:

$$FOR \quad I = ALL(QUANTY)\$$$

If we use this, the TRIVIAL compiler will obtain the necessary information from the compool and set up the three fields of initial, increment, and final.

It frequently occurs that we would like to have the FOR statement apply to several TRIVIAL statements following it. This can be accomplished by enclosing the statements by the words BEGIN and END. Suppose, for example, that we wished to set all items QUANTY to 9, all items MAKE to FORD, and all items COLOR to RED. We could write:

```
EOR   I = ALL(QUANTY)$
BEGIN   QUANTY($I$) = 9$   MAKE($I$) =
   V(FORD)$   COLOR($I$) = V(RED)$   END
```

The three TRIVIAL statements enclosed by the BEGIN and END make what is called a *compound statement*.

The expression to the right of the equal sign in a TRIVIAL statement can be quite complex. Should we wish to set item QUANTY to the value $5\left(\frac{9+3}{2}\right)^4$ we could write:

$$QUANTY(I) = 5*((9 + 3)/2)(*4*)\$$$

V. DECISION MAKING

Decision making is done in TRIVIAL by an IF statement for yes-no types of decisions. A statement to be tested has an IF attached to its beginning. If the statement is true, the statement immediately following the IF statement is performed. If the statement is false, the first statement following the IF statement is skipped and control goes to the second statement.

Suppose we wish to write a program which will count how many items
QUANTY contain the value 0, and we wish to maintain this count in an item
called TALLY. We could write:

TALLY = 0$ Clear TALLY initially.
FOR   I = ALL(QUANTY)$ Prepare to cycle thru table.
BEGIN
  IF   QUANTY(I)   EQ   0$ Test the item for zero.
    TALLY = TALLY + 1 $ If item contains zero, con-
                                        trol goes here.
      TALLY = TALLY $ ⎧If item does not contain
                            ⎨ zero, control goes here.
END   ⎪Thus, TALLY is not in-
                                     ⎩creased.

The IF statement may be quite complex. It may involve the Boolean algebra
"and," "or," and "not," along with six different types of relational operators.
We may, for example, have:

  IF   QUANTY(I)   GR 9 AND   MAKE(I)   EQ
      V(FORD)   OR   COLOR(I)   EQ   V(RED)$

This statement would be considered true if COLOR contained the status
RED. It would also be considered true if *both* QUANTY were greater than
9 *and* MAKE contained the status FORD.

If several things are to be done in the event of the IF statement being true,
the several statements following the IF statement may be enclosed by the
brackets BEGIN and END making a *compound statement*. Then, in the event
of the IF statement being false, the entire compound statement is skipped
and control given to the first statement following the compound statement.

The EQ and GR used above are called *relational operators*. TRIVIAL
contains six of these.

EQ	Equal to
NQ	Not Equal to
GR	Greater than
GQ	Greater than or equal to
LS	Less than
LQ	Less than or equal to

VI. SWITCHES

A SWITCH in TRIVIAL enables a programmer to make a multiple
branch in his program. For example, if an item can contain one of a possible

five values, a programmer could use a SWITCH with this item and cause control to be transferred to one of five different places in his program, depending upon the value of the item. A SWITCH consists of two parts, a definition and a call. The definition is made at the beginning of the program along with item and table definitions. The call is one of the dynamic TRIVIAL statements and is included in the main body of the program. An example of a particular call is GOTO ALPHA $. Here the name of the SWITCH is ALPHA. The term GOTO is required before the call name. The definition of this particular SWITCH might appear as follows:

SWITCH ALPHA(ABLE(I))
   = (WHITE = AA, BLACK = BB, GREEN = CC)$

Here the word SWITCH declares this to be a SWITCH definition statement. The name that this particular SWITCH has been given is ALPHA. ALPHA is a SWITCH which switches according to the contents of item ABLE of the entry as is specified by the subscript I. If the value of the item is WHITE, control is transferred automatically to a TRIVIAL program statement labeled AA. If it is BLACK, control goes to a statement labeled BB. Similarly, control goes to CC if the item contains the value GREEN.

VII. STATEMENT LABELS AND GOTO STATEMENTS

A TRIVIAL statement may be labeled by a label consisting of from two to six alphanumeric characters. These must be followed by a period. The reason for labeling a statement is the same as it was in programming the EX-1; namely, so that control can be transferred to a statement from a sequence changing statement. The sequence changing statement in TRIVIAL is called a GOTO statement. It consists of the term GOTO followed by a statement label without a period, Let us look at an example.

```
                     ALPHA = BETA   $
                     IF  ALPHA  EQ  0 $
                        GOTO   BB$                    Sequence
                        ALPHA = ALPHA + 1$             changing
Statement labels  →AA.  STOP   $                       statement
                   BB.  ALPHA = 2 + BETA
                        − GAMMA   $
                     EPSLON = ALPHA(*2*)$
                     GOTO   AA$                        Sequence
                                                        changing
                                                        statement
```

VII. PROCEDURES

A *procedure* in TRIVIAL essentially enables a programmer to call a group of TRIVIAL statements by a single name, Then, using this name in various places throughout his program, he can accomplish the function achieved by the procedure. A procedure performs the same function in TRIVIAL as a subroutine does for the EX-1.

IX. IN CONCLUSION

The objective of this chapter has been to give some slight insight into what TRIVIAL (and hence a higher level language) achieves in the way of programming ease. Consequently, only the main features of the language have been presented.

Problem 11.1

Given item ALPHA in table TABLEA and item BETA in table TABLEB. Each are fixed length tables of 9 entries. Write a TRIVIAL program which will transfer all of the ALPHA information to the respective BETA items.

Problem 11.2

Write a TRIVIAL program which will add 6 to the contents of each entry of item GAMMA. GAMMA is an item in the fixed length table PLUSIX. Table PLUSIX contains 14 entries.

Problem 11.3

Write a TRIVIAL program which will replace every other entry of item USQARE with its square. Start with entry 0. USQARE is an item of fixed length table FIXUP which contains 29 entries.

Problem 11.4

Write a TRIVIAL program which will examine each item CHECK of 20 entry table DATA and change each entry as follows:
1. Add 3 to each entry which contains 3.
2. Add 4 to all other entries.

Problem 11.5

Given a fixed length table SWOP of 35 entries (each entry consists of items INFOA and INFOB), write a TRIVIAL program which will exchange the contents of INFOA and INFOB. Assume that you have a single item TEMP at your disposal.

Problem 11.6

Write a **TRIVIAL** program which will examine item **MAYBE** of each entry of fixed length table **QESTON**. **QESTON** contains 30 entries. If an entry of item **MAYBE** satisfies the condition that $3 \leq$ |contents of **MAYBE** | < 9, the contents of the item is to be tripled and increased by 5. Otherwise, the contents of the item should just be increased by 7.

Problem 11.7

Write a **TRIVIAL** program which will move the contents of every entry of item **BOLTS** in 10 entry table **MOVUP** up one entry. Move the contents of the 1st entry to the last. Assume that the single item **TEMP** is at your disposal.

CHAPTER TWELVE

Programming Systems

Computer programs can usually be classified as belonging to one of two broad categories. These categories are:

1. Operational Programs
2. Utility Programs

Given a function to be automated or programmed, the programs which achieve this automation can be called the *operational programs*. The programs which aid the writing and "putting on the air" of the operational programs are called *utility programs*. An assembler is a good example of a utility program.

Frequently the program solution to a given problem becomes so large and complex that the solution is broken down into smaller units. These smaller units are then called programs and the totality of the interrelated programs is called a system.

This can be carried even further and we can get a system consisting of subsystems, where each subsystem consists of programs. Each system and subsystem, as a rule, has a program acting as control for the entire system or subsystem.

There are no hard and fast rules as to how one initially subdivides a system into subsystems or programs. It is usually done in some convenient arbitrary manner. For example, the system may be divided so that each program is small enough to be the responsibility of one programmer. Or the system may consist of a set of separate functions and each function may be performed by one program. Or the machine might be able to hold 10,000 computer instructions, plus data, in it at one time, hence, each program would be about 10,000 instructions long. Meetings are held by the programming supervisors (who are preferably experienced programmers) and the subdivisions are made.

Since the utility programs aid in the writing and checking out of the operational programs, the utility programs are written first. While a group of personnel is writing utility programs, a team of system analysts can be studying the requirements of the operational system and planning its design.

Usually, a set of utility programs is provided as a package by the manufacturer of the computer. However, in very large program systems, these must usually be supplemented in order to deal with special features of the operational system. For example, the manufacturer will almost always supply an assembler for changing symbolic machine instructions to binary, but perhaps not a compiler for a higher level language, although supplying the latter also appears to be the trend. Utility tools for testing the operational system are generally produced by the developer of the operational system.

Utility programs usually take easily constructed human inputs and produce machine-usable inputs or take machine-produced outputs and produce easily understood outputs for humans. Examples would be assemblers, compilers, compool assemblers, tape handlers, data insertion programs for use in testing, and data printing routines for use in testing.

The work on the development of a control program for a large system usually gets under way at the very beginning of a project. This is so because its development depends heavily upon the characteristics of the computer involved and its associated I/O equipment. The particular computer to be used in a particular project for automation is generally chosen at the very first—before the design of the system. This is not to say that this is the way is should be done, or always will be done, but it seems to have been historically the case.

A control program can usually be classified as being of one of two types. It controls either a "demand" type of system or a "cyclic" type of system.

A *demand type of system* is one where the control program must be capable of bringing in and operating at a moment's notice any of the many possible programs.

A *cyclic system*, as opposed to a demand system, is one where the sequence of program operation is determined prior to the installation of the system in the machine.

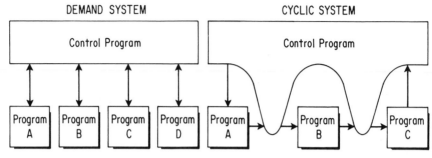

DEMAND SYSTEM

CYCLIC SYSTEM

Any program may follow or precede any other one

The programs always operate in the sequence A, B, C, etc.

Since the control program attempts to keep I/O operations going on continuously while operating a program, one program will be in core memory operating, while a previously operated one and its data are being read out of core memory, and a future one and its data are being read into core memory.

If we employ a demand type of system and also the philosophy of any three programs and their data in core at the same time, the control program must dynamically assign core memory locations to each program just prior to read-in from auxiliary storage. It must, likewise, dynamically assign core memory locations to the environment (tables and items) of a program and then communicate the whereabouts of these data to the using program. Dynamic allocation adds greatly to the complexity of a control program.

The process of developing a program system is quite variable as far as subdivisions of the process are concerned. Also, the terminology varies from system to system, but essentially the system documentation is as follows:

1. Feasibility Studies
2. Scope Documents (describe the extent or capabilities of the system)
3. Operational Design Requirements (describe the methods used to achieve the automation)
   a. Operational Program Requirements (describe the functions performed by the machine)
   b. Human Action Requirements (describe the functions performed by users of the system)
4. Program System Specifications
5. Program Specifications
6. Test Specifications

The first three stages produce documents that are oriented in terms of the operational system. That is, the documents are written to contain descriptions in English of procedures and mathematical formulae to be used in the automation of the particular problem at hand.

The last three stages are written making use of specific computer terminology and machine capability. It is the author's belief that the individuals taking part in any of the above stages should have written a computer program (be it ever so small) at one time in their career. This is so because the system-designer should have some "feel" for the consequences in machine programming involved to achieve his prose descriptions.

The proliferation in the number of stages of system design as the automation job increases in scope is somewhat appalling. This undoubtedly is connected in some way to Parkinson's Law.[1]

A good approach to system design and development seems to be to do the job in teams. Each team should be composed of members from the customer or user group and members from the system design and development group. The individuals comprising the customer component of the team should each have had about three to six months of programming experience or training. The individuals comprising the system development component of the team should have had a period of about equal time to study the user's current manual process. This tends to reduce the tendency towards a lopsided and unrealistic approach.

In extremely large systems, it is generally desirable to make a first pass at the design with a limited system capability. Much education on the part of all concerned takes place and many unforeseeable problems arise.

A second pass at the design can then be made with improved capability and wiser designers.

It would seem that a good way to train system developers might be to select a fairly good, responsible programmer and give him an assignment to automate some small function—for example, inventory records at the local supermarket. Then, four months later, after he has done this all by himself, give him a larger assignment, such as automating school bus scheduling at the local high school. For this, give him a subordinate. After six months and with this job solved, assign him to perhaps automating the billing at the county hospital or automation of records at the police depeatment. For this, give him four or five programmers.

All of these assignments are jobs that should be contracted for and, thus, be real jobs, not just make-believe. After a company had five or ten of these competent teams, the company might tackle automating the United Nations, or some other such gigantic function. But this idea may be like building a tree house—workable in theory, but not always practical.

---

[1] Parkinson's Law states something to the effect that work expands to fill the time allotted.

Management control and guidance are extremely important but difficult areas of system design and development. The difficulty seems to increase exponentially with the size of the system. This is probably due to the number of people involved, their lack of experience, and the complexity of the work.

Two fairly recent developments in computer systems are *timesharing* and *general purpose data management systems.*

Timesharing refers to having several users tied into a computer through remote consoles. These remote consoles are of a keyboard-input type (a teletype machine is in common use). Although all of the users are not really using the computer simultaneously, the machine is completely at their disposal.

Programmers in the early days of computing worked physically with their computers quite regularly. With the advance in the state of the art, more and more work was done in a "closed shop." This meant that programs were sent to the computer room once or twice a day and *computer operators* ran the jobs in what is called *batch processing.* In Batch processing you save up jobs and run many—one after the other. Turn-around-time in batch processing can sometimes be too slow.

Hopefully with timesharing, both programmer and computer user will find the machine more accessible.

Data Management systems are program systems that enable a user (non-programmer) to define the data that his organization users. Then, he can query his data, change it, rearrange it, and produce reports based upon it. With a data management system the user is provided with the software that enables him to manage and control his organization by making decisions based on computer output.

Both timesharing of computers and general purpose data management systems have been around a few years but still are so relatively new that they can be considered to be in the developmental stage.

It will be interesting to learn what the future holds as regards standardization of technology for large-scale system development.

Let me conclude with a bit of good system philosophy: It is true that the best laid plans of mice and men often go awry; but, of course, that does not mean that one should stop trying.

APPENDIX ONE

I. REVIEW OF OPERATIONS WITH EXPONENTS

When a factor in a product is repeated several times, it is possible to write the expression more concisely using an exponent.

Thus, $2 \times 2 \times 2 \times 2 \times 2$ may be written as 2^5. The 2 is called the base and the 5 is called the exponent.

An *exponent* indicates the number of times that the *base* appears as a factor in a product.

If a number does not appear as a factor in a product, it may still be indicated, but with an exponent of 0. Any base with an exponent of 0 is defined to be equal to 1. Thus,

$$2^0 = 1$$
$$3^0 = 1$$
$$8^0 = 1$$
$$N^0 = 1$$

Two numbers with equal bases may be multiplied by simply adding the exponents:

$$2^5 \times 2^3 = (2 \times 2 \times 2 \times 2 \times 2) \times (2 \times 2 \times 2) = 2^{5+3} = 2^8$$

Two numbers of equal bases may be divided by simply subtracting the exponent of the divisor from the exponent of the dividend:

$$\frac{2^5}{2^3} = \frac{2 \times 2 \times \cancel{2} \times \cancel{2} \times \cancel{2}}{\cancel{2} \times \cancel{2} \times \cancel{2}} = \frac{2 \times 2}{1} = 2^{5-3} = 2^2$$

This rule is consistent with the one about zero exponents.

$$\frac{5^2}{5^2} = 1 \quad \text{and} \quad \frac{5^2}{5^2} = 5^{2-2} = 5^0 = 1$$

A base with a negative exponent is defined to be the reciprocal of the base with a positive exponent:

$$2^{-3} = \frac{1}{2^3}$$

A base and its exponent may be transferred across the division line by changing the sign of the exponent. This is true as long as the numbers are factors and not terms. A factor is connected by multiplication; a term is connected by addition or subtraction.

$$\frac{2^{-4}}{3^{-5}} = \frac{3^5}{2^4}$$

Actually what we have done is multiply both numerator and denominator by 2^4 and 3^5.

$$\frac{2^{-4}}{3^{-5}} \times \frac{2^4}{2^4} \times \frac{3^5}{3^5} = \frac{2^{4-4} \times 3^5}{3^{5-5} \times 2^4} = \frac{2^0 \times 3^5}{3^0 \times 2^4} = \frac{3^5}{2^4}$$

A number such as $(2^3)^2$ is equivalent to 2^6. In other words, the exponents multiply when in the above form. This is because

$$(2^3)^2 = (2^3) \times (2^3) = 2^{3+3} = 2^6$$

II. REVIEW OF ABSOLUTE MAGNITUDE AND RELATION SYMBOLS

Signed numbers are considered to get larger the farther right they are found on the number line.

Thus $+4$ is greater than $+3$, and -3 is greater than -4.

The following relational symbols are used in mathematics:

> $>$ is the symbol for "greater than"
> $<$ is the symbol for "less than"
> $=$ is the symbol for "equal to"
> $\neq$ is the symbol for "not equal to"

$\geq$ is the symbol for "greater than or equal to"

$\leq$ is the symbol for "less than or equal to"

$\approx$ is the symbol for "approximately equal to"

Thus, we can say $+3 > -3$, or $-3 < +3$. A good memory device for remembering $>$ and $<$ is to think of these symbols as arrow heads that always point toward the smaller of the two quantities.

We note that $+2$ is greater than $+1$ and less than $+3$. This can be expressed as

$$+1 < +2 < +3$$

This also states that $+2$ lies between $+1$ and $+3$ on the number line.

If we wish to use the magnitude of a number (the value of the number without regard to sign) we may enclose the quantity with two vertical bars.

$$|+6| = 6 \qquad |-6| = 6$$

The magnitude is also called the *absolute magnitude*.

III. MATHEMATICAL INSIGHTS INTO CONVERSION RULES

A. Reason why dividing by 8 works in converting decimal integers to octal integers:

Since 1 is the same in all systems; or in other words,

$$1_n = 1_{n-1} = \cdots 1_{10} = 1_8 = 1_2$$

any quantity less than one (a fraction) in one system, is less than one (a fraction) in any other system.

Thus, if the following fractions are in lowest terms, whenever

$$\left(XY + \frac{W}{Z}\right)_r = \left(PQ + \frac{M}{N}\right)_s$$

then

$$(XY)_r = (PQ)_s \quad \text{and} \quad \left(\frac{W}{Z}\right)_r = \left(\frac{M}{N}\right)_s$$

where X, Y, W, Z and P, Q, M, N are digits in the base r and s respectively.

That is to say,

THEOREM: If a number in one number system equals a number in another system, the integral parts in the two systems are equal and the fractional parts are equal.

Let

$$N_{\cdot 10} = A_n A_{n-1} + \cdots + A_2 A_1 A_0$$

or

$$N_{\cdot 10} = A_n 8^n + A_{n-1} 8^{n-1} + \cdots + A_2 8^2 + A_1 8^1 + A_0 8^0$$

where N is a number in base 10 and the A_is are digits in the octal system. The problem is to determine each A_i.

Dividing both sides by 8 gives

$$\text{Quotient} + \frac{R_1}{8} = A_n 8^{n-1} + A_{n-1} 8^{n-2} + \cdots + A_2 8 + A_1 + \frac{A_0}{8}$$

from the previous theorem, we known that

$$\frac{R_1}{8} = \frac{A_0}{8} \quad \text{hence, } R_1 = A_0$$

Dividing the integral parts on each side of the equation again gives $R_2 = A_1$. Repeating the procedure gives all the A_is.

Thus, we derive the rule that *dividing the decimal number* (integer) *by 8 gives us the octal number* (integer) *via remainders reversed.*

B. Reason why multiplying by 8 works in converting decimal fractions to octal fractions:

The reasoning is similar to (A) above.

Let

$$.N_{10} = .A_0 A_1 \cdots A_{n-1} A_n$$

then

$$.N_{10} = \frac{A_0}{8} + \frac{A_1}{8^2} + \cdots \frac{A_{n-2}}{8^{n-1}} + \frac{A_{n-1}}{8^n}$$

Multiplying both sides by 8 gives

$$I_1 + \text{fraction} = A_0 + \frac{A_1}{8} + \cdots \frac{A_{n-2}}{8^{n-2}} \frac{A_{n-1}}{8^{n-1}}$$

where I_1 is either an integer or zero.

Hence, by the theorem stated previously,

$$I_1 = A_0$$

Repeated multiplications of the fractions on both sides of the equation give

$$I_2 = A_1, I_3 = A_2 \quad \text{etc.}$$

C. Reason why three binary digits may be replaced by one octal digit: Let $b_5b_4b_3b_2b_1b_0$ be a binary number where each b_i is either a zero or a one. Then $b_5b_4b_3b_2b_1b_0$ may be expressed as,

$$b_5 \times 2^5 + b_4 \times 2^4 + b_3 + 2^3 + b_2 \times 2^2 + b_1 \times 2^1 + b_0 \times 2^0$$

and factoring gives

$$(b_5 \times 2^2 + b_4 \times 2^1 + b_3 \times 2^0) \times 2^3$$
$$+(b_2 \times 2^2 + b_1 \times 2^1 + b_0 \times 2^0) \times 2^0$$
$$= (b_5 \times 2^2 + b_4 \times 2^1 + b_3 \times 2^0) \times 8^1$$
$$+(b_2 \times 2^2 + b_1 \times 2^1 + b_0 \times 2^0) \times 8^0$$

Since the modulus of three binary positions is 8 and the modulus of one octal position is also 8, the three-bit binary number in each of the parenthetical expressions may be replaced by the appropriate octal digit E_i giving:

$$E_1 \times 8^1 + E_0 \times 8^0 = E_1 E_0$$

This concludes our mathematical insights into the conversion rules.

APPENDIX TWO

Powers of 2

2^{30}	=	1,073,741,824	2^{12} =	4,096
2^{29}	=	536,870,912	2^{11} =	2,048
2^{28}	=	268,435,456	2^{10} =	1,024
2^{27}	=	134,217,728	2^{9} =	512
2^{26}	=	67,108,864	2^{8} =	256
2^{25}	=	33,554,432	2^{7} =	128
2^{24}	=	16,777,216	2^{6} =	64
2^{23}	=	8,388,608	2^{5} =	32
2^{22}	=	4,194,304	2^{4} =	16
2^{21}	=	2,097,152	2^{3} =	8
2^{20}	=	1,048,576	2^{2} =	4
2^{19}	=	524,288	2^{1} =	2
2^{18}	=	262,144	2^{0} =	1
2^{17}	=	131,072	2^{-1} =	1/2
2^{16}	=	65,536	2^{-2} =	1/4
2^{15}	=	32,768	2^{-3} =	1/8
2^{14}	=	16,384	2^{-4} =	1/16
2^{13}	=	8,192		

EX-1 Instruction List

Mnemonic	Octal Code	Interpretation	Function
* ADD	422	ADD	Adds to the contents of the accumulator, the contents of the core memory location specified by the director. Leaves the result in the accumulator. Does not change the contents of the core memory location.
AXD	563	ADD INDEX TO DIRECTOR	Adds the contents of the specified index register (present count) to the director (not the contents of the memory location specified by the director) and places the result in mask register. The accumulator is not affected.
COB	706	CHECK ONE BIT	Checks the contents of the bit position of accumulator as specified by the director. If the specified bit position contains a 1, skip the next instruction. If the specified bit position contains a 0, does not skip the next instruction. In either case, the contents of the accumulator are not

---

* Means that the director may be modified by the contents of an index register.

	Octal		
Mnemonic	Code	Interpretation	Function

affected. The director is specified in decimal.

CTB	707	CHECK TWO BITS

Checks the contents of the two bit positions of the accumulator as specified by the director. The director coded in decimal specifies the rightmost of the pair. If the specified bit positions contain 00, 01, 10, or 11, skip, none, one, two, or three instructions accordingly. In any case, the contents of the accumulator are not affected.

CYL	101	CYCLE

Moves all of the bits in the accumulator as many places to the left as is specified by the director. Those bits leaving the sign position are re-entered at the rightmost accumulator bit position. No bits are lost. The director is specified in decimal on EX-1 coding paper.

* DEP	534	DEPOSIT

For each bit position in the mask register which contains a 1, replaces the contents of the corresponding bit position of the core memory location specified by the director with the contents of the corresponding bit position of the accumulator. Does not affect the other bit positions in the core memory location. Does not affect contents of the accumulator or mask register.

* DIV	502	DIVIDE

Divides the contents of the combined accumulator and mask register by the contents of the core memory location specified by the director. Leaves the quotient in the accumulator. The core memory location is not affected.

Mnemonic	Octal Code	Interpretation	Function
EXT	533	EXTRACT	Takes no director. For each bit position in the mask register which contains a zero, replaces the corresponding bit position of the accumulator with a zero. Does not affect other accumulator bit portions. Does not affect mask register.
* FAD	722	FLOATING ADD	The contents of the core memory location specified by the director are added in a floating point manner to the contents of the accumulator. The results are left in normalized form in the accumulator. The core memory location is not affected. A floating point zero consists of a word of all zeros.
* FDV	503	FLOATING DIVIDE	The contents of the accumulator are divided in a floating point manner by the contents of the core memory location specified by the director. The results are left in normalized form in the accumulator. The core memory location is not affected.
* FMU	762	FLOATING MULTIPLY	The contents of the accumulator are multiplied in a floating point manner by the contents of the core memory location specified by the director. The results are left in normalized form in the accumulator. The core memory location is not affected.
* FSB	742	FLOATING SUBTRACT	The contents of the core memory location specified by the director are subtracted in a floating point manner from the contents of the accumulator. The results are left in normalized form in the accumulator. The core memory location is not affected. A floating point zero consists of a word of all zeros.

Mnemonic	Octal Code	Interpretation	Function
* GET	402	GET	Clears the accumulator and brings contents of core memory location specified by the director into accumulator. Does not change the core memory location.
HLT	000	HALT	Stops the machine. Program counter will then be one more than location of this instruction. Accumulator not affected.
JGN	705	JUMP ON GREEN LIGHT	If the green light is on, jumps to operate the instruction specified by the director. If the green light is not on, does not jump, but continues with the next instruction. If a jump occurs, turns off the light and saves the instruction location of what would have been the next step (had the jump not occurred) in the mask register. Whether or not a jump occurs, the contents of the accumulator are not affected.
JIX	701	JUMP ON INDEX	Adds the increment to the present count of the index registers and then checks to see if present count is less than the final count. If it is, jumps to operate the instruction specified by the director. If it is not, does not jump but continues with the next instruction in sequence. If a jump occurs, saves the instruction location (contents of program counter) of what would have been the next step (had the jump not occurred) in the mask register. Whether or not a jump actually occurs, the contents of accumulator are not affected.

Mnemonic	Octal Code	Interpretation	Function
JMP	705	JUMP	Transfers controls to the address specified in the director field. Saves the instruction location (current contents of program counter) of what would have been the next instruction (had the jump not occurred) in the mask register. Does not distub contents of the accumulator.
JOV	421	JUMP ON OVERFLOW	If the overflow light is on, jumps to operate the instruction at the location specified by the director. If the overflow light is not on, does not jump, but continues with the next instruction.
			If a jump occurs, saves the instruction location of what would have been the next step (had the jump not occurred) in the mask register. A jump also turns off the light.
			Whether or not a jump occurs, the contents of the accumulator are not affected.
JPO	703	JUMP ON POSITIVE	If accumulator sign is 0, jumps to operate the instruction at location specified by director.
			If accumulator sign is 1, does not jump, but continues on with next instruction in sequence.
			If a jump occurs, save the instruction location (contents of program counter) of what would have been the next step (had the jump not occurred) in the mask register.
			Whether or not a jump actually occurs, the contents of the accumulator are not affected.

Mnemonic	Octal Code	Interpretation	Function
JRD	704	JUMP ON RED LIGHT	If the red light is on, jumps to operate the instruction specified by the director. If the red light is not on, does not jump, but continues with the next instruction. If a jump occurs, turns off the light and save the instruction location of what would have been the next step (had the jump not occurred) in the mask register. Whether or not a jump occurs, the contents of the accumulator are not affected.
JZE	702	JUMP ON ZERO	If the accumulator is positive or negative zero, jumps to operate instruction at location specified by director. If accumulator is not zero, does not jump, but continues on with next instruction in sequence. If a jump occurs, saves the instruction location (contents of program-counter) of what would have been the next step (had the jump not occurred) in the mask register. Whether or not a jump actually occurs, the contents of the accumulator are not affected.
* MUL	462	MULTIPLY	Multiplies the contents of the accumulator by the contents of the core memory location specified by the director. The result will be left in the combined accumulator and mask register. The most significant bits of the product will be in the accumulator. The core memory location is not affected.
* PAD	766	PUT ADDRESS	Takes contents of bits 16-24 (address field) from mask register and places these contents in bits 16-24 of the core memory location specified by director.

Mnemonic	Octal Code	Interpretation	Function
			Does not affect accumulator or mask register. Does not affect contents of bits S–15 of core memory location specified by director.
PCD	132	PUNCH A CARD	Electrically selects the card punch and punches 1 card. The card will be punched in columns 1 through 25 corresponding to bit positions 1 through 25 of core memory locations 30_8 through 43_8. Row 9 will correspond to core location 30_8. Row 8 will correspond to core location 31_8, etc.
* PIM	767	PUT IN MASK	Clears the mask register and brings the contents of the core memory location specified by the director into the mask register. Does not affect specified core memory location or accumulator.
* PUT	202	PUT	Replaces the contents of the core memory register specified by director with the contents of the accumulator. Does not change contents of accumulator. Destroys previous contents of core memory register.
RCD	130	READ A CARD	Electrically selects the card reader and reads columns 1 through 25 of 1 card into core. Row 9 will go into core location 0. Row 8 will go into core location 1, etc.
SAL	102	SHIFT ACCUMULATOR LEFT	All bits in the accumulator with the exception of the sign bit are moved as many places to the left as is specified by the director. Bits leaving bit position 1 are lost. Vacancies caused by bits moving left, out of the rightmost position of the accumulator are filled in with duplicates of the sign bit. The sign bit is not affected. The director is specified in decimal on EX-1 coding paper.

Mnemonic	Octal Code	Interpretation	Function
SAR	103	SHIFT ACCUMULATOR RIGHT	All bits in the accumulator with the exception of the sign bit are moved as many places to the right as is specified by the director. Bits leaving the rightmost bit position are lost. Vacancies caused by bits moving right out of bit position 1 are filled with duplicates of the sign bit. The sign bit is not affected. The director is specified in decimal on EX-1 coding paper.
SBL	021	SHIFT BOTH LEFT	All bits in the combined accumulator and mask register with the exception of the accumulator sign bit are moved as many places to the left as is specified by the director. Bits leaving bit position 1 are lost. Vacancies caused by bits moving left out of the rightmost position of the mask register are filled in with duplicates of the accumulator sign bit. The sign bit is not affected. The director is specified in decimal on EX-1 coding paper.
SBR	022	SHIFT BOTH RIGHT	All bits in the combined accumulator and mask register with the exception of the accumulator sign bit are moved as many places to the right as is specified by the director. Bits leaving the rightmost bit position of the mask register are lost. Vacancies caused by bits moving right out of bit position 1 are filled in with duplicates of the accumulator sign bit. The sign bit is not affected. The director is specified in decimal on EX-1 coding paper.
SIN	566	SET INDEX	Sets the final count of the indicated index register to the amount specified by the director. Sets the present count to zero. Accumulator contents are not affected.

Mnemonic	Octal Code	Interpretation	Function
			If there is a value of from 1 to 6 in the increment field, it will cause the present count to be set to the increment value and the final count to the director value.
			If there is a value of 7 in the increment field, it will cause both the present and final count to be set to the director value. The director is specified in decimal on the EX-1 coding paper.
* SUB	442	SUBTRACT	Subtracts from the contents of the accumulator the contents of the core memory location specified by the director. Leaves result in accumulator. Does not change the specified core memory location.
TAR	126	TAPE READ	Electrically selects the magnetic tape drive and reads (transfer from tape to core memory) as many words as are specified in the associated control word. There are two control words associated with a TAR instruction. The first control word is specified by the director of the TAR. The second control word follows the first. The first control word specifies the number of 25-bit tape words to read into core. The second control word specifies the starting core location into which to start their transfer.
TAW	146	TAPE WRITE	Electrically selects the magnetic tape drive and writes (transfer from core memory to tape) as many words as is specified in the associated control word. There are two control words associated with a TAW instruction. The first control word is specified by the director of the TAW. The second control word follows the first.

Mnemonic	Octal Code	Interpretation	Function
			The first control word specifies the number of 25-bit tape words to write from core. The second control word specifies the starting core location from which to start their transfer.
TON	232	TURN ON	Energizes the specified electrical device (bell, red light, or green light). Turning off of the bell is done manually. The lights can be turned off manually or by the appropriate jump instruction.
TRW	136	TAPE REWIND	Electrically selects the tape drive and rewinds it to load point.
WRT	131	WRITE ON PRINTER	Electrically selects the printer and prints 1 line. Prints the 12-bit hollerith found column-wise in columns 1 through 25 of core memory locations 14_8 through 27_8. Row 9 will correspond to core location 14. Row 8 will correspond to core location 15, etc.

COLLEGE of Programming

THE GRAND SEAL

date_____

Know ye all men that

_____

knows and understands programming.

INSTRUCTOR _____

CUT HERE

If you have conscientiously worked all of the problems in this text and if you believe that you have a firm grasp on the material, please feel free to detach the following certificate and fill it in appropriately. Congratulations.

Answers to Problems

Problem 1.1

List left to student research.

Problem 2.1

1 =	1	17 =	10001	33 =	100001
2 =	10	18 =	10010	34 =	100010
3 =	11	19 =	10011	35 =	100011
4 =	100	20 =	10100	36 =	100100
5 =	101	21 =	10101	37 =	100101
6 =	110	22 =	10110	38 =	100110
7 =	111	23 =	10111	39 =	100111
8 =	1000	24 =	11000	40 =	101000
9 =	1001	25 =	11001	41 =	101001
10 =	1010	26 =	11010	42 =	101010
11 =	1011	27 =	11011	43 =	101011
12 =	1100	28 =	11100	44 =	101100
13 =	1101	29 =	11101	45 =	101101
14 =	1110	30 =	11110	46 =	101110
15 =	1111	31 =	11111	47 =	101111
16 =	10000	32 =	100000	48 =	110000

$$49 = 110001 \qquad 53 = 110101 \qquad 57 = 111001$$
$$50 = 110010 \qquad 54 = 110110 \qquad 58 = 111010$$
$$51 = 110011 \qquad 55 = 110111 \qquad 59 = 111011$$
$$52 = 110100 \qquad 56 = 111000 \qquad 60 = 111100$$

Problem 2.2

1. $7_{10} = 7_8 = 111_2$
2. $14_{10} = 16_8 = 1110_2$
3. $30_{10} = 36_8 = 11110_2$

Problem 2.3

$1000000_2 = 64_{10}$. Thus, a binary millionare would have 64 dollars.

Problem 2.4

Twindred Twosand, Twindred Twin One.

Problem 2.5

1. 551_8
2. 3270_8
3. 656_8
4. 167421_8
5. 1737_8
6. 10000_8

Problem 2.6

1. 114_{10}
2. 179_{10}
3. 8192_{10}
4. 643_{10}
5. 8192_{10}
6. 7_{10}
7. No. There can be no 8's or 9's in an octal number.

Problem 2.7

1. 111100.010
2. 1000000000.
3. 110.010000100
4. 0.101111111000100
5. 11101101101000.
6. 110111.101010001
7. 10010010010010.
8. 10011.
9. 1010100.111101
10. 110101111100001.
11. 10011000.000100
12. 111111111111001
13. 100100100110011.
14. 1.011100110000
15. 1010011100101110.

Problem 2.8

1. 3750.	6. 17.144	11. 6314.
2. 6.071	7. 21.624	12. 3247.
3. 10.604	8. 5532.	13. 4665.
4. 261.70	9. 3320.0	14. 1743.
5. 0.1111	10. 0.2225	15. 126.

Problem 2.9

1. 0.256_8 or 0.26_8
2. 0.624_8 or 0.63_8
3. 0.4_8
4. 0.53111_8 or 0.5311_8

Problem 2.10

1. $\dfrac{19}{32} = 0.593_{10} = 0.59_{10}$

2. $\dfrac{5}{64} = 0.078_{10} = 0.08_{10}$

3. $\dfrac{226}{512} = \dfrac{113}{256} = 0.4414_{10} = 0.441_{10}$

4. $\dfrac{498}{512} = \dfrac{249}{256} = 0.9726_{10} = 0.973_{10}$

Problem 2.11

1. 33.2_8
2. 554.1_8

Problem 2.12

1. D83A
2. 57BF2

Problem 2.13

1. 0010100110101011
1. 111100001001101101110

Problem 2.14

1. 14
2. 41
3. 2622

Problem 2.15

1. 4B
2. B9

Problem 2.16

1. Modulus is $100,000_{10}$ and range is 0 through 99,999.
2. Modulus is 64_{10} and range is 0 through 63.
3. Modulus is 4096_{10} and range is 0 through 4095_{10}.

Problem 2.17

1. 01101100	4. 567411
2. 01000110	5. 4789056
3. 350746	6. 6119709

Problem 2.18

$$0_\triangle 0111. = 7$$
$$\underline{0_\triangle 0010. = 2}$$
$$0_\triangle 1001. = 9$$

Problem 2.19

1. $+5_{10}$ or $+5_8$
2. -4_{10} or -4_8
3' $+14_{10}$ or $+16_8$
4. -15_{10} or -17_8

Problem 2.20

1. 664277 and 604312
2. $0_\triangle 00002064$ and $1_\triangle 77773447$

Problem 2.21

1. One
2. N
3. Ten
4. Dividing, 1000
5. Mutliplying, 2
6. Dividing, 8
7. 64
8. One, three
9. A high base has a greater number of symbols and number facts to memorize.
   A low base requires a large number of positions to represent a relatively small number.
10. Because of the electrical (on-off) bi-state nature of computer circuits.
11. 1000001 and 110000

Problem 2.22

I have found that giving this set of problems as homework one day and then discussing it properly the next day provides an excellent way to open up a class and get students to talk and participate.

The instructor, however, has the important responsibility to see that no students are frightened off by this assignment. Most students will consider themselves fairly expert in this area of mathematics and will dig into the problems in delight. However, there will always be one or two conscientious students who will look upon these problems as being strictly in the realm of Einsteinian mathematics.

It is important, therefore, for the instructor to make clear that although he wants these problems done, if there be those that absolutely cannot do them because of lack of mathematical knowledge, those people definitely should not worry too much about it. The problems are for interest, motivation, and understanding and are not important for what is to follow in the text.

1. The students will find fault with this number system. The lack of zero and the lack of a way to represent numbers less than unity bothers them.

The instructor should remain neutral as to pro or con for this system being a number system.

He might ask if $\pm^1_1$ has answered itself. In other words, could the absence of a symbol denote zero? Of course the answer is "No" because then we would have "1's" and the "absence of 1's" in our system, and hence, we would not have a unitary system but rather a binary one.

The instructor might ask if the following representation would suffice:

In Unitary		In Binary
$1 = 0_{10}$		$0 = 0_{10}$
$11 = 1_{10}$		$1 = 1_{10}$
$111 = 2_{10}$	similar to	$10 = 2_{10}$
$1111 = 3_{10}$		$11 = 3_{10}$
$11111 = 4_{10}$		$100 = 4_{10}$
etc		etc

Then our unitary arithmetic would be like this:

$$3 - 3 = 0 \quad \text{or} \quad 3 - 2 = 1$$
$$1111 - 1111 = 1 \quad 1111 - 111 = 11$$

Fractions might be $\frac{1}{2} = \frac{11}{111}$ and $\frac{2}{3} = \frac{111}{11111}$, etc.

The conclusion finally drawn will probably be that, although the unitary number system might be usable by employing gimmicks, it is certainly different from and more awkward than the others of base 2 and up. Thus, base 2 is probably the lowest practical number system base.

2. (a) The modulus (or number of possible different license plates) is $26^3 \cdot 10^3$ $= 260^3 = 17,576,000.$

   (b) $17,576,000 - 1,000,000$ or $16,576,000$

   (c) The answer to this question can be arrived at either in an empirical manner or by a college algebra formula for permutations. In an empirical manner (trial and error) the following permutations can be obtained:

L L L D D D	D D D L L L	Since there are 20 of these permuta-
L L D D D L	D D L L L D	tions and, as we saw from the answer
L L D D L D	D D L L D L	to (a) above, each permutation gives a
L L D L D D	D D L D L L	modulus of 260^3, the number of plates
L D D D L L	D L L L D D	which could be represented is 20.260^3
L D D L D L	D L L D L D	$= 351,520,000.$
L D L D D L	D L D L L D	Note: L represents a letter and D repre-
L D D L L D	D L L D D L	sents a digit.
L D L D L D	D L D L D L	
L D L L D D	D L D D L L	

You might ask the students how this number compares with the population of the United States.

Each different arrangement which can be made of all or part of a number of things is called a *Permutation*.

This is not a problem in *Combinations* as LLLDDD and DDDLLL are considered the same combination (namely 3L's and 3D's).

THEOREM: If P is the number of permutations of n things taken all at a time of which n_1 are alike, n_2 others alike, n_3 others alike, and so on, then

$$P = \frac{n!}{n_1! \, n_2! \, n_3! \ldots}$$

Applying this to our problem we get

$$P = \frac{6!}{3!3!} = \frac{1 \cdot 2 \cdot 3 \cdot 4 \cdot 5 \cdot 6}{1 \cdot 2 \cdot 3 \cdot 1 \cdot 2 \cdot 3} = 20$$

3. (a)

$$\overset{\displaystyle C \quad\quad E \quad\quad G}{2 \times 26^2 + 4 \times 26^1 + 6 \times 26^0}$$

$$1352 + 104 + 6 = 1462_{10}$$

(b)

$$
\begin{array}{r}
471 \\
26\overline{)\,12248} \\
104 \\
\hline
184 \\
182 \\
\hline
28 \\
26 \\
\hline
\boxed{2}
\end{array}
\qquad
\begin{array}{r}
18 \\
26\overline{)\,471} \\
26 \\
\hline
211 \\
208 \\
\hline
\boxed{3}
\end{array}
\qquad
\begin{array}{r}
0 \\
26\overline{)\,18} \\
0 \\
\hline
\boxed{18}
\end{array}
$$

Since $18 = $ S
$3 = $ D
$2 = $ C
$12248_{10} = $ SDC$_{\text{literal}}$

4.

$$
\begin{array}{r}
54 \\
12_8\,\overline{)\,701_8} \\
62 \\
\hline
61 \\
50 \\
\hline
11_8 = 9_{10}
\end{array}
\qquad
\begin{array}{r}
4 \\
12_8\,\overline{)\,54_8} \\
50_8 \\
\hline
4
\end{array}
\qquad
\begin{array}{r}
0 \\
12_8\,\overline{)\,4} \\
0 \\
\hline
4
\end{array}
$$

hence $701_8 = 449_{10}$

5. By dividing by 3 as many times as necessary and observing the remainders as to whether they are 1 or 0 (they will never be 2 because of the number used), one can obtain the following as an answer.

$$3^0 \quad \boxed{3^1} \quad \boxed{3^2} \quad 3^3 \quad \boxed{3^4} \quad 3^5 \quad \boxed{3^6} \quad \boxed{3^7} \quad 3^8 \quad 3^9 \quad \boxed{3^{10}}$$

$$0 \quad 1 \quad 1 \quad 0 \quad 1 \quad 0 \quad 1 \quad 1 \quad 0 \quad 0 \quad 1$$

6. 14_{10}

7. It is possible to have different bases in different positions. The Mayan Indians, for instance, had a base 20 in their "units" columns and a base 18 in their "tens" column; then 20 in all of the others. This handled their year of 360 days nicely.

The English system of measures can be thought of as having different bases in different positions.

Rods	Yards	Feet	Inches
	0 through 1759	0 through 2	0 through 11
	base 1760	base 3	base 12

Of course, there are two positions required to represent inches, however, this would not be the case in a duodecimal system (base 12).

Of course, there are two positions required to represent inches, however, this would not be the case in a duodecimal system (base 12).

The number system of license plates can be considered a system of various bases.

It is apparent that performing arithmetic in number systems of this type presents some problems.

Take for example the following number system:

"ten's" position	**"unit's" position**
base 10	base 8
symbols 0 through 9	symbols 0 through 7
$D_{10} \cdot 10^1$	$D_8 \cdot 8^0$

How does one represent 8 or 9 in the above system?

(You cannot)

Or look at this system:

"ten's" position	**"unit's" position**
base 8	base 10
symbols 0 through 7	symbols 0 through 9
$D_8 \cdot 8^1$	$D_{10} \cdot 10^0$

How does one represent 9 in the above system?

We have two representations—namely, 11 or 9.

These gaps and duplications can be eliminated by combining bases:

"hundred's" position	**"ten's" position**	**"unit's" position**
base 8	base 10	base 8
symbols 0 through 7	symbols 0 through 9	symbols 0 through 7
$D_8 \cdot 10^1 \cdot 8^1$	$D_{10} \cdot 10 \cdot {}^0 \cdot 8^1$	$D_8 \cdot 8^0$

Note: D_8 stands for any octal digit.

D_{10} stands for any decimal digit.

8. Since 29_r stands for $2 \cdot r + 9$ and since the smallest two digit perfect square in decimal ending in 9 is 49, then $2 \cdot r \cdot 9 = 49$ and therefore, $r = 20$, and the Integral square root of 29_{20} is 7.

9. Since $36_r = 3r + 6$ we see that the number is already divisible by 3 regardless of what r is. Therefore, the number 36_r is divisible by a number other than 1 and itself and hence, is not prime.

CHAPTER 3

Problem 3.1

The message: HELP, I AM BEING HELD PRISONER IN THE ACCUMULATOR

Problem 3.2

1. One could call it MONEY. The name given is arbitrary.

2. Since 200 pennies is $310_8 = 11001000_2$, it is necessary to allocate at least 8 bit positions.

3. Any 8 positions would do, however we probably would want to keep the item out of the sign bit since we might desire to perform arithmetic operations with the item. If a 1 is in the sign position during an arithmetic operation, the quantity will be treated as negative. Although, if the item were in positions through 7, we could use it by isolating it first, and moving it into the rightmost eight positions of the accumulator before using it.

Problem 3.3

1. An item name of GRADE would seem a logical choice.

2. Since I want to represent the statuses A through F (six statuses), I will require room for numbers 0 through 5, or 000_2 through 101_2, therefore, three bit positions will be required.

3. Any three positions will do—for example, bit positions 22, 23, and 24.

4. Probably the following:

$$
\begin{aligned}
000 &= A \\
001 &= B \\
010 &= C \\
011 &= D \\
100 &= E \\
101 &= F
\end{aligned}
$$

Problem 3.4

1. AEN, WPY, JFC, QTA, HUG, JZF

2. HUG is not happy.

3. $\$470_8 = \$312_{10}$.

4. $27_8 = 23_{10}$.

5. $SALRY_0$ contains the larger amount.

6. AGE_4 contains $34_8 = 28_{10}$.

7. When $i = 1$ the combined salary is $\$622_8 = \$402_{10}$.

   When $i = 3$, the combined salary is $\$10.50_8 = \$552_{10}$.

8. Most of the six employees are happy—namely, 4.

9. JZF is the oldest employee.

CHAPTER 4

Problem 4.1

BETA will contain 17_{10}

Problem 4.2

One possible solution follows:

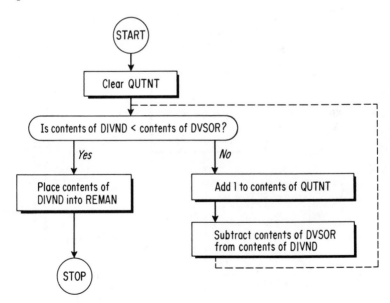

Problem 4.3

One possible solution follows:

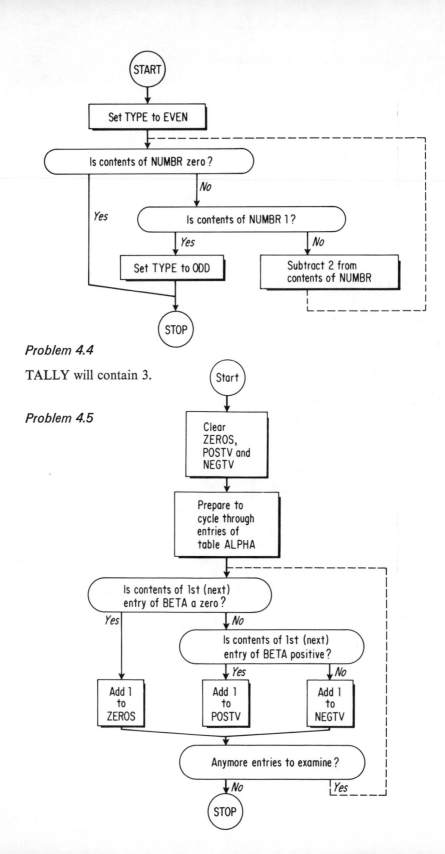

Problem 4.4

TALLY will contain 3.

Problem 4.5

Problem 4.6

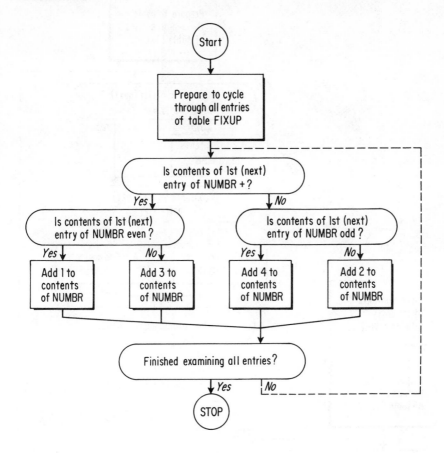

Following is one of the many possible alternate solutions for this problem if wording is unrestricted.

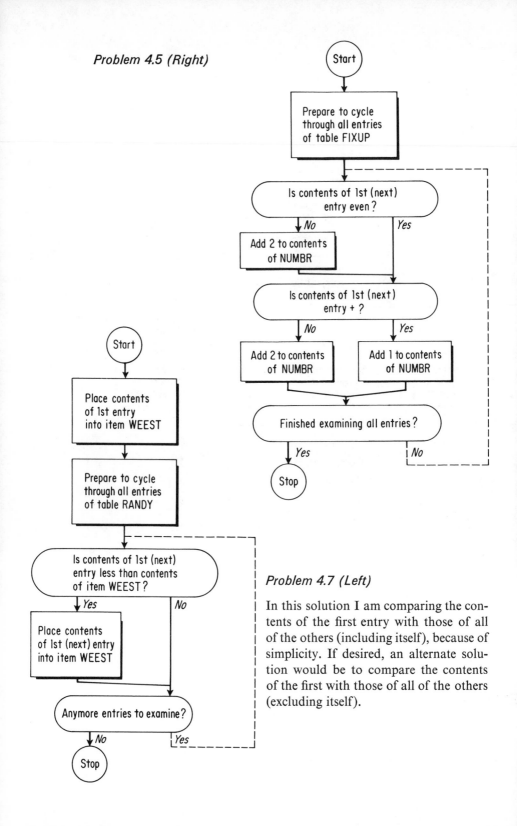

Problem 4.5 (Right)

Start

Prepare to cycle
through all entries
of table FIXUP

Is contents of 1st (next)
entry even?

No → Add 2 to contents
of NUMBR

Yes

Is contents of 1st (next)
entry + ?

No → Add 2 to contents
of NUMBR

Yes → Add 1 to contents
of NUMBR

Finished examining all entries?

Yes

Stop

No

Start

Place contents
of 1st entry
into item WEEST

Prepare to cycle
through all entries
of table RANDY

Is contents of 1st (next)
entry less than contents
of item WEEST?

Yes → Place contents
of 1st (next) entry
into item WEEST

No

Anymore entries to examine?

No

Stop

Yes

Problem 4.7 (Left)

In this solution I am comparing the contents of the first entry with those of all
of the others (including itself), because of
simplicity. If desired, an alternate solution would be to compare the contents
of the first with those of all of the others
(excluding itself).

Problem 4.8

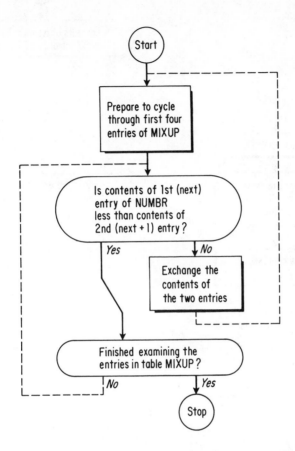

Also, you may refer to pages 144 through 152 which concern sorting.

Note: I wish to cycle through only the first four entries because on the last pass if "next" is the next to last entry, then "next + 1" is the last entry. In other words we do not wish "next" to become the last entry because "next + 1" would be outside of the table.

Problem 4.9

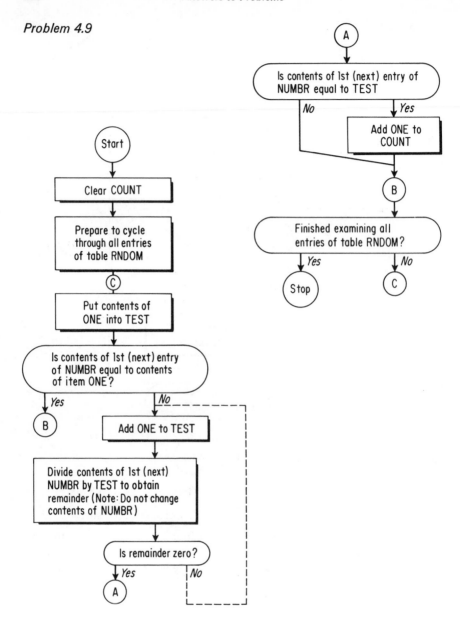

Note: A check could be built into the solution to examine a number only unit TEST equals half of the number. If a number is prime to this point, it will remain so.

An even more accurate check would be to continue only as a long as the divisor is less than or equal to the quotient.

Problem 4.10

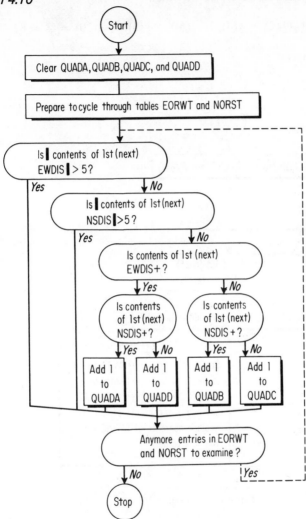

Note: The bars in the first two decision boxes denote absolute magnitude. Also, since the two tables are parallel in construction, a single "Prepare to cycle" and "Finished examining" are possible.

Problem 4.11

It does not do the job. In the first place, it does not disregard the first entry if it is zero; secondly, it does not result in obtaining the average. For example, if the numbers involved are 2,4,6,8, and 10, the average is 6; that is (2 + 4 + 6 + 8 + 10) ÷ 6.

The flow diagram, however, would obtain

$$\tfrac{1}{2}(\tfrac{1}{2}(\tfrac{1}{2}(\tfrac{1}{2}(2) + \tfrac{1}{2}(4)) + \tfrac{1}{2}(6)) + \tfrac{1}{2}(8)) + \tfrac{1}{2}(10) = \tfrac{65}{8} = 8\tfrac{1}{8}$$

which is incorrect.

Problem 4.12

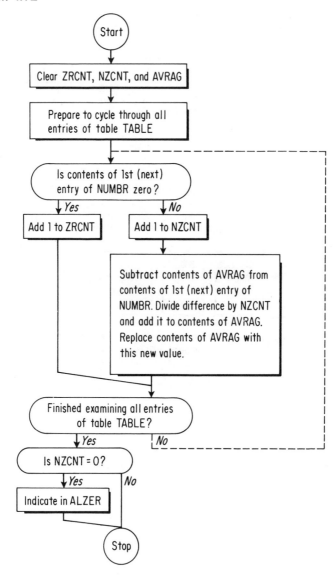

Problem 4.13

$1 = \text{NONE}$	$6 = 2\,\text{PAR}$	$11 = 2\,\text{PAR}$
$2 = 1\,\text{PAR}$	$7 = 3\,\text{KND}$	$12 = \text{FHSE}$
$3 = 1\,\text{PAR}$	$8 = 4\,\text{KND}$	$13 = 3\,\text{KND}$
$4 = 3\,\text{KND}$	$9 = 1\,\text{PAR}$	$14 = \text{FHSE}$
$5 = 1\,\text{PAR}$	$10 = 2\,\text{PAR}$	$15 = 4\,\text{KND}$

Problem 4.14

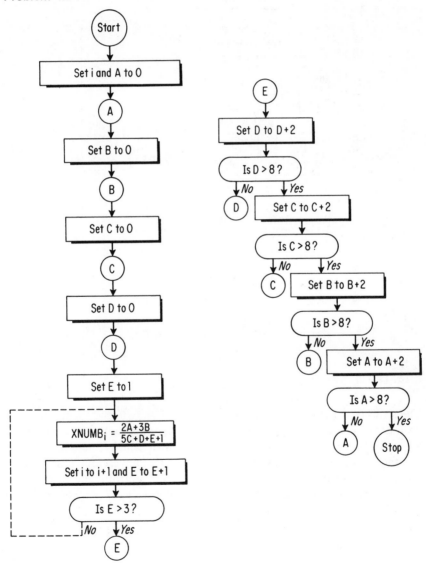

Problem 4.15

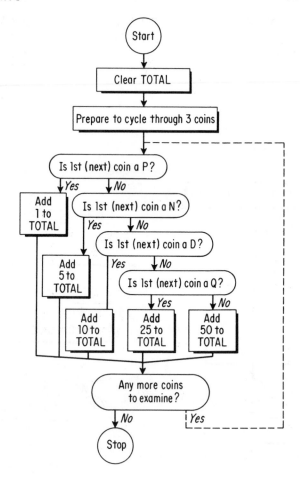

CHAPTER 5

The series of cartoon drawings on pages 66 through 76 lend themselves very well as visual aids. I have taught this particular area many times and I use a board with nails, cards, and a homemade timer which I manually rotate. On the blackboard I draw a program counter, an accumulator, and an arithmetic element. I then play the part of Mr. Control going through the actual steps depicted in the 11 drawings. It seems to work out very well and easily gets across the several basic concepts.

Also, it is at this point in the course that a supply of EX-1 coding paper should be supplied.

Problem 5.1

∅.∅∅∅∅1234 ⟵ Contents of core memory location 105
∅.62∅∅17∅2 ⟵ Contents of core memory location 106
─────────────
∅.62∅∅3136
1.47774563 ⟵ Computer complements (because of SUB) and adds
─────────────
1∅.31777721
└────────→1 ⟵ Automatic end-around-carry
─────────────
∅.31777722 ⟵ Answer

Problem 5.2

1∅∅	∅.∅4∅2∅1∅5
1∅1	∅.∅422∅1∅6
1∅2	∅.∅442∅1∅7
1∅3	∅.∅2∅2∅11∅
1∅4	∅.∅∅∅∅∅∅∅∅
1∅5	∅.∅∅∅∅1234
1∅6	∅.62∅∅17∅2
1∅7	∅.3∅∅∅3214
11∅	∅.∅∅∅∅∅∅∅∅

Problem 5.3

1.7321∅∅∅∅
1.47774563   Complement of core memory location 205
─────────────
11.432∅4563
          1
─────────────
1.432∅4564

Problem 5.4

LOCATION						S I G N	I N D E X	INSTRUCTION			I N C R M T	DIRECTOR				
1	2	3	4	5		8	9	10	11	12	13	14	15	16	17	18
			3	∅				G	E	T						5
			3	1				P	U	T					⊥	2
			3	2				G	E	T						6
			3	3				P	U	T					⊥	3
			3	4				H	L	T						

Problem 5.5

LOCATION						S I G N	I N D E X	INSTRUCTION			I N C R M T	DIRECTOR				
1	2	3	4	5		8	9	10	11	12	13	14	15	16	17	18
		5	Ø	Ø				G	E	T				3	Ø	1
		5	Ø	1				A	D	D				3	Ø	2
		5	Ø	2				P	U	T				4	Ø	7
		5	Ø	3				H	L	T						

It is probably clear that we could also have written GET 3Ø2 and ADD 3Ø1.

Problem 5.6

LOCATION						S I G N	I N D E X	INSTRUCTION			I N C R M T	DIRECTOR				
1	2	3	4	5		8	9	10	11	12	13	14	15	16	17	18
			1	Ø				G	E	T				1	Ø	Ø
			1	1				A	D	D					1	7
			1	2				P	U	T				1	Ø	Ø
			1	3				G	E	T				1	Ø	1
			1	4				A	D	D					1	7
			1	5				P	U	T				1	Ø	1
			1	6				H	L	T						
			1	7		Ø	Ø	Ø	Ø	Ø	Ø	Ø	Ø	1		

Problem 5.7

Accumulator contains Ø.ØØØØØØ14

Problem 5.8

400	0.04020412
401	0.04420413
402	0.02020412
403	0.07030406
404	0.04020414
405	0.00000000
406	0.04020414
407	0.04220413
410	0.02020414
411	0.07050400
412	0.00000007
413	0.00000002
414	0.00000006

Problem 5.9

600	G E T	617
601	P U T	152
602	G E T	151
603	S U B	150
604	J P O	614
605	G E T	152
606	A D D	620
607	P U T	152
610	G E T	150
611	S U B	151
612	P U T	150
613	J M P	602
614	G E T	150
615	P U T	153
616	H L T	
617	0.00000000	
620	0.00000001	

Problem 5.10

The present count of Index Register 1 is set to zero and the final count is set to 9.

Problem 5.11

1. 2SIN3 17 will result in the present count of Index Register 2 being set to 3 and the final count being set to 17.

2. 2SIN7 19 will result in both the present and final count of Index Register 2 being set to 19.

Problem 5.12

The final accumulator contents are ∅.1321∅6421.

Problem 5.13

20	2 S I N	9
21	2 G E T	6∅
22	2 P U T	12∅
23	2 J I X1	21
24	H L T	

Problem 5.14

2∅∅	2 S I N	15
2∅1	2 G E T	3∅∅
2∅2	A D D	2∅6
2∅3	2 P U T	3∅∅
2∅4	2 J I X1	2∅1
2∅5	H L T	
206	0.∅∅∅∅∅∅∅3	

Note that the Add instruction at location 202 does not have an Index Register specified. This is because only two elements are involved; namely, the accumulator and the contents of location 206, whereas, with the GET and PUT a table is involved.

Problem 5.15

One possibility is

3∅∅	G E T	11∅	since	110—1st
				101—2nd
				102—3rd
				103—4th
				104—5th
				105—6th
				106—7th
				107—8th
				110—9th

Another possibility:

3ØØ	2 S I N7	8
3Ø1	2 G E T	1ØØ

A third could be

3ØØ	2 S I N6	5Ø
3Ø1	2 J I X2	3Ø2
3Ø2	2 G E T	1ØØ

Problem 5.16

4ØØ	G E T	6ØØ
4Ø1	P U T	411
4Ø2	2 S I N	17
4Ø3	2 G E T	6Ø1
4Ø4	2 P U T	6ØØ
4Ø5	2 J I X1	4Ø3
4Ø6	G E T	411
4Ø7	P U T	621
41Ø	H L T	
411	Ø.ØØØØØØØØ	

Problem 5.17

4ØØ	2 S I N	17
4Ø1	2 G E T	6Ø1
4Ø2	P U T	411
4Ø3	G E T	6ØØ
4Ø4	2 P U T	6Ø1
4Ø5	G E T	411
4Ø6	P U T	6ØØ
4Ø7	2 J I X1	4Ø1
41Ø	H L T	
411	Ø.ØØØØØØØØ	

Problem 5.18

5Ø	G E T	64
51	P U T	4Ø
52	2 S I N	99
53	2 G E T	2ØØ
54	J Z E	57

55	2 J I X2	53
56	H L T	
57	G E T	40
60	A D D	63
61	P U T	40
62	J M P	55
63	0.00000001	
64	0.00000000	

Problem 5.19

150	2 S I N	29
151	2 G E T	300
152	J P O	155
153	G E T	157
154	2 P U T	300
155	2 J I X1	151
156	H L T	
157	0.00000000	

Problem 5.20

LOCATION						SIGN	INDEX	INSTRUCTION			INCRMT	DIRECTOR				
1	2	3	4	5		8	9	10	11	12	13	14	15	16	17	18
								B	E	G				2	0	0
								G	E	T		Z	E	R	0	
								P	U	T					5	0
							2	S	I	N					1	5
M	O	R	E				2	G	E	T				3	0	0
								J	P	O		T	A	L	L	Y
A	N	Y	M	O			2	J	I	X	1	M	O	R	E	
								H	L	T						
T	A	L	L	Y				G	E	T					5	0
								A	D	D		O	N	E		
								P	U	T					5	0
								J	M	P		A	N	Y	M	O
Z	E	R	O			0	0	0	0	0	0	0	0	0		
O	N	E				0	0	0	0	0	0	0	0	1		
								E	N	D						

Problem 5.21

200	0.04020213
201	0.02020050
202	0.25660017
203	0.24020300
204	0.07030207
205	0.27011203
206	0.00000000
207	0.04020050
210	0.04220214
211	0.02020050
212	0.07050205
213	0.00000000
214	0.00000001

Problem 5.22

```
              B E G        5 0
            2 S I N          9
AGAIN         G E T    Z E R O
            2 S U B      1 5 0
            2 P U T      1 5 0
            2 J I X 1 AGAIN
              H L T
ZERO    0 . 0 0 0 0 0 0 0 0
              E N D
```

Problem 5.23

200	0.04020213
201	0.02020050
202	0.25660017
203	0.24020300
204	0.07030207
205	0.27011203
206	0.00000000
207	0.04020050
210	0.04220214
211	0.02020050
212	0.07050205
213	0.00000000
214	0.00000001

Problem 5.24

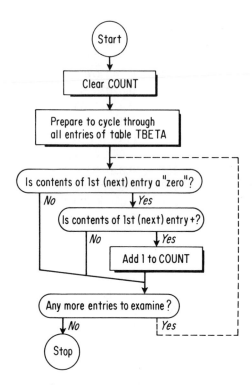

```
                    BEG          3 Ø
                    GET      ZERO
                    PUT      COUNT
                    2SIN     TBETA
AGAIN               2GET     TBETA
                    JZE      CKPOS
ANYMO               2JIX1AGAIN
ZERO                HLT
CKPOS               JPO      TALLY
                    JMP      ANYMO
TALLY               GET      COUNT
                    ADD      ONE
                    PUT      COUNT
                    JMP      ANYMO
ONE        Ø . Ø Ø Ø Ø Ø Ø Ø 1
                    END
```

Problem 5.25

30	0.04020036
31	0.02020250
32	0.25660034
33	0.24020100
34	0.07020037
35	0.27011033
36	0.00000000
37	0.07030041
40	0.07050035
41	0.04020250
42	0.04220045
43	0.02020250
44	0.07050035
45	0.00000001

Problem 5.26

```
          BEG        1 2 5
          2 S I N    GAMMA
AGAIN     2 GET      GAMMA
          SUB        NINE
          JZE        ADSIX
          GET        FIVE
STORE     2 PUT      GAMMA
          2 JIX 1 AGAIN
          HLT
ADSIX     GET        FIFTN
          JMP        STORE
FIVE      0 . 0 0 0 0 0 0 0 5     Note the octal equivalent of 9.
NINE      0 . 0 0 0 0 0 0 1 1     Note the octal equivalent of 15.
FIFTN     0 . 0 0 0 0 0 0 1 7
          END
```

Problem 5.27

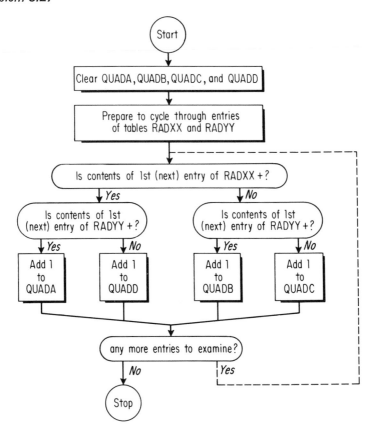

LOCATION					SIGN	INDEX	INSTRUCTION			INCRMT	DIRECTOR				
1	2	3	4	5	8	9	10	11	12	13	14	15	16	17	18
							B	E	G				2	5	Ø
							G	E	T		Z	E	R	O	
							P	U	T		Q	U	A	D	A
							P	U	T		Q	U	A	D	B
							P	U	T		Q	U	A	D	C
							P	U	T		Q	U	A	D	D
						2	S	I	N		R	A	D	X	X
A	G	A	I	N		2	G	E	T		R	A	D	X	X
							J	P	O		C	H	E	K	Y
						2	G	E	T		R	A	D	Y	Y
							J	P	O		U	P	Q	D	B
							G	E	T		Q	U	A	D	C
							A	D	D		O	N	E		
							P	U	T		Q	U	A	D	C
A	N	Y	M	O		2	J	I	X	⊥	A	G	A	I	N
Z	E	R	O				H	L	T						
C	H	E	K	Y		2	G	E	T		R	A	D	Y	Y
							J	P	O		U	P	Q	D	A
							G	E	T		Q	U	A	D	D
							A	D	D		O	N	E		
							P	U	T		Q	U	A	D	D
							J	I	X		A	N	Y	M	O
U	P	Q	D	B			G	E	T		Q	U	A	D	B
							A	D	D		O	N	E		
							P	U	T		Q	U	A	D	B
							J	M	P		A	N	Y	M	O
U	P	Q	D	A			G	E	T		Q	U	A	D	A
							A	D	D		O	N	E		
							P	U	T		Q	U	A	D	A
							J	M	P		A	N	Y	M	O
O	N	E			Ø	Ø	Ø	Ø	Ø	Ø	Ø	Ø	⊥		
							E	N	D						

Problem 5.28

```
                    B E G           7 7
                  2 S I N     T N U M B
A G A I N         2 G E T     T N U M B
                    J P O     A N Y M O
                    G E T     Z E R O
                  2 S U B     T N U M B
                  2 P U T     T N U M B
A N Y M O         2 J I X 1 A G A I N
Z E R O             H L T
                    E N D
```

Problem 5.29

```
                    B E G           2 Ø Ø
O V E R           2 S I N               4
                  1 S I N 1             5
A G A I N         2 G E T     M I X E D
                  1 S U B     M I X E D
                    J P O     E X C N G
                  1 J I X 1 N E X T
N E X T           2 J I X 1 A G A I N
                    H L T
E X C N G         2 G E T     M I X E D
                    P U T     T E M P
                  1 G E T     M I X E D
                  2 P U T     M I X E D
                    G E T     T E M P
                  1 P U T     M I X E D
                    J M P     O V E R
T E M P     Ø . Ø Ø Ø Ø Ø Ø Ø Ø
                    E N D
```

Note that two entries containing equal values will result in a $-\emptyset$ (negative zero), hence, the solution should be programmed so as not to get into a perpetual loop when there are two equal values, and the subtraction results in a $-\emptyset$.

Also see pages 144 – 152 of textbook.

Problem 5.30

```
                    B E G           3 5
                    G E T     Z E R O
                    P U T     N G S U M
                    P U T     P O S U M
                  2 S I N     R A N D Y
```

```
AGAIN   2GET   RANDY
        JPO    ADPOS
        ADD    NGSUM
        PUT    NGSUM
ANYMO   2JIX1AGAIN
        HLT
ADPOS   ADD    POSUM
        PUT    POSUM
        JIX    ANYMO
ZERO    Ø.ØØØØØØØØ
        END
```

CHAPTER 6

Problem 6.1

1. 3742.6000

   6.60

   .064000000

   −23777.7

   1770.

   ---

2. B9

   B3

   B3

   B-6

   B4

   ---

3. 0.02564000

   0.75000000

   1.35420000

   0.65300000

   0.64000000

Problem 6.2

```
GET   NUMBA
SAR      2
PUT   ANSER     Temp Storage
GET   NUMBB
SAR      3
ADD   ANSER
```

```
PUT   ANSER
GET   NUMBC
SAR        1
ADD   ANSER
PUT   ANSER
HLT
```

Since the answer may be as large as 109_{10} or 155_8, we see that 7 binary places are required for the whole number portion of the answer. In other words the answer must be scaled B7.

Problem 6.3

```
GET   NUMBA
MUL   NUMBB
SBL        6
PUT   ANSER
HLT
```

$47.5 \times 429 = 20357.5_{10} = 47605.4_8$

therefore, accumulator scaled B21 will be 0.00476054.

Problem 6.4

```
GET   XNUMB
SBR        4
DIV   YNUMB
PUT   ZNUMB
HLT
```
Z will be scaled B9 in ZNUMB.

Problem 6.5

1. $9.5_{10} = 11.4_8 = 1001.1_2 = 0.10011_2 \times 2^4 = 0.10011_2$ B4
therefore $= 0.40446000$

2. $68.125_{10} = 104.1_8 = 1000100.001_2 = 0.1000100001_2 \times 2^7$
$= 0.1000100001_2$ B7
therefore $= 0.40742040$

3. $0.0055_{10} = 0.00264162_8 = 0.00000001011010000111 0010_2$
$= 0.10110100001110010 \times 2^{-7}$ or B-7
therefore $= 0.37155034$

4. $-9.25_{10} = -11.2_8 = -1001.01_2 = -0.100101_2 \times 2^4$ or B4
therefore $=$ complement of 0.40445000 or 1.37332777

5. $-0.00005_{10} = -0.0000150667_8$
$= -0.0000000000000001101000110110111_2$
$= -0.1101000110110111_2 \times 2^{-14}$ or B-14
therefore $=$ complement of 0.36264333 or 1.41513444

Problem 6.6

```
        GET   XNUMB
        FMU   YNUMB
        FAD   CONST
        FDV   ZNUMB
        PUT   WNUMB
        HLT
CONST   FLO   9 . 6 7 5
```

CHAPTER 7

Problem 7.1

```
              BEG        1 ∅ ∅
              GET    ZERO
              PUT    INCSE
              PIM    SALRY
             2SIN    EMPLY
NEXT         2GET    EMPLY
              EXT
              SUB    SIXHD
              JPO    MAYBE
ANYMO        2JIX1NEXT
ZERO          HLT
MAYBE         SUB    TWOFY
              JPO    ANYMO
              JZE    ANYMO
             2GET    EMPLY
              ADD    FIFTY
             2PUT    EMPLY
              GET    INCSE
              ADD    SOME
              PUT    INCSE
              JMP    ANYMO
SIXHD    ∅ . ∅ 1 1 3 ∅ ∅ ∅
TWOFY    ∅ . ∅ ∅ 3 7 2 ∅ ∅ ∅
FIFTY    ∅ . ∅ ∅ ∅ 6 2 ∅ ∅ ∅
SOME     ∅ . ∅ ∅ ∅ ∅ ∅ 6 2
SALRY    1 . 7 7 7 7 7 ∅ ∅ ∅
              END
```

Problem 7.2

```
      GET   NUMBR
    3 GET   ROOTS
      PUT   SQRUT
      HLT
```

In this solution the number is obtained in the accumulator. Then, this number is used to index down into the table ROOTS to pickup the correct square root, which is then placed into SQRUT.

Problem 7.3

Since N can be 100_{10}, the N can be a maximum of 10 and the ANSWER will need to be scaled to hold a maximum of $100 + 20 + 29$ or $149_{10} = 225_8$; therefore, we will need the answer scaled B8.

```
         BEG      1 Ø Ø
         GET   NMBER
       3 GET   ROOTS
         SAR        3 ←——— This scales the square root B8.
         PUT   ANSER      It is already B4 so 4 moves
         GET   NMBER      right will scale it B8 and 1
         SAL        1 6   move left willdouble it. This
         ADD   ANSER      dual shift (4 right and 1 left)
         ADD   TWNIN      is accomplished by moving 3
         PUT   ANSER      places to the right.
         HLT
 TWNIN  Ø . Ø 7 2 Ø Ø Ø Ø Ø
         END
```

Problem 7.4

```
         BEG      1 Ø Ø
         PIM   RECOR
         PAD   LGADA ⎫
         PAD   LGADB ⎬←—— Store "leg" table address
         SBR        1 2
         PAD   LGLNA ⎫
         PAD   LGLNB ⎬←—— Store length of tables
         PIM   POLAR
         PAD   HPADA ⎫
         PAD   HPADB ⎪
         PAD   HPADC ⎬←—— Store "hypotenuse-angle"
         PAD   HPADD ⎭      table address
```

```
L G L N A    1 S I N                 Ø    Prepare to cycle through 1st, 3rd,
                                          5th etc., registers.
L G L N B    2 S I N 1               Ø    Prepare to cycle through 2nd, 4th,
                                          6th etc., registers.
H P A D A    1 G E T                 Ø    Obtain 1st (next) angle.
             3 G E T    C O S N  S         Obtain cosine of 1st (next) angle
H P A D B    2 M U L                 Ø    Multiply by 1st (next) hypotenuse.
             S B R                   3    Scale adjacent leg in quarter inches.
L G A D A    1 P U T                 Ø    Store in 1st (next) "adjacent leg"
                                          register.
H P A D C    1 G E T                 Ø    Obtain 1st (next) angle.
             3 G E T    S I N E  S         Obtain sine of 1st (next) angle.
H P A D D    2 M U L                 Ø    Multiply by 1st (next) hypotenuse.
             S B R                   3    Scale opposite leg in quarter inches.
L G A D B    2 P U T                 Ø    Store in 1st (next) "opposite leg"
                                          register.
             1 J I X 2 N E X T
N E X T      2 J I X 2 H P A D A
             H L T
             E N D
```

Problem 7.5

```
                   2 S I N    A L P H A
         A G A I N    2 G E T    A L P H A
                   S U B     G A M M A
                   J Z E     G O T I T
                   2 J I X 1 A G A I N
                   H L T
         G O T I T    2 A X D                Ø
                   P A D     G A M M A
                   H L T
```

Problem 7.6

```
         B E G        1 Ø Ø
         1 S I N    E M P L Y
         2 S I N 1 E M P L Y
         P I M     S A L R Y
         1 G E T    E M P L Y
         E X T
         S U B     S I X H D
         J P O     F O R L T    First one is closest.
```

```
AGAIN   2 GET   EMPLY
        EXT
        SUB    SIXHD
        JPO    GOTIT
       1 JIX 1  NEXT
NEXT    2 JIX 1 AGAIN     Fall-through means last is closest.
FORLT  1 GET    EMPLY
        PIM    EMNUM
        DEP    CLOSE
       1 AXD        0
        PAD    CLOSE
        HLT
GOTIT   PUT    TEMP
        GET    SIXHD
       1 SUB   EMPLY
        SUB    TEMP
        JPO    SECND      Current entry is closest.
        JMP    FORLT      Previous entry is closest.
SECND   2 GET   EMPLY
        PIM    EMNUM
        DEP    CLOSE
       2 AXD        0
        PAD    CLOSE
        HLT
SALRY   0 . 0 0 0 0 7 7 7 7
SIXHD   0 . 0 0 0 0 1 1 3 0
EMNUM   1 . 7 7 7 7 0 0 0 0
TEMP    0 . 0 0 0 0 0 0 0 0
        END
```

Problem 7.7

This is based on $|R_0 - R_1| < .0001$ since we are undoubtedly assuming a positive n, and hence, R_0 and R_1 will always be positive.

```
        BEG        1 0 0
        GET    NUMBR
        FDV    TWO
MORE    PUT    RZERO
        GET    NUMBR
        FDV    RZERO
        FAD    RZERO
```

```
          F D V    T W O
          P U T    R O N E
          G E T    R Z E R O
          F S B    R O N E
          J P O    T E S T        Already in absolute value form
          P U T    T E M P ⎫
          G E T    Z E R O ⎬ ◄── Obtain | R₀ − R₁ |
          F S B    T E M P ⎭
T E S T   F S B    C O N S T
          J P O    A G A I N
          G E T    R O N E
          P U T    R Z U L T
Z E R O   H L T
A G A I N G E T    R O N E
          J M P    M O R E
T W O     F L O    2 . 0 0 0
C O N S T F L O    . 0 0 0 1
T E M P   0 . 0 0 0 0 0 0 0 0
R O N E   0 . 0 0 0 0 0 0 0 0
R Z E R O 0 . 0 0 0 0 0 0 0 0
              E N D
```

The "Obtain | R₀ − R₁ |" annotation in LaTeX: Obtain $|R_0 - R_1|$

Problem 7.8

Since $0 \leq n \leq 100$, then $\sqrt{n} \leq 10_{10}$. Thus, since $10_{10} = 12_8 = 1010_2$, four places will be required for the whole number part which scales ANSER as B4.

Since we will use $\frac{n}{2}$ as our first approximation, we will need to allow $\frac{100}{2} = 50_{10} = 62_8 = 110010_2$ or six bits for the whole number part of R_0, and we can also use that scaling, B6, for R_1. Thus, R_0 and R_1 will be scaled B6.

Since the quantity in parentheses $\left(R_0 + \frac{n}{R_0} \right)$ can be $\left(50_{10} + \frac{100}{50_{10}} 10 \right)$ or 52_{10}, six bits is still adequate.

Furthermore, the constant $.0001_{10} = .0000321_8$ and, if we scale it B6 for comparison with $|R_0 - R_1|$, we get as an octal computer word 0.00000032.

```
          B E G      1 0 0
          G E T    Z E R O
          P U T    A N S E R
          G E T    N U M B R
```

```
              J Z E    E X I T
              S A L          1 7 ◄──── Scale B6 and also divide by 2
A G A I N     P U T    R Z E R O          for first approximation.
                                          Scale n as B12 (dividend must
              G E T    N U M B R ⎫        appear smaller than divisor)
              S A L          1 2 ⎪◄──     and thus result will be scaled
              D I V    R Z E R O ⎪        B12—B6 (same scaling as $R_0$)
              A D D    R Z E R O ⎭        to be a scaling of B6 so that
                                          $R_0$ can be added.
              S B R            1 ◄──── Divide by 2.
              P U T    R O N E
              G E T    R Z E R O
              S U B    R O N E
              J P O    T E S T ◄──────── Jump here indicates $R_0 - R_1$
                                          already positive.
              P U T    T E M P   ⎫
              G E T    Z E R O   ⎬◄── Obtain $|R_0 - R_1|$ when $R_0 -$
              S U B    T E M P   ⎭     $R_1$ is negative.
T E S T       S U B    C O N S T
              J P O    M O R E
              G E T    R O N E
              S E L            2 ◄──── Scale result to B4.
              P U T    A N S E R
E X I T       H L T
M O R E       G E T    R O N E
              J M P    A G A I N
Z E R O    0 . 0 0 0 0 0 0 0 0
C O N S T  0 . 0 0 0 0 0 0 3 2
R Z E R O  0 . 0 0 0 0 0 0 0 0
R O N E    0 . 0 0 0 0 0 0 0 0
T E M P    0 . 0 0 0 0 0 0 0 0
              E N D
```

Problem 7.9

Since π is 3.14. ... I chose to scale PYE as B2 for maximum precision. Also, my solution is based upon the fact that every denominator in the formula is 1 greater than the previous numerator, and every numerator is 1 greater than the previous denominator. Furthermore, each factor in the product alternates between numbers less than 1, and numbers greater than 1 but less than 2.

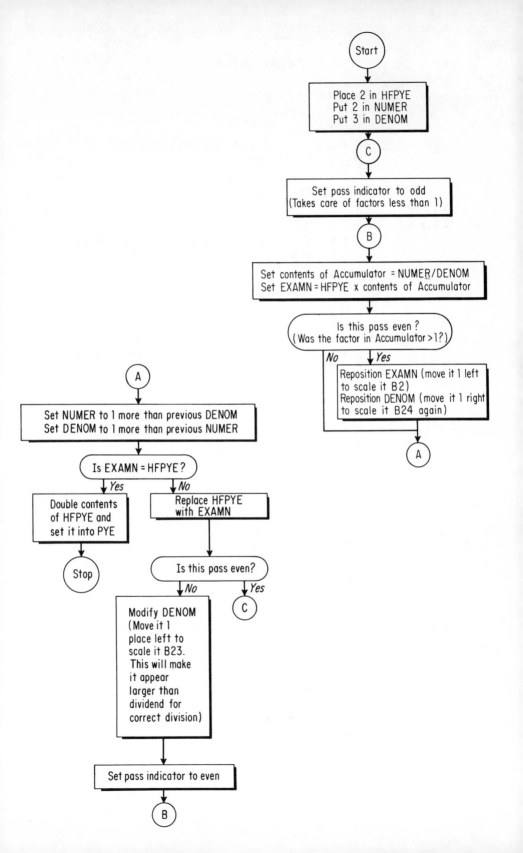

```
            B E G        1 0 0
            G E T     T W O
            P U T     N U M E R
            S A L            2 2        HFPYE scaled B2.
            P U T     H F P Y E
            G E T     T H R E E
            P U T     D E N O M
O V E R    2 S I N              1        Present count of 0 for odd passes.
N E X T     G E T     N U M E R         Scaled B24.
            D I V     D E N O M         Denominator scaled B23 or B24.
            M U L     H F P Y E         Results scaled B2 or B3.
            P U T     E X A M N
           2 J I X 0 O D D
            S B L            1           Scale result B2—was B3.
            P U T     E X A M N
            G E T     D E N O M
            S A R            1           Scale demonimator B24—was B23.
            P U T     D E N O M
O D D       G E T     N U M E R  ⎫
            A D D     O N E      ⎪
            P U T     T E M P    ⎪
            G E T     D E N O M  ⎬ Modify numerator and denomi-
            A D D     O N E      ⎪ nator for next pass.
            P U T     N U M E R  ⎪
            G E T     T E M P    ⎪
            P U T     D E N O M  ⎭
            G E T     E X A M N
            S U B     H F P Y E
            J Z E     G O T I T
            G E T     E X A M N
            P U T     H F P Y E
           2 J I X 0 O D D P A
            J M P     O V E R
O D D P A   G E T     D E N O M ⎫ Scale denominator B23 for proper
            S A L            1  ⎬←division for next pass (even
            P U T     D E N O M ⎭ pass).
           2 J I X 2 N E X T
            J M P     N E X T
G O T I T   G E T     H F P Y E
            A D D     H F P Y E
            P U T     P Y E
            H L T
```

```
EXAMN 0 . 0 0 0 0 0 0 0 0
HFPYE 0 . 0 0 0 0 0 0 0 0
NUMER 0 . 0 0 0 0 0 0 0 0
DENOM 0 . 0 0 0 0 0 0 0 0
ONE    0 . 0 0 0 0 0 0 0 1
TWO    0 . 0 0 0 0 0 0 0 2
THREE 0 . 0 0 0 0 0 0 0 3
TEMP   0 . 0 0 0 0 0 0 0 0
            END
```

Problem 7.10

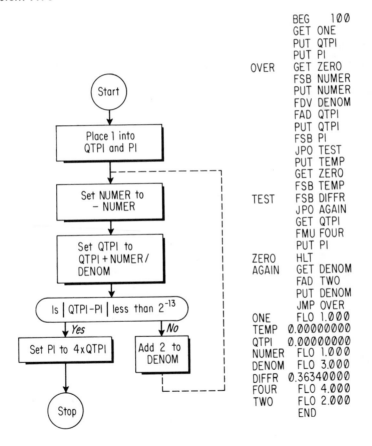

```
            BEG   100
            GET   ONE
            PUT   QTPI
            PUT   PI
OVER        GET   ZERO
            FSB   NUMER
            PUT   NUMER
            FDV   DENOM
            FAD   QTPI
            PUT   QTPI
            FSB   PI
            JPO   TEST
            PUT   TEMP
            GET   ZERO
            FSB   TEMP
TEST        FSB   DIFFR
            JPO   AGAIN
            GET   QTPI
            FMU   FOUR
            PUT   PI
ZERO        HLT
AGAIN       GET   DENOM
            FAD   TWO
            PUT   DENOM
            JMP   OVER
ONE   FLO 1.000
TEMP  0.00000000
QTPI  0.00000000
NUMER FLO 1.000
DENOM FLO 3.000
DIFFR 0.36340000
FOUR  FLO 4.000
TWO   FLO 2.000
      END
```

Note: I have arbitrarily decided that the answer is sufficiently accurate if one iteration differs from the next by less than 2^{-13} or 0.36340000.

Problem 7.11

For the student to answer.

Problem 7.12

For the student to answer.

Problem 7.13

No, we would have to housekeep the instruction addresses that we have modified before the subroutine would operate correctly a second or third time.

Problem 7.14

It would be helpful to have a "store index" instruction, and "add to index" instruction, and perhaps several others.

Problem 7.15

```
FACTO      PUT   TEST
           PUT   TEMPA
           PAD   NEXT
           GET   NEXT
           ADD   ONEA
           SBR        2 5
           PAD   GOBAK
NEXT       GET          Ø
           SBR        2 5
           PAD   STORE
AGAIN      GET   TEST
           FSB   ONE
           PUT   TEST
           JZE   DONE
           FMU   TEMPA
           PUT   TEMPA
           JMP   AGAIN
DONE       GET   TEMPA
STORE      PUT          Ø
GOBAK      JMP          Ø
TEST       Ø . Ø Ø Ø Ø Ø Ø Ø
TEMPA      Ø . Ø Ø Ø Ø Ø Ø Ø
ONEA       Ø . Ø Ø Ø Ø Ø Ø 1
ONE        FLO   1 . Ø Ø Ø
           END
```

Problem 7.16

Basically, we would have to housekeep the instructions that the program modifies.

Problem 7.17

```
            P I M   N E N T  ⎫   Isolate number of entries.
            G E T   E M P L Y ⎬
            E X T            ⎭
            J Z E   O U T        There are no employees.
            S A L           1    Double to obtain number of
                                 locations.

            S U B   T W O    ⎫   Determine if only one employee.
            J Z E   O U T    ⎬
            A D D   T W O    ⎭
            S B R           2 5
            P A D   C Y C U P
            P A D   C Y C L O
CYCUP   1 S I N 1         ∅
CYCLO   2 S I N 3         ∅
            P I M   E M P N O
AGAIN   2 G E T   E M P L Y
            E X T
            P U T   T E M P
        1 G E T   E M P L Y
            E X T
            S U B   T E M P
            J P O   X C H N G
        1 J I X 2 N E X T
NEXT    2 J I X 2 A G A I N
OUT         H L T
XCHNG   1 G E T   E M P L Y
            P U T   T E M P
        2 G E T   E M P L Y
        1 P U T   E M P L Y
            G E T   T E M P
        2 P U T   E M P L Y
        1 J I X 1 N E X T A
NEXTA   2 J I X 1 N E X T B
NEXTB   1 G E T   E M P L Y
            P U T   T E M P
        2 G E T   E M P L Y
        1 P U T   E M P L Y
```

```
          GET   TEMP
        2 PUT   EMPLY
          JMP   CYCUP
NEXT    0 . 0 0 0 0 0 7 7 7
TWO     0 . 0 0 0 0 0 0 0 2
TEMP    0 . 0 0 0 0 0 0 0 0
EMPNO   0 . 0 0 0 1 7 7 7 7
```

Problem 7.18

```
                    GET   ZERO
                    PUT   BCNT
                    GET   CYCLE
                    SUB   ONE
                    PUT   CYCLE
                    GET   LOWER
                    ADD   ONE
                    SBR        2 5
                    PAD   LOWER
                    PAD   UNDER
                    PAD   LESSA
                    PAD   LESSB
CYCLE   1 S I N   NUMBR
AGAIN   1 GET   NUMBR
LOWER   1 SUB   NUMBR
                    J P O   XCHNG
ANYMO   1 J I X 1 NEXT
ZERO            HLT
NEXT            GET   BCNT
                    ADD   ONE
                    PUT   BCNT
                    JMP   AGAIN
XCHNG           GET   BCNT
                    PUT   TEMPA
MORE            SBR        2 5
                    PAD   BCYC
BCYC    2 S I N 7        0
                  2 GET   NUMBR
UNDER   2 SUB   NUMBR
                    J Z E   ANYMO
                    J P O   XAGIN
                    JMP   ANYMO
XAGIN   2 GET   NUMBR
                    PUT   TEMP
```

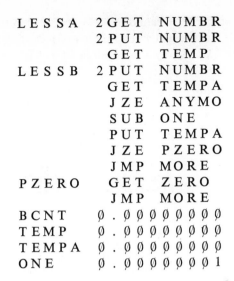

```
LESSA    2GET    NUMBR
         2PUT    NUMBR
          GET    TEMP
LESSB    2PUT    NUMBR
          GET    TEMPA
          JZE    ANYMO
          SUB    ONE
          PUT    TEMPA
          JZE    PZERO
          JMP    MORE
PZERO     GET    ZERO
          JMP    MORE
BCNT     0 . 0 0 0 0 0 0 0 0
TEMP     0 . 0 0 0 0 0 0 0 0
TEMPA    0 . 0 0 0 0 0 0 0 0
ONE      0 . 0 0 0 0 0 0 0 1
```

Problem 7.19

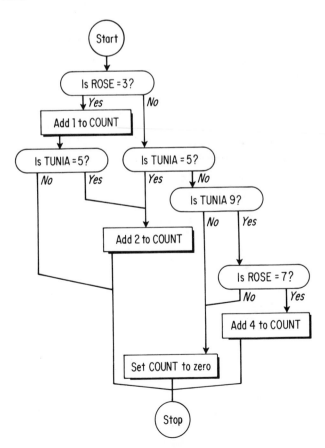

Note that in this problem we cannot set COUNT to ∅ initially, as we want to *increase* COUNT if the given conditions are met. There is a difference between increasing COUNT by 1 and setting COUNT to 1.

An alternate logic follows:

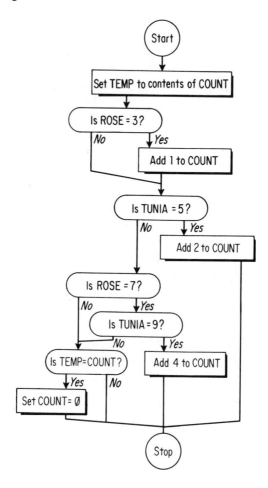

```
              GET   ROSE
              SUB   THREE
              JZE   ADONE
              GET   TUNIA
              SUB   FIVE
              JZE   ADTWO
              SUB   FOUR
              JZE   CKRSE
SETZE         GET   ZERO
              PUT   COUNT
ZERO          HLT
ADONE         GET   ONE
              ADD   COUNT
              PUT   COUNT
              GET   TUNIA
              SUB   FIVE
              JZE   ADTWO
              JMP   ZERO
ADTWO         GET   TWO
              ADD   COUNT
              PUT   COUNT
              JMP   ZERO
CKRSE         GET   ROSE
              SUB   SEVEN
              JZE   ADFOR
              JMP   SETZE
ADFOR         GET   COUNT
              ADD   FOUR
              PUT   COUNT
              JMP   ZERO
ONE           0 . 0 0 0 0 0 0 0 1
TWO           0 . 0 0 0 0 0 0 0 2
THREE         0 . 0 0 0 0 0 0 0 3
FOUR          0 . 0 0 0 0 0 0 0 4
FIVE          0 . 0 0 0 0 0 0 0 5
SEVEN         0 . 0 0 0 0 0 0 0 7
```

Note: Be sure to use the test matrix to verify your flow diagram and coding.

CHAPTER 8

Problem 8.1

This problem is left for student research and opinion.

Problem 8.2

0	0.00000050
1	0.04020064
2	0.02020040
3	0.15660143
4	0.14020200
5	0.07020057
6	0.17011053
7	0.00000000
10	0.04020040
11	0.04220063
12	0.02020040
13	0.07010055

Problem 8.3

0	0.00000000
1	0.00000000
2	0.00020000
3	0.00000000
4	0.00040400
5	0.00000000
6	0.00000000
7	0.00100000
10	0.00000000
11	0.00000200
12	0.00000000
13	0.00160000

Problem 8.4

```
        JRD   MORE        Initially, be sure lite is off.
MORE    RCD               Read Card.
        JRD   GO          Jump here indicates no more
                          cards.
        GET   TEMP
        SUB        0
        JPO   REPLA
        GET        0
```

```
PLACE      SBR        2 5
           PAD  STORE          Store starting address this
                               card.
      2 S I N        1 1
AGAIN 2 G E T          1        Place 11 words on this binary
STORE 2 P U T          Ø   ⟵── card into proper core memory
      2 J I X 1 A G A I N       locations.
           JMP  MORE
REPLA      GET          Ø
           PUT  TEMP
           JMP  PLACE
GO         GET  TEMP
           SBR        2 5
           PAD  JUMP
JUMP       JMP          Ø       Jump to 1st instruction in
                               program.

TEMP  Ø . Ø Ø Ø Ø Ø Ø Ø Ø
```

Problem 8.5

```
           GET  TERM
           PUT  COUNT
           JRD  READ
READ       RCD
           JRD  ERROR          An Error routine. No END
                               card.
      2 S I N        1 2
AGAIN 2 G E T          Ø
STORE 2 P U T        3 Ø Ø
      2 J I X 1 A G A I N
           GET  COUNT
           ADD  TWLVE
           PUT  COUNT
           GET  STORE
           ADD  TWLVE
           PUT  STORE
      2 S I N        1 2
OVER  2 G E T          Ø
      2 S U B  TERM
           JZE  GOOD
           JMP  READ
GOOD  2 J I X 1 O V E R
           JMP  CTROL
```

```
T E R M        0 . 0 0 0 0 0 0 0 0 ⎫
               0 . 0 0 0 0 0 0 0 0 ⎪
               0 . 0 0 0 0 0 0 0 0 ⎪
               0 . 0 0 0 0 0 0 0 0 ⎪
               0 . 0 0 0 2 0 0 0 0 ⎪
               0 . 0 0 1 4 0 0 0 0 ⎬   Image of END card
               0 . 0 0 0 0 0 0 0 0 ⎪
               0 . 0 0 0 0 0 0 0 0 ⎪
               0 . 0 0 0 0 0 0 0 0 ⎪
               0 . 0 0 0 0 0 0 0 0 ⎪
               0 . 0 0 0 4 0 0 0 0 ⎪
               0 . 0 0 1 2 0 0 0 0 ⎭
T W L V E      0 . 0 0 0 0 0 0 1 4
```

Problem 8.6

```
                   J R D    N E X T
       N E X T     R C D
                   J R D    O U T
                   2 S I N            1 2
       A G A I N   2 G E T               0
                   2 P U T            3 0
                   2 J I X 1 A G A I N
                   P C D
                   J M P    N E X T
       O U T       H L T
```

Problem 8.7

```
       14     0.00000000
       15     0.00000000
       16     0.00000000
       17     0.00000000
       20     0.00000000
       21     0.00000000
       22     0.00000000
       23     0.00000000
       24     1.00000000
       25     0.77777777
       26     0.00000000
       27     1.00000000
```

Problem 8.8

```
          2 S I N          1 2
AGAIN     2 GET   NAME
          2 PUT            1 4
          2 J I X 1 AGAIN
          WRT
          HLT
NAME    0 . 0 0 0 4 0 0 0 0
        0 . 0 0 0 0 0 0 0 0
        0 . 0 0 0 0 0 0 0 0
        0 . 2 0 0 0 0 0 0 0
        0 . 1 0 1 0 0 0 0 0
        0 . 4 1 0 0 0 0 0 0
        0 . 0 2 6 0 0 0 0 0
        0 . 0 0 0 0 0 0 0 0
        0 . 0 0 0 0 0 0 0 0
        0 . 0 1 4 0 0 0 0 0
        0 . 3 0 2 4 0 0 0 0
        0 . 4 2 1 0 0 0 0 0
```

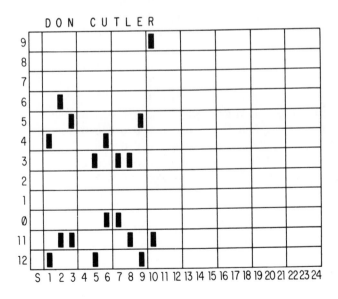

Problem 8.9

```
                 GET   ZERO
              2 S I N            1 2
MORE          2 P U T            1 4
              2 J I X 1 MORE
              1 S I N               8
AGAIN         P I M   MASK
              GET   ALPHA
CYCLE         CYL               2 5
              EXT
              PUT   TEMP
              GET   TWFIV
              SUB   TEMP
              SBR               2 5
              PAD   OBTAN
              PAD   RETRN
OBTAN         GET                 Ø
              ADD   BIT
RETRN         PUT                 Ø
              GET   BIT
              SAL                 1
              PUT   BIT
              GET   CYCLE
              SUB   THREE
              PUT   CYCLE
              1 J I X 1 AGAIN
              WRT
ZERO          HLT
TEMP      Ø . Ø Ø Ø Ø Ø Ø Ø Ø
THREE     Ø . Ø Ø Ø Ø Ø Ø Ø 3
BIT       Ø . Ø Ø Ø Ø Ø Ø Ø 1
TWFIV     Ø . Ø Ø Ø Ø Ø Ø 2 5
MASK      Ø . Ø Ø Ø Ø Ø Ø Ø 7
```

Problem 8.10

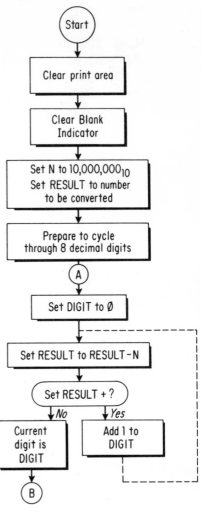

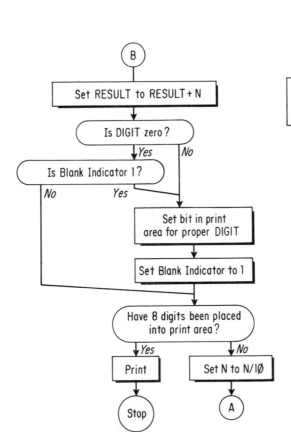

Note: $N = 10,000,000_{10}$ initially, because the EX-1 computer is 25 bits and, hence, may have as a maximum number $2^{24} - 1$ or 16,777,215.

```
            GET   ZERO
            2 S I N        1 2
NEXT        2 P U T        1 4
            2 J I X 1 N E X T
            1 S I N          8
            GET   ZERO
            PUT   BLKIN
MORE        PUT   DIGIT
            GET   ALPHA
            SUB   CONST
            PUT   ALPHA
            JPO   UPDIG
            ADD   CONST
            PUT   ALPHA
            GET   TWFIV
            SUB   DIGIT
            SBR           2 5
            PAD   OBTAN
            PAD   RETRN
            GET   DIGIT
            JZE   CKBLK
OBTAN       GET            0
            ADD   BIT
RETRN       PUT            0
            GET   ONE
            PUT   BLKIN
BLANK       GET   BIT
            SAR            1
            PUT   BIT
            1 J I X 1 A G A I N
            WRT
ZERO        HLT
AGAIN       1 G E T   CONST
            PUT   CONST
            GET   ZERO
            JMP   MORE
UPDIG       GET   DIGIT
            ADD   ONE
            JMP   MORE
```

```
CKBLK      GET    BLKIN
           JZE    BLANK
           GET    DIGIT
           JMP    OBTAN
BIT        0.00000200
DIGIT      0.00000000
ONE        0.00000001
BLKIN      0.00000000
TWFIV      0.00000025
CONST      0.46113200  ◄──── 10,000,000₁₀
           0.03641100  ◄──── 1,000,000₁₀
           0.00303240  ◄──── 100,000₁₀
           0.00023420  ◄──── 10,000₁₀
           0.00001750  ◄──── 1,000₁₀
           0.00000144  ◄──── 100₁₀
           0.00000012  ◄──── 10₁₀
           0.00000001  ◄──── 1₁₀
```

Problem 8.11

```
                  TAW   DATA
DATA       0.00000031
           0.00000050
```

Problem 8.12

```
                  2SIN        10
AGAIN             TAW   DATAA
                  GET   DATAB
                  ADD   DATAA
                  PUT   DATAB
                  2JIX1AGAIN
                  HLT
DATAA      0.00000024
DATAB      0.00000300
```

Problem 8.13

```
                  TAR   DATA
                  GET   NOREC
                  SBR        25
                  PAD   NEXT
                  TRW
```

```
                    GET   NOREC
                    ADD   DATA
                    PUT   NOREC
                    TAW   DATA
        NEXT      2 SIN            Ø
        AGAIN       TAR   TEN
                    2 JIX1AGAIN
                    TAW   NEWDA
                    HLT
        NEWDA     Ø . Ø Ø Ø Ø Ø Ø 1 2
                    HLT   HIRED
        DATA      Ø . Ø Ø Ø Ø Ø Ø Ø 1
                    HLT   NOREC
        NOREC     Ø . Ø Ø Ø Ø Ø Ø Ø Ø
        TEN       Ø . Ø Ø Ø Ø Ø Ø 1 2
                    HLT   TABLE
        TABLE     Ø . Ø Ø Ø Ø Ø Ø Ø Ø
                  Ø . Ø Ø Ø Ø Ø Ø Ø Ø
                  Ø . Ø Ø Ø Ø Ø Ø Ø Ø
                  Ø . Ø Ø Ø Ø Ø Ø Ø Ø
                  Ø . Ø Ø Ø Ø Ø Ø Ø Ø
                  Ø . Ø Ø Ø Ø Ø Ø Ø Ø
                  Ø . Ø Ø Ø Ø Ø Ø Ø Ø
                  Ø . Ø Ø Ø Ø Ø Ø Ø Ø
                  Ø . Ø Ø Ø Ø Ø Ø Ø Ø
                  Ø . Ø Ø Ø Ø Ø Ø Ø Ø
```

Problem 8.14

```
            TAR   DATA
            GET   NOREC        Obtain number of records.
            SBR      2 5
            PAD   NEXT
            GET   NOREC ⎤
            SUB   DATA  ⎬←—Reduce number of records by 1.
            PUT   NOREC ⎦
            SBR      2 5
            PAD   MORE
NEXT      2 SIN            Ø
AGAIN       TAR   INFOA       Read 1st (next) employee record.
INSTR       GET      3 Ø Ø
            SUB   QUIT
            JZE   GOTIT
```

```
              GET     INSTR
              ADD     INFOA
              PUT     INSTR
              GET     INFOB
              ADD     INFOA
              PUT     INFOB
GOTIT    2 J I X 1 AGAIN
              TRW
              TAW     DATA           Write number of records.
MORE     1 S I N            ∅
              GET     THRHD
              PUT     INFOB
OVER         TAW     INFOA          Write 1st (next) employee record.
              GET     INFOB
              ADD     INFOA
              PUT     INFOB
         1 J I X 1 OVER
              HLT
DATA     ∅ . ∅ ∅ ∅ ∅ ∅ ∅ ∅ 1
              HLT     NOREC
NOREC    ∅ . ∅ ∅ ∅ ∅ ∅ ∅ ∅ ∅
INFOA    ∅ . ∅ ∅ ∅ ∅ ∅ ∅ 1 2
INFOB    ∅ . ∅ ∅ ∅ ∅ ∅ 3 ∅ ∅
THRHD    ∅ . ∅ ∅ ∅ ∅ ∅ 3 ∅ ∅
```

Note: I am assuming that I have available a block of locations in core memory from 300 up into which I can write the tape records.

Problem 8.15

```
              GET     ZERO
              PUT     ALPHA
              PIM     MASK
OVER         TAR     DATA           Read 1st (next) 20-word record.
         2 S I N            2 ∅     Prepare to cycle through 20 words.
MORE     1 S I N            4        Prepare to cycle through 4 letters.
         2 GET            3 ∅ ∅
AGAIN        EXT
              SUB     LETTA
              JZE     UPALP          Jump if 1st (next) letter is letter A.
REPET    2 GET            3 ∅ ∅  ⎫
              SAR              6   ⎬ ←─Modify to obtain next letter.
         2 PUT            3 ∅ ∅  ⎭
```

```
            1 J I X 1 A G A I N ←── Have 4 letters been examined this
                                       location?
            2 J I X 1 M O R E ←──── Have 20 locations been examined?
              G E T   C O U N T
              S U B   O N E
              P U T   C O U N T
              J Z E   Z E R O ←──── Jump if three 20 word records
                                       have been processed.
              J M P   O V E R
U P A L P     G E T   A L P H A
              A D D   O N E
              P U T   A L P H A
              J M P   R E P E T
Z E R O       H L T
C O U N T     0 . 0 0 0 0 0 0 3
O N E         0 . 0 0 0 0 0 0 1
D A T A       0 . 0 0 0 0 0 2 4
              0 . 0 0 0 0 3 0 0
M A S K       0 . 0 0 0 0 0 7 7    Mask for right-most 6-bits.
L E T T A     0 . 0 0 0 0 0 2 1    6-bit hollerith for letter A.
```

Problem 8.16

```
              J R D   N E X T A    Make sure Red Light is off.
N E X T A     J G N   N E X T B    Make sure Green Light is off.
N E X T B     G E T       7 7 7    Obtain number set in Console
                                     Switches.
              S U B   S E V E N
              J P O   G O O D A    Number > 7
Z E R O       H L T
G O O D A     S U B   T N Y O N
              J P O   G O O D B    Number ≥ 29
              T O N 2              Turn on Green Light.
              J M P   Z E R O
G O O D B     S U B   F R T E N
              J P O   G O O D C    Number > 42
              J M P   Z E R O
G O O D C     S U B   T N Y O N
              J P O   G O O D D    Number ≥ 64
              T O N 1              Turn on Red Light.
              J M P   Z E R O
G O O D D     S U B   T W L V E
              J P O   G O O D E    Number > 75
              J M P   Z E R O
```

```
GOODE      SUB   FOUR
           JPO   ZERO        Number ≥ 80.
           TON 3             Ring the Bell.
           JMP   ZERO
FOUR       Ø . Ø Ø Ø Ø Ø Ø Ø 4
SEVEN      Ø . Ø Ø Ø Ø Ø Ø Ø 7
TWLVE      Ø . Ø Ø Ø Ø Ø Ø 1 4
FRTEN      Ø . Ø Ø Ø Ø Ø Ø 1 6
TNYON      Ø . Ø Ø Ø Ø Ø Ø 2 5
```

CHAPTER 9

Problem 9.1

1. 265.4ØØØØ
   17.457ØØØ
   Ø.Ø165222ØØ
   −6Ø17Ø.ØØ
   6243667ØØ.
2. 2^9
   2^3
   2^3
   2^{-6}
   2^{10}
3. Ø.1243ØØØØ
   Ø.3ØØØØØØØ
   1.2651ØØØØ
   Ø.425ØØØØØ
   Ø.7ØØØØØØØ

Problem 9.2

1. X̄ is .ØØØØØØ37.
   X is 3.7.
2. X̄ is −Ø.ØØØØ4112.
   X is −41.12
3. $|3| = 3, |−3| = 3, |9| = 9, |−17| = 17$
4. $|X| \leq 7$
5. Three binary places would be required for the integral portion of the largest X.
6. The scale factor is 2^{21}.
7. Yes.

Problem 9.3

$$|Z| < 121 + 31$$
$$|Z| < 152$$
$$|Z| < 2^8 \quad \text{therefore, } Z = 2^8 Z$$
$$2^8 \bar{Z} = 2^7 \bar{X} + 2^5 \bar{Y}$$
$$\bar{Z} = 2^{-1} \bar{X} + 2^{-3} \bar{Y}$$

```
GET   XNUMB
SAR        1
PUT   ANSER      Store 2⁻¹X̄ temporarily.
GET   YNUMB
SAR        3
ADD   ANSER
PUT   ANSER
HLT
```

Problem 9.4

$$X = 2^{14} \bar{X} \text{ as is given}$$
$$Y = 2^8 \bar{Y} \text{ as is given}$$
$$|Z| \leq 499 + 199$$
$$|Z| \leq 698$$
$$|Z| < 2^{10}$$

And since problem requests $Z = 2^{24-14}\bar{Z}$ or $Z = 2^{10}\bar{Z}$,

$$2^{10} \bar{Z} = 2^{14} \bar{X} + 2^8 \bar{Y}$$
$$\bar{Z} = 2^4 \bar{X} + 2^{-2} \bar{Y}$$

```
GET   XNUMB
SAL        4
PUT   ANSER      Store 2⁴X̄ temporarily.
GET   YNUMB
SAR        2
ADD   ANSER
PUT   ANSER
HLT
```

Problem 9.5

$$r = 2^5 \bar{r}$$
$$s = 2^5 \bar{s}$$
$$|t| < 32 + 32$$
$$|t| < 64$$

$$|t| < 2^6$$
$$t = 2^6\bar{t}$$
$$2^6\bar{t} = 2^5\bar{r} + 2^5\bar{s}$$
$$\bar{t} = 2^{-1}\bar{r} + 2^{-1}\bar{s}$$

```
GET   RSTOR
SAR        1
PUT   TSTOR      Store 2⁻¹r temporarily.
GET   SSTOR
SAR        1
ADD   TSTOR
PUT   TSTOR
HLT
```

Since r and s are in RSTOR and SSTOR scaled in maximum precision, we cannot add them first and then shift. If we did, we could get overflow depending upon the specific values involved. Hence, the programming should not be done according to

$$\bar{t} = 2^{-1}(\bar{r} + \bar{s})$$

but rather

$$\bar{t} = 2^{-1}\bar{r} + 2^{-1}\bar{s}$$

It is necessary for the programmer to always be fully aware of the results of his actions, and never blindly apply what appear on the surface to be logical maneuvers.

Problem 9.6

Since c may be -31, the formula $d = a + b - c$ may read $d = 63 + 128 - (-31)$ and hence, $|d| \leq 63 + 128 + 31$

$$|d| \leq 222 \qquad |d| < 2^8$$
$$d = 2^8\bar{d}$$
$$2^8\bar{d} = 2^6\bar{a} + 2^8\bar{b} - 2^5\bar{c}$$
$$\bar{d} = 2^{-2}\bar{a} + \bar{b} - 2^{-3}\bar{c}$$

```
GET   ZERO
SUB   CNUMB
SAR        3
ADD   BNUMB
PUT   RESLT      Store temporarily.
GET   ANUMB
SAR        2
```

```
        ADD   RESLT
        PUT   RESLT
ZERO    HLT
```

Problem 9.7

$$|W_i| < 700 + 320 + 9$$
$$|W_i| < 1029$$
$$|W_i| < 2^{11}$$
$$W_i = 2^{11}\bar{W}_i$$
$$2^{11}\bar{W}_i = 2^{11}\bar{X}_i + 2^9\bar{Y}_i - 2^{14}\bar{Z}_i$$
$$\bar{W}_i = \bar{X}_i + 2^{-2}\bar{Y}_i - 2^3\bar{Z}_i$$

```
        2 SIN   TABLX
AGAIN     GET   ZERO
        2 SUB   TABLZ
          SAL        3
        2 PUT   TABLW      Store $-2^3\bar{Z}_i$ temporarily.
        2 GET   TABLY
          SAR        2
        2 ADD   TABLX
        2 ADD   TABLW
        2 PUT   TABLW
        2 JIX1  AGAIN
ZERO      HLT
```

Problem 9.8

$$|X| < 2^7 \qquad |Y| < 2^3$$
$$X = 2^7\bar{X} \qquad Y = 2^3\bar{Y}$$
$$|Z| < 66 \cdot 5$$
$$|Z| < 330$$
$$|Z| < 2^9$$
$$Z = 2^9\bar{Z}$$
$$2^9\bar{Z} = 2^7\bar{X}2^3\bar{Y}$$
$$\bar{Z} = 2^1\bar{X}\bar{Y}$$

```
        GET   XNUMB
        MUL   YNUMB
        SBL        1
        PUT   ZNUMB
        HLT
```

Problem 9.9

$$|a| < 2^7 \qquad |b| < 16$$
$$a = 2^7\bar{a} \qquad b = 2^4\bar{b}$$
$$C = 2^{14}\bar{C} \text{ as is given}$$
$$2^{14}\bar{C} = 2^7\bar{a}2^4\bar{b}$$
$$\bar{C} = 2^{-3}\bar{a}\bar{b}$$

```
GET   TESTA
MUL   TESTB
SAR        3
PUT   RZULT
HLT
```

Problem 9.10

$$a = 2^5\bar{a}$$
$$b = 2^4\bar{b}$$
$$c = 2^8\bar{c}$$
$$|d| < 31 \cdot 16 + 249$$
$$|d| < 745$$
$$|d| < 2^{10}$$
$$d = 2^{10}\bar{d}$$
$$2^{10}\bar{d} = 2^5\bar{a}2^4\bar{b} + 2^8\bar{c}$$
$$\bar{d} = 2^{-1}\bar{a}\bar{b} + 2^{-2}\bar{c}$$

```
GET   ANUMB
MUL   BNUMB
SAR        1
PUT   DNUMB        Store 2⁻¹ āb̄ temporarily.
GET   CNUMB
SAR        2
ADD   DNUMB
PUT   DNUMB
HLT
```

Store 2^{-1} $\bar{a}\bar{b}$ temporarily.

Problem 9.11

$$X = 2^6\bar{X}$$
$$Y = 2^{10}\bar{Y}$$
$$Z = 2^5\bar{Z}$$
$$W = X(Y - Z) \text{ by factoring}$$

$$|W| < 60(1024 + 31)$$
$$|W| < 63{,}300$$
$$W = 2^{16}\bar{W}$$

Let $T = Y - Z$

$$|T| < 1024 + 31 \text{ since } Z \text{ may be negative}$$
$$|T| < 1055$$
$$|T| < 2^{11}$$
$$T = 2^{11}\bar{T}$$
$$2^{11}\bar{T} = 2^{10}\bar{Y} - 2^5\bar{Z}$$
$$\bar{T} = 2^{-1}\bar{Y} - 2^{-6}\bar{Z}$$

Substituting back into original equation:

$$2^{16}\bar{W} = 2^6\bar{X}(2^{10}\bar{Y} - 2^5\bar{Z})$$
$$2^{16}\bar{W} = 2^6\bar{X}2^{11}\bar{T}$$
$$\bar{W} = 2^1\bar{X}\bar{T}$$

GET	ZNUMB	Obtain $\bar{Z}$.
SAR	6	Otbain $2^{-6}\bar{Z}$.
PUT	WNUMB	Store $2^{-6}\bar{Z}$ temporarily.
GET	YNUMB	Obtain $\bar{Y}$.
SAR	1	Obtain $2^{-1}\bar{Y}$.
SUB	WNUMB	Obtain $2^{-1}\bar{Y} - 2^{-6}\bar{Z}$ or $\bar{T}$.
MUL	XNUMB	Obtain $\bar{X}\bar{T}$.
SBL	1	Obtain $2^1\bar{X}\bar{T}$ or $\bar{W}$.
PUT	WNUMB	Store $\bar{W}$.
HLT		

Problem 9.12

$$
\begin{array}{r}
.23_8 \\
.205_8 \\
\hline
137 \\
460 \\
\hline
.04737_8
\end{array} = 0.\underline{000} \quad \underbrace{100} \quad 111 \quad 011 \quad 111
$$

SBL 5 will lose these five bits (rather illogical since the 1 is significant) to give:

$$0.35740000$$

Problem 9.13

$$|X| < 2^7 \qquad X = 2^7\bar{X}$$
$$|Y| < 2^{10} \qquad Y = 2^{10}\bar{Y}$$
$$|Z| < 2^{13} \qquad Z = 2^{13}\bar{Z}$$
$$|W| < 2^{10} \qquad W = 2^{10}\bar{W}$$
$$|V| < \frac{98 \cdot 98 + 98 \cdot 1000 + 5000}{8}$$
$$|V| < 14{,}075.5$$
$$|V| < 2^{14}$$
$$V = 2^{14}\bar{V}$$

Factoring gives:

$$V = \frac{X(X + Y) - Z}{W}$$

$$\text{Let } T = X + Y$$
$$|T| < 1098$$
$$|T| < 2^{11}$$
$$T = 2^{11}\bar{T}$$
$$2^{11}\bar{T} = 2^7\bar{X} + 2^{10}\bar{Y}$$
$$\bar{T} = 2^{-4}\bar{X} + 2^{-1}\bar{Y}$$
$$2^{14}V = \frac{2^7\bar{X}(2^7\bar{X} + 2^{10}\bar{Y}) - 2^{13}\bar{Z}}{2^{10}\bar{W}}$$
$$2^{14}\bar{V} = \frac{2^7\bar{X}2^{11}\bar{T} - 2^{13}\bar{Z}}{2^{10}W}$$
$$\bar{V} = \frac{2^{-6}\bar{X}\bar{T} - 2^{-11}\bar{Z}}{\bar{W}}$$

G E T	X N U M B	Obtain $\bar{X}$.
S A R	4	Obtain $2^{-4}\bar{X}$.
P U T	V N U M B	Store $2^{-4}\bar{X}$ temporarily.
G E T	Y N U M B	Obtain $\bar{Y}$.
S A R	1	Obtain $2^{-1}\bar{Y}$.
A D D	V N U M B	Obtain $2^{-4}\bar{X} + 2^{-1}\bar{Y}$ or $\bar{T}$.
M U L	X N U M B	Obtain $\bar{X}\bar{T}$.
S A R	6	Obtain $2^{-6}\bar{X}\bar{T}$.
P U T	V N U M B	Store $2^{-6}\bar{X}\bar{T}$ temporarily.
G E T	Z E R O	
S U B	Z N U M B	Obtain $-\bar{Z}$.

```
        S A R          1 1      Obtain −2⁻¹¹Z̄.
        A D D   V N U M B      Obtain 2⁻⁶X̄T − 2⁻¹¹Z̄.
        D I V   W N U M B      Obtain V.
        P U T   V N U M B
ZERO   HLT
```

Problem 9.14

$$|X| < 2^9 \qquad X = 2^9 \bar{X}$$

Note that since X can equal 256 or 2^8 we must allow 9 places for the integral portion of X, hence, $X = 2^9 \bar{X}$.

$$|Y| < 2^{13} \qquad Y = 2^{13} \bar{Y}$$

$$|Z| < 2^{14} \qquad Z = 2^{14} \bar{Z}$$

Since $W = \dfrac{8(X + Y) - 7Z + 9}{Y}$, we see that $W = \dfrac{8X}{Y} + 8 - \dfrac{7Z}{Y} + \dfrac{9}{Y}$ and hence, W is a maximum when Y is a minimum.

Thus: $\quad |W| < \dfrac{8(256 + 1) + 7 \cdot 10000 + 9}{1}$

$$|W| < 72{,}065$$

$$|W| < 2^{17}$$

$$W = 2^{17} \bar{W}$$

Let $T = X + Y$

$$|T| < 256 + 7500$$

$$|T| < 7756$$

$$|T| < 2^{13}$$

$$T = 2^{13} \bar{T}$$

$$2^{13} \bar{T} = 2^9 \bar{X} + 2^{13} \bar{Y}$$

$$\bar{T} = 2^{-4} \bar{X} + 2^0 \bar{Y}$$

$$2^{17} \bar{W} = \frac{2^3(2^9 X + 2^{13} Y) - 2^? 7 2^{14} \bar{Z} + 2^? 9}{2^{13} Y}$$

Note that I have replaced 8 with 2^3.

$$\bar{W} = \frac{2^3 2^{13} \bar{T} - 2^{? + 14} 7 \bar{Z} + 2^? 9}{2^{30} \bar{Y}}$$

$$\bar{W} = \frac{2^{-14} \bar{T} - 2^{? + 14 - 30} 7 \bar{Z} + 2^{? - 30} 9}{\bar{Y}}$$

We see that if we scale 7 as $7 = 2^{16} \bar{7}$, then the power of 2 in the middle term will be $2^{16 + 14 - 30}$ or 2^0 and, hence, simplify things a little.

Since the most that we can scale 9 is $9 = 2^{24}\bar{9}$, we cannot likewise get $2^{?-30}$ to 2^0.

Therefore, let us consider the constants scaled thus:

$$7 = 2^{16}\bar{7} \quad \text{and} \quad 9 = 2^{24}\bar{9}$$

then our equation is

$$\bar{W} = \frac{2^{-18}\bar{T} - \bar{7}\bar{Z} + 2^{-6}\bar{9}}{\bar{Y}}$$

Observe that if $\bar{9}$ is scaled 2^{24}, it appears as NINE 0.00000011 and a shift of 6 to the right will eliminate it.

Thus, if we wish to have 9 in the calculation we had best compute the numerator separately.

$$\begin{aligned}
\text{Let } N &= 8(X + Y) - 7Z + 9 \\
|N| &< 8(256 + 7500) + 7 \cdot 10{,}000 + 9 \\
|N| &< 132{,}057 \\
|N| &< 2^{18} \\
N &= 2^{18}\bar{N} \\
2^{18}\bar{N} &= 2^3(2^9\bar{X} + 2^{13}\bar{Y}) - 2^?\bar{7}2^{14}\bar{Z} + 2^?\bar{9} \\
2^{18}\bar{N} &= 2^3 2^{13}\bar{T} - 2^{?+14}\bar{7}\bar{Z} + 2^?\bar{9} \\
\bar{N} &= 2^{-2}\bar{T} - 2^{?-4}\bar{7}\bar{Z} + 2^{?-18}\bar{9}
\end{aligned}$$

Here we see that we should scale $7 = 2^4\bar{7}$ and $9 = 2^{18}\bar{9}$ to get

$$N = 2^{-2}\bar{T} - \bar{7}\bar{Z} + \bar{9}$$

$$2^{17}\bar{W} = \frac{2^{18}\bar{N}}{{}^{13}\bar{Y}}$$

Finally,

$$\bar{W} = \frac{2^{-12}\bar{N}}{\bar{Y}}$$

We are now ready to code.

GET	XNUMB	Obtain $\bar{X}$.
SAR	4	Obtain $2^{-4}\bar{X}$.
ADD	YNUMB	Obtain $2^{-4}\bar{X} + \bar{Y}$ or $\bar{T}$.
SAR	2	Obtain $2^{-2}\bar{T}$.

```
          P U T   W N U M B      Store 2⁻²T̄ temporarily.
          G E T   Z E R O
          S U B   Z N U M B      Obtain −Z̄.
          M U L   S E V E N      Obtain −7̄Z̄.
          A D D   N I N E        Obtain −7̄Z̄ + 9̄.
          A D D   W N U M B      Obtain 2⁻²T̄ − 7̄Z̄ + 9̄ or N̄.
          S B R         1 2      Obtain 2⁻¹²N̄.
          D I V   Y N U M B      Obtain W̄.
          P U T   W N U M B      Store W̄.
Z E R O   H L T
S E V E N  0 . 3 4 0 0 0 0 0 0   Seven scaled 2⁴
N I N E    0 . 0 0 0 0 1 1 0 0   Nine scaled 2¹⁸
```

Note that I used S B R 12 to obtain $2^{-12}\bar{N}$. I did this to get the shifted numerator to go into the Mask Register since the D I V considers the combined Accumulator-Mask Register as the dividend.

CHAPTER 11

Problem 11.1

```
F O R   I = A L L ( T A B L E A ) $
B E T A ( $ I $ ) = A L P H A ( $ I $ ) $
S T O P $
```

Alternate solution:

```
F O R   J = 0, 1, 8 $
B E T A ( $ J $ ) = A L P H A ( $ J $ ) $
S T O P $
```

Problem 11.2

```
F O R   R = A L L ( P L U S I X ) $
G A M M A ( $ R $ ) = G A M M A ( $ R $ ) + 6 $
S T O P   $
```

Alternate solution:

```
F O R   K = 0, 1, 13  $
G A M M A ( $ K $ ) = G A M M A ( $ K $ ) + 6   $
```

Problem 11.3

```
F O R   T = 0, 2, 28  $
U S Q A R E ( $ T $ ) = U S Q A R E ( $ T $ ) ( * 2 * )   $
S T O P   $
```

Alternate solution:

```
F O R   Q = 0, 2, 28   $
U S Q A R E($Q$) = U S Q A R E($Q$)*U S Q A R E($Q$)   $
S T O P   $
```

Problem 11.4

```
F O R   I = A L L(D A T A)   $
B E G I N
   I F   C H E C K($I $)   N Q 3   $
       C H E C K($I $) = C H E C K($I $) + 1   $
       C H E C K($I $) = C H E C K($I $) + 3   $
E N D
S T O P   $
```

Observe thet if an entry of CHECK contains a number other than 3, both the +1 and +3 will be performed giving a result of adding 4 to non-3 entries.

Problem 11.5

```
F O R   M = A L L(S W O P)   $
B E G I N
  T E M P = I N F O A($M$)   $
  I N F O A($M$) = I N F O B($M$)   $
  I N F O B($M$) = T E M P   $
E N D
S T O P   $
```

Alternate solution:

```
F O R   P = 0, 1, 34   $
B E G I N
  T E M P = I N F O B($P$)   $
  I N F O B($P$) = I N F O A($P$)   $
  I N F O A($P$) = T E M P   $
E N D
S T O P   $
```

Problem 11.6

```
F O R   L = A L L(Q E S T O N)   $
B E G I N
I F   A B S(M A Y B E($L $))   G Q 3 A N D   A B S(M A Y B E
    ($L $))L S 9   $
```

```
BEGIN
  MAYBE($L$) = 3*MAYBE($L$) + 5   $
  GOTO  DUMMY   $
END
  MAYBE($L$) = MAYBE($L$) + 7   $
DUMMY.    MAYBE($L$) = MAYBE($L$)   $
END
STOP   $
```

Problem 11.7

```
TEMP = BOLTS($0$)   $
FOR   I = 0, 1, 8   $
BOLTS($I$) = BOLTS($I + 1$)   $
BOLTS($9$) = TEMP   $
STOP   $
```

Note that I placed an 8 in the C factor of the FOR statement since, when subscript I is 8, the expression $I + 1$ will be 9 and I will be setting entry #8 with entry #9 (which is the tenth entry).

This concludes the answers for the book *Introduction to Computer Programming.*

Having mastered the contents therein please be encouraged to continue your studies with the sequel, *The Return of the EX-1.*

GLOSSARY

accumulator—A computer register used for accumulating sums and for holding numbers and information while it is being operated upon.

analog computer—A computer which represents numbers by forming analogies between numbers and continuously varying physical quantities such as voltages, lengths, etc. It operates on the principle of measurement, like a slide rule.

assembler—A computer program which translates the symbolic machine code of an intermediate level language into the binary of a low level language. Usually one instruction of the intermediate language is translated into one instruction of the low level language.

batch processing—Saving up jobs and processing them one after the other.

binary number system—A number system employing the two symbols, 0 and 1. It is the number system most frequently used with digital computers because digital computers are composed of electrical components—and electrical components are either on (1) or off (0).

bit—Abbreviation for binary digit, the symbol 0 or 1 in the binary number system.

byte—A group of bits, most commonly a group of 6 bits or 8 bits depending upon the computer involved.

compiler—A computer program which translates the program statements of a higher level language into the binary of a low level language. Usually one statement of the high level language is translated into several or many instructions of the low level language.

complement—As used in computer work it is usually the representation of the negative of a number. Computers use complements for subtraction.

compool—A dictionary-like table which an assembler or compiler uses when translating a symbolic program deck into a binary object deck. It is used to define items and tables by giving their sizes and absolute addresses.

core memory word—The contents of a computer memory location.

data management system—A software system (program system) that enables a non-programmer to define data and retrieve it, change it, and print out reports.

debugging—Trouble-shooting a computer program or program system.

digital computer—A computer which represents numbers by discrete quantities such as numbers of pulses, cogs on a gear, etc. It operates on the principle of counting, like an abacus.

EBCDIC—A commonly used 8-bit code used to represent hollerith information. The letters stand for Extended Binary Coded Decimal Interchange Code.

end-around-carry—The automatic process of adding 1 to the right of the contents of the accumulator when a 1 is lost on the left due to the modulus of the machine.

entry—A grouping of items in a table which relate to each other in some manner. For example, the items in an entry may describe one specific object, and a subsequent entry may describe a different specific object.

exponent—A representation of the number of times that a number appears as a factor in a product.

fixed point arithmetic—This is a type of computer arithmetic in which the programmer must keep track of the real point. No bits in the computer word are allotted for describing the location of the real point. Scaling equations are often used in programming for fixed point arithmetic.

fixed-word-length machine—A computer whose operations or instructions always work with the same number of bits.

floating point arithmetic—This is a type of computer arithmetic in which the computer itself automatically keeps track of the real point. Certain bit positions in the computer word are required to describe the location of the real point. This leaves fewer bit positions for the significant bits of the number, but simplifies programming considerably.

garbage—Undesirable information in a computer register left over from a previous operation. Usually removed by the process of clearing called initializing or housekeeping.

hardware—Computer equipment. The feature of an automated system that cannot be easily modified.

hollerith code—A binary code used for representing letters, numbers, and special characters on punched cards, magnetic tape, and other computer storage media.

index register—A special register used by computers for keeping track of passes in the process called looping. The contents of an index register are used for address modification when processing tables.

initializing—Clearing out undesirable information from computer registers prior to processing, or the setting up of initial environment prior to processing.

item—A unit of information contained in a group of adjacent bit positions in a computer word. It may be as little as 1 bit or as large as a full computer word. An item has a name and it has a value. The information in it may be coded in several different ways.

machine point—An imaginary point which separates the sign bit from the magnitude bits in a computer word. In the text it is represented by Δ where extreme clarity is required and by · where no confusion will result.

maximum precision— Placing a number in a computer register so as to have the largest possible number of bit positions available for the fractional part of the number without losing any of the integer bits.

mnemonic—An abbreviation of a computer instruction which the programmer may use when writing a program and which the assembler can recognize and translate into an instruction in binary.

multiprocessing—The operation of more than one program in a computer. Operation is simultaneous and is possible because the computer is a 3rd generation machine with more than one C.P.U. (Central Processing Unit).

octal number system—A number system employing the 8 symbols, 0 through 7. It is used a great deal by computer programmers because of the extremely easy conversion of numbers between it and the binary number system.

operational program—A program which automates a manually performed task. A program which computes paychecks is an example of an operational program.

program counter—A computer register which contains the location of the next instruction to be performed.

random access storage—Storage from which the computer can obtain information directly without waiting for the information to pass by. Magnetic core storage is an example of random access storage. Magnetic tape and magnetic drum are examples of storage devices not randomly accessible.

real point—The point which separates the whole number part of a number from the fractional part. In the decimal system it is called the decimal point. In the octal system it is called the octal point. In the binary system it is called the binary point.

real time system—An automated system which can react to its environment. It must be fast enough and designed in such a way that it can supply information on demand. A system which controls airline reservations is an example of a real time system.

scale factor—A number (expressed as a power of 2) needed to multiply the computer word (expressed as a fraction with real point at the machine point) in order to get the actual number desired (expressed as an octal number with the real point in its correct place).

serial access storage—Storage-like magnetic tapes through which records must be passed to arrive at the information desired.

significant digit—A singnificant digit is the leftmost non-zero digit in a number and any zero or non-zero digit following it.

software—Computer programs. The feature of an automated system that can be "easily" modified.

source deck—The symbolic program deck that is submitted to the compiler or assembler.

specific precision—Placing a number in a computer register so that the fractional portion of the number occupies a specific given number of bit positions.

table—A consecutive group of computer storage registers. Tables are made of entries, entries, and entries contain items of a related nature.

test matrix—A table of sample inputs to be hand tested with a program to compare expected inputs with actual inputs.

USASCII—An 8-bit code used to represent hollerith information. The letters stand for USA Standard Code for Information Interchange.

utility program—A program which aids the writing and production of an operational program. Assemblers and compilers are examples of utility programs.

variable-word-length machine—A computer that works with information fields of varying length.

time-sharing—A computer system whereby several users can use a computer at the same time. A number of input/output devices are attached to the machine. The system responds to each user one at a time but, since it is so fast, the effect is as if the user had complete use of the machine alone.

Index